AF658843

Innovative Technology for Production and Postharvest Management of Vegetables

The Editor

Dr. Udit Kumar, working as Assistant Professor (SS), Department of Horticulture, Faculty of Agriculture, Dr. Rajendra Prasad Central Agricultural University, Pusa and honored his Ph.D. degree in Horticulture (Vegetable Science) from G.B. Pant University of Agriculture and Technology, Pantnagar (Uttarakhand). Dr Kumar has also completed PG Diploma in Agriculture Extension Management from MANAGE, Hyderabad. He has also served as Subject Matter Specialist (Horticulture) at Krishi Vigyan Kendra of Birsa Agricultural University, Ranchi (Jharkhand).

Thirty one full length research papers in national, international and foreign reputed Journals, 21 abstract, 21 book chapters and 29 Hindi and 7 English popular articles and 2 extension bulletins/book to his credit. He has also edited one books related to the field of Horticulture. Dr Kumar is the recipient of prestigious awards namely 'Excellence in teaching Award' in the year 2014 by the Society for Recent Development in Agriculture, Meerut(UP) and 'Young Scientist Award' for the year 2015 conferred by the G.K.V. Society, Agra(UP).

Founder member of the Bihar Horticulture Society, Pusa, Bihar credited to him and was honoured for his outstanding contributions in strengthening the cause of the society. He is life member of nine national and international professional bodies and societies. Dr Kumar was also recognized by many national and international prestigious societies exist as member of editorial board of Journal of Hill Agriculture and The Asian Journal of Horticulture, published by Indian Society of Hill Agriculture and Hind Agri-Hoticultural Society respectively. He has over twelve years experience in teaching, research and extension in the field of Horticulture and handled projects as Principal Investigator like AICRP on Vegetable Crops, AINRP on Onion and Garlic, NHM (Vegetable Seed Production Programme), etc. More than 12 courses have been taught by him at Under Graduate and Post Graduate level.

Innovative Technology for Production and Postharvest Management of Vegetables

Dr. Udit Kumar

Department of Horticulture
Faculty of Agriculture
Dr. Rajendra Prasad Central Agricultural University,
PUSA, Samastipur - 848125 (BIHAR)

BIOTECH

2021

BIOTECH BOOKS®

© 2021 AUTHOR
ISBN 978-81-7622-479-6

All rights reserved. Including the right to translate or to reproduce this book or parts thereof except for brief quotations in critical reviews.

Published by: **BIOTECH BOOKS**®
4762-63/23, Ansari Road, Darya Ganj,
New Delhi - 110 002
Phone: 09899295259, 011-43003222
E-mail: biotechbooks@yahoo.co.in
Website: www.biotechbooks.in

Typeset at: **Classic Computer Services**
Delhi - 110 035

Printed at: **Replika Press Pvt. Ltd.**

PRINTED IN INDIA

Preface

Horticulture sector encompasses a wide range of crops namely fruits, vegetables, ornamental, medicinal and aromatic, spices along with plantation crops. Besides providing nutritional security, horticulture is the prime engine that provides relatively more income as well as employment opportunity in rural areas. Technology breakthrough in vegetable crops has improved the quality and yield considerably, besides, bringing higher income to the farmers leading to crop diversification. Over the years, vegetable has emerged as one of the potential agricultural enterprise in accelerating the growth of economy. Its role in the country's nutritional security, poverty alleviation and employment generation programmes is becoming increasingly important. It offers not only a wide range of options to the farmers for crop diversification, but also provides ample scope for sustaining large number of agro-industries which generate huge employment opportunities. India has emerged as a major producer of vegetable crops and is placed second after China. Also vegetable in India with its higher annual growth rate has become a major contributor to growth of horticulture. It is, therefore, important that technology management is given more emphasis so that it could sustain the desired growth rate in horticulture sector and provide job opportunities to the ever increasing youth. Vegetbale growth and development needs to be inclusive to benefit various stakeholders in the system. Hence, it is essential to reassess our programmes and devise overall strategies to make this sector more inclusive under the rapidly changing consumer and market driven economy and rapidly depleting environmental conditions. Today, the challenges are many namely, nutritional security, threat of climate change, need for new plant genotypes for diversified end uses, production deficit and gluts, lack of infrastructure in commodity value-chain, retail chains and organized market systems, farmer producer companies, and export promotion. It is, therefore, necessary that modern horticulture technology gears to meet new challenges in horticulture management leading to restructuring the role and goals in research, production, education, extension and human resource development to boost production, productivity, processing and export of fresh and processed horticultural produce and products.

This book endeavor try to keep the pace with somewhat rapid intervention in modern technology for enhancing production, quality education along with fresh and processed quality produce. Here the efforts have been made to compile near to complete coverage of new aspect of technology management which is practiced in the field as well as teaching, research, extension and allied processing industries.

Dr. Udit Kumar

Contents

Chapter 1

Perennial Vegetables

Those vegetable crops which live for more than two year and repeat the vegetative-reproductive cycle annually are called perennial vegetables. Such crops remain for a number of years in the field. Therefore, the location should be selected in a such a way that they do not interfere with culture operation for other crops. The upper portion of perennial vegetable during severe cold winter period and again sprout in the spring season to produce edible portion.

Common Name	*Botanical Name*	*Family*	*Edible Part*	*Chromosome Number (2n)*
Asparagus	*Asparagus officinalis* L.	Liliaceae	Spears	20
Globe artichoke	*Cynara scolymus* L.	Compositae	Flower buds	34
Jerusalem artichoke	*Helianthus tuberosus*	Compositae	Root tuber	102 (6x)
Rhubarb	*Rheum rhaponticum* L.	Polygonaceae	Large, thick leaf stalks.	44 (4x)
Curry leaf	*Murraya keinigii* (L.) Spreng	Rutaceae	Leaves	18
Drumstick	*Moringa oleifera* L.	Moringaceae	Green pods and sometimes leaves	28
Agathi	*Sesbaria grandiflora* (L.) Poir.	Leguminosae	Leaves and flowers	24

ASPARAGUS

Asparagus (*Asparagus officinalis* L.) is an important herbaceous perennial plant and known as Shatawar in hindi. It is grown for tender succulent shoots known as 'spears' which are used as vegetable and in the preparation of soup. The canned and frozen spears are also used as processed foods. The tender shoots contain a white crystalline substance, asparagine, which is used in medicine as diuretic in cardiac dropsy and chronic gout. It has a good potential for export as fresh vegetable.

Origin and Botany

Asparagus is a monocot of the family Liliaceae. The chromosome number of *A. officinalis* is 2n=20. There are more than 150 species under the genus *Asparagus,* including the ornamental foliage types, like *A. densiflorus, A. falcatus, A.myriocladus* and *A. setaceus*. However, the related species are *A. cochinchinensis* with edible tubers and *A. racemosus* having edible roots. It had its origin between the eastern Mediterranean and temperate Europe and Asia. It was perhaps introduced in India during the early British period. Asparagus is a perennial dioecious herb with erect branches and growing to a height of 1-3m. The roots are tuberous, occur horizontally inside the soil and serve as storage organs. The leaves are narrow and needle-like. The crown is made up of roots and rhizomes. The aerial stem (spear) arises from a bud on the rhizome. The male flowers are yellowish-green and conspicuous, while female flowers are less conspicuous, while female plants produce berries with one to three seeds per fruit.

Varieties

They are broadly divided into two groups:

1. Varieties which produce green coloured spears are more popular and mainly used in fresh market.
2. White or light green coloured asparagus mainly used for processing.

Variety	*Important Characteristic*
Perfection	An early, uniform and delicious with high food value. The spears are large, green, succulent and light tipped. Yield is 80-100q/ha.
Selection-841	Busy type, medium, uniform and productive. The spears are 15-20 cm long, succulent tender and green with better flavor. Suitable for soup preparation. Yields 90-110 q spears/ha.

Soil and Climate

Asparagus prefers sandy loam or alluvial soils with organic matter. The optimum pH is 6.0-7.0. The soil should be deep with good drainage. It is a temperate crop and requires a temperature of 15.5p- 23.8°C for most of the growing season for spear production. A lower temperature is necessary for about 60-90 days during dormant season. It tolerates frost to some extent. Continuous freezing temperatures, however, are harmful. For economic yields, an elevation of above 1,000m is ideal.

Field Preparation

Asparagus is propagated through seed and crown. Two to three kilograms of seed would be required to raise seedling for planting one hectare. Seeds are sown in nursery beds but before sowing these are soaked in water for about 3-4 days. Seedling 10-12 weeks old are transplanted in the field at a distance of 20-50 cm in a row and 1.0-2.0m between rows. Planting can be done in double rows also but at slightly wider spacing. Seeds are also sown directly at the bottom of 15-20cm deep furrow and covered with 3-5cm of soil. This method of seed sowing is practiced for production of white or blanched spears. Another method is to be use crowns from one-year old plants for propagation of asparagus. Seed sowing or planting can be done during July to November in the plains and in March-May in the hills.

Manure and Fertilizers

About 30-40 tonnes of FYM are applied to the soil in one hectare at the time of field preparation. Fertilizers, 80-120kg N, 80-100kg P and 60-80 kg K per hectare are also incorporated into the soil before planting. Nitrogen should be applied in 3-4 split doses during and first harvest. The first harvesting of spears is two years after planting or seed sowing. After harvesting, every year about 20-30kg N per hectare should be applied for better plant growth.

Irrigation

The first irrigation is given at the time of planting and thereafter at 10-15 day intervals. The water is allowed to stand in furrows to facilities percolation. Excess irrigation should be avoided and proper drainage provided. Under temperate conditions, the crown become dormant during winter and formation of spears starts in the beginning of spring. In mild climatic conditions, the dormancy is not distinct. Weeds between the rows can be kept under control by shallow hoeing so that the young sprouts are not damaged.

Blanching

Mounding the soil to a height of 25-30cm over is practiced to blanch the young spears and get 'white asparagus' for canning. After harvesting the green asparagus sent fresh market, blanching is normally done to produce white asparagus.

Harvesting and Yield

Tender spears, about 10-15cm long, are harvested by cutting 3-4cm below the surface of the soil using a special kind of knife which has a wide chisel- like blade. The spears can be stored at 2° and more than 95 per cent relative humidity for about 10-14 days. The yield increased upto 6-7 years, remain constant upto 12 years and then start to gradual decline. However, the crop between 4-10 years produces best quality spears. On an average crop yield about 25-30 q/ha.

Insect-Pests and Diseases

Asparagus Beetle (*Crioceris asparagi*)

Beetle feed on spears and foliage resulting in crooked and dull spears.

Control

i. Cut the affected spears at every 3 to 5 days.

ii. Spray insecticides like chloropyriphos 50 EC or quinolphos 25 per cent EC 2 ml/lit of water.

Garden Centipede (*Scutigerella immaculata*)

The pest makes the small and round holes in the spears below the ground surface and makes them unfit for consumption.

Control

i. Remove the affected plants.
ii. Flooding the field.

Fungal Diseases

Asparagus Rust (*Puccinia asparagi*)

The small reddish yellow spots appear on the main stem, branches and leaves. Finally, they turn in reddish-yellow colour. The top of the plant is destroyed.

Control

i. Destroy debris of the previous crops.
ii. Locate to resistant varieties.
iii. Uproot affected plants and destroy them.
iv. Spray Dithane M-45 @ 0.2 per cent.

Fusarium Wilt (*Fusarium* spp.)

The fungus is soil borne. The affected spears remain stunted, show brown discolouration and finally wilt.

Control

i. Follow crop rotation.
ii. Use disease free planting material.
iii. Remove affected plants and destroy.
iv. Spray Diathane M-45 @ 0.2 per cent.

GLOBE ARTICHOKE

Globe artichoke, *Cynara scolymus* L., is an herbaceous perennial but grown as an annual having edible young flower heads or buds (*capitulum*). In the heads harvested early at young immature stage, the receptacle, fleshy inner bracts and choke (immature flower buds, pappus and bristles) are edible. It is eaten row or cooked as boiled or steamed and also processed, mainly for canning and freezing. The flower heads are considered useful in the dietary of diabetics. The leaves are bitter and considered to be useful in dropsy and rheumatism. The main artichoke growing countries are Spain, Italy and France in Europe and Argentina in South America.

Origin, Distribution and Botany

The globe artichoke originated from the Mediterranean region. Wild form and wide range of variation occur in southern Europe and northern Africa. The globe artichoke, *Cynara scolymus* L., a diploid (2n=2x=34) belongs to the tribe *Cynarae* of the family Astraceae. Its progenitor species are *C. cardunculus* L. distributed in Spain, Morocco, Algeria and Sicily and *C. syriaca* found in Palestine. Another species, *C. sibthorpiana* Boiss and Heldr. occure in the Peloponnese, Angeanv Islands and Cyrenaica. Globe artichoke (*C. scolymus* L.), *C. cardunculus* and *C. syriaca* are crossable with each other and produce fertile hybrids.

Globe artichoke is a perennial herb reaching a height of 1-1.5m. The shoots produce a rosette of deeply cut pinnatified, wooly leaves of 5-8cm long. The flowers are borne terminally on the main stem and laterals. The edible portion consists of immature tender bases of scale-like leaves as well as receptacle or fleshy base upon which the flower buds are borne. These heads range from 2.5-10.0cm in diameter. The flower head is large and composed of many florets which are fertile. The above ground portion dies every year during winter and the crown of individual plant decays after a year's growth. New growth emerges in spring renewed by offshoots from the rootstocks.

Varieties

Very little work has been done on crop improvement and it is considered a largely unexploited genetic source. Green Globe and Purple Globe are popular cultivar, while fresh market cultivars like Violet de Provence, Catanese and Spinosa Sarda and processing varieties Bianco Tarantino and Precoce di Jesi are also under cultivation. Other cultivars include Bull, Tudella, E 15, Brindisino and Romonesco.

Soil and Climate

Globe artichoke grows on many types of soil but deep, sandy, well-drained soil with adequate organic matter is ideal. The optimum soil pH is 6-7.5. It is a cool season crop that can be grown successfully at a temperature of 12-18°. The temperature above 22° results in tough buds and tendency to spread. The root can tolerate and survive freezing temperature, while aerial portion are injured. A light frost may not destroy the edible quality of the bud, but causes blistered appearance, which will affect the marketability. Freezing temperature (-2° to 1°) prior to harvest kills the buds and above ground growths. This will result in delayed harvest up to 6-8 weeks.

Field Preparation and Manuring

The field is brought to fine tilth by repeated ploughings and beds or ridges are formed at a spacing of 2.4m. A basal dose of 25 tonnes of FYM and 60-100kg/ha of N, 50-60kg/ha of P and 150-200kg/ha of K are applied. The planting of suckers or off-shoots is taken up along the rows at spacing of 1.8m during February-March, when they come out of dormancy and start new growth. The plants are set at a depth of 15-20cm.

Propagation and Planting

The plants are propagated by seeds or by suckers or off-shoots from the older plants in November and stored in cool moist place to prevent drying till February. Sometimes even the old crown is split into several pieces each with a stem. Plants raised from seeds are highly variable and thus less popular. Hence uniform crops can be raised from suckers or off-shoots obtained from selected plants. The suckers or off-shoots are removed when they are 30-45cm high. For seed propagation, raised seed beds are prepared, seeds broadcast and seedlings of 10-12.5cm height are used for planting.

Irrigation

A soaking irrigation is given at the time of planting and in early stages frequent irrigation are necessary for good establishment of crop. After each irrigation, interspaces between the rows are hoed for control of weeds. Application of Trifluralin 1.2kg + Diuron 1kg/ha before planting gives good control of broad leaves grass leaves and stems are cut off below the ground level and allowed to decompose in the soil.

Harvesting and Yield

Plants grown from seeds come to bearing in about 8 months, while in plants raised from suckers, the first harvest commences 6-7 months after planting. The harvesting season start from September-October. A mature plant will produce 12 or more stems and 40-50 edible buds. The harvesting continues throughout the winter season. The buds are selected for harvest on the basis of compactness, size and age. Buds which are old and compact become fibrous and inedible. Though each stem has several buds, the terminal one is the most desirable. Each bud is cut along with 2-2.5cm long stem.The average yield is 10-12 tonnes/ha.

Storage

The bud can be stored at 0° and 90-95 per cent relative humidity for a period of 3-4 weeks. Precooling of buds at 5°C is practiced to achieve lesser weight loss, discolouration and incidence of decay than buds that buds that are not precooled.

Physiological Disorder

i. Scuffing
ii. Split bracts
iii. Detached epidermis
iv. Bracket wilting

} All are marketing disorders

DRUMSTICK

The Moringaceae is a single genus family with 14 known species. Of these, *Moringa oleifera* Lam. belonging to the family Moringaceae is a soft wood tree, native of India,occurring wild in the sub-Himalayan regions of Northern India and now grown worldwide in the tropics and sub-tropics. In India it is grown all over the subcontinent for its tender pods and also for its leaves and flowers. The pod of moringa is a very popular vegetable in South Indian cuisine and valued for their distinctly inviting flavour. It is commonly called 'horse radish' tree (arising from the taste of a condiment prepared from the roots) or drumstick (arising from the shape of a pod), or ben oil tree (arising from the ben oil extracted from seed) and has a host of other country specific vernacular names.

Nutritive Value and Uses

Drumstick is grown for its nutrient rich tender, but full-grown pods, leaves and flowers which are used for culinary preparations. Fruits are rich in vitamin C(120 mg/100g), carotene (110 mg), phosphorus (110 mg) and minerals like magnesium (28mg), potassium (259mg), sulphur (137mg), chlorine (423mg) *etc.* The crop is grown in homesteads for family use or cultivated commercially for market. Tender leaves and flowers are comparable to that of colocasia in vitamins and minerals and have great role for combating malnutrition of urban and rural masses. Certain moringa types principally grown for its foliage are reported from West Indies. Drumstick roots are good substitute for horse radish. Root, bark and seed have many industrial uses also.

Botany

Drumstick is a small or medium sized perennial tree of about 10 m height with fragile and corky stem. The leaves are usually tri-pinnate with elliptic leaflets. Pods are pendulous and length ranges from 20 cm to 100cm. Seeds are trigonous with wings on angles. Flowers are produced on current season growth on large and erect panicles or monocladial cyme. Flowers were yellowish creamy white and sweet smelling. Individual flowers are bisexual, zygomorphic and pedicellate. Calyx and corolla consist of five sepals and petals. Androecium also has five stamens alternating with five stamindodes. Gynoecium has a superior, one celled and three carpelled ovary containing many ovules on parietal placentation. Stigma is truncate. Flowering in drumstick varies from place to place and is greatly influenced by rain, temperature, humidity,wind, soil temperature, soil moisture *etc.* Under South Indian condition, one or two distinct peak periods of flowering noticed. Peak period of flowering in central parts of Kerala is December-January while in southern part it is February-March and July-August with maximum flowering in February-March. Under Coimbatore and Bangalore conditions, flowering seasons are March-May and July-September respectively. Anthesis continues throughout the day. Two anthesis peaks *i.e.,* 2.00 pm and 4.00 am. are noticed at Thiruvannthapuram. In most parts of Tamil Nadu, flowering is from 4.30 am. to 6.30 p.m. In southern part of Kerala, stigma becomes receptive one day prior to flower opening and continues with maximum receptivity on the day of opening and a sudden decline thereafter.

Varieties

PKM-1

This "seed moringa", propagated through seeds is developed at Horticultural Research Station, TNAU, Periyakulam. Plants grow to a height of 4-6m and come to flower in 90-100 days after planting. The first harvest starts 160-170 days after planting and on an average each tree bears 200-225 fruits/year. Pods are 65-70 cm long with 6.3cm girth and 150g weight. Fruits are green coloured and highly pulpy.

PKM-2

This "seed moringa", propagated through seeds, is also developed at Horticultural Research Station, TNAU, Periyakulam. Pods are extra-long (125-130 cm), pulpy and suitable for homesteads.

Dhanraj

This is also an annual drumstick propagated through seeds and is evolved at KRC College of Agriculture, UAS, Arabhavi, Karnataka.

KM-1 (Kudumianmalai 1)

Bushy variety propagated through seeds. Plants come to bear 6 months after planting and can be rationed for 2-3 years. Productivity 400-500 fruits/year. Developed at Anna Pannai, Kudumianmalai of Pudukottai.

Local Cultivars	*Description*
Jaffna moringa	A perennial type which bares 60-90cm long pods with soft flesh and good taste.
Chavakacheri muringa	A perennial type producing 90-120 cm long pods.
Chemmuringa	This perennial type flowers throughout year and bears red tipped fruits.
Yazhpanam muringa	A perennial type which bares 60-90cm long pods with soft flesh and good taste.
Pal muringai	Pods having thicker pulp and better taste
Puna muringa	Thinner fruits.
Kodikal muringa	produces short pods of 15-20cm long and is sued as support for betel vine plants. Propagated by seeds.

Climate and Soil

Drumstick is predominantly a crop of dry and arid tracts. However intensive cultivation with good irrigation and systematic cultural practices will give good yield especially for annual type. The plant put forth luxuriant growth at 25-30°. Higher temperature results in heavy flower shedding. Crop is also injured severely by frost. Though the crop comes up well in all types of soil, performance is better in sandy loam rich in organic matter. A pH range of 6.0–6.72 is most ideal.

Propagation

Perennial types are propagated through limb cutting of 90-100cm length and 5-8cm diameter. Annual types are propagated by seeds. Average seed weight is 0.288 g and 10 g contain 35 seeds. Seeds @ 625 g/ha can be either sown in pits or transplanted after raising seedlings in polythene bags. Transplanting of seedlings can be made one month after sowing. It is always advisable to raise a few plants additionally in polythene bags for purpose of gap filling. Time of sowing of seeds for annual seed drumstick or planting of limb cuttings varies from region to region depending on receipt of monsoon.

Field Preparation

Field is ploughed 3-4 times. Apply FYM @ 20 t/ha at last ploughing. Take pits of size 45 x 45 x 45 cm at a spacing of 6.0 x 6.0m for perennial types and 2.5 x 2.5 m for annual types, apply 10 kg FYM and fill up pits.

Intercultural, Manure and Fertilizers

To facilitate side branches, shoot may be nipped off when the seedlings are at 75 cm height. Apply 100g Urea, 100g Super phosphate and 50 g MOP and irrigate heavily. Top dress plants with 100g Urea again 3 months after first application. Provide light irrigation for early emergence of seedlings for annual type.After harvest of main crop, annual types are cut back to one-meter height from ground level for rationing. These rationed plants develop new shoots and start bearing four to five months after rationing. Likewise, about three ratoon crops can be taken. At each and every ratoon crop, plants are supplied with N, P and K nutrients as already mentioned along with 20-35kg of FYM and irrigate.

Harvesting and Yield

After 6 months of planting, harvesting it can be done. On average 200 fruits could be obtained. After harvesting, pruning of plants is done to get more branches and fruits in the next season.From the vegetative propagation tall plants are obtained. Therefore, after harvesting, branches have to be axed. Initially, about 90 fruits per plants are obtained but with the passage of times about 800 - 1000 drumstick are obtained per plant.

Insect-Pest and their Management

Bud Worm (*Noorda moringae*)

The Larva bores into flower buds and causes shedding to alarge extent. *N. moringae*occured in South India which caused 78 per cent bud damage when the infestation was severe. Adults are small sized moths with dark brown forewings and white hind wings withdark brown border. Creamy oval eggs are laid in singly or in groups on buds. Fecundity is 248 eggs/female. The larva is dirty brown with a prominent mid dorsal stripe and black head. It pupates in soil or on the ground surface in earthern cocoon.

Management

i. Plough around trees to expose and kill pupae

ii. Collect and destroy damaged buds along with caterpillar

iii. Set up light trap @ 1/ha.

iv. Spray insecticides like chloropyriphos 50 EC or quinolphos 25 per cent EC 2 ml/lit of water.

Leaf Caterpillar (*Noorda blitealis*)

The caterpillars build silken webs by joining the ventral side of the adjacent leaflets and remain inside the web on the leaves and make them papery. Severe infestation causes complete defoliation.

Management

i. Plough around trees to expose and kill pupae.

ii. Collect and destroy silken webs and caterpillars in the initial stages of infestation.

iii. Set up light trap @ 1/ha.

iv. Spray insecticides like chloropyriphos 50 EC or quinolphos 25 per cent EC 2 ml/lit of water.

Diseases and their Management

Brown Leaf Spot (*Cercospora* spp.)

The symptoms appear as scattered brown spots appear onthe leaves and then spread to cover them entirely. Coalescing of spots leads to irregular and blighted appearance of the leaves. The leaves turn yellow and fall off prematurely.

Management

Foliar sprays of Carbendazim, Difolatan, mancozeb,maneb, zineb, metiram have been reported effective for the control of the disease.

Septoria Leaf Spot (*Septoria lycopersici*)

Circular spots with whitish grey centre and dark brownmargins are seen on the leaves, stem and calyx. Centre of the spots shows minute black glistening pin head sized pycinida. Severe infection causes defoliation during rainy season.

Management

Spray applications of various fungicides such as carbendazim, mancozeb, copper oxychloride, is found to be effective against the disease.

Powdery Mildew (*Leveillula taurica*)

The symptoms appear as white to light grey powdery growthon the under surface of the leaves and the corresponding upper surface exhibits yellow lesions with brown necrotic centres. Affected leaves curl upwards and shed profusely. Affected plants lose their vigour and remain barren. Yield is very much reduced.

Management

Spraying wettable sulphur 0.2 per cent at gives better control.

Dust Sulphur 25 kg/ha or spray Dinocap 2 ml/lit or Tridemorph 0.5 ml/lit or Carbendazim 1 g/lit or Wettable sulphur 2 g/lit immediately after noticing the disease and repeat after 15 days or four sprays of Triademorph (0.5 per cent) at 10 days interval from 30 days after sowing.

RHUBARB

Rhubarb, or "pie plant," (*Rheum rhabarbarum* L.) is a perennial of the Polygonaceae family. The economic part is the large thick leafstalk or petiole. Petioles may be green, pink, or white depending on the variety. The plant is a herbaceous perennial with large fleshy underground rhizome having a fibrous root system.

Origin, Distribution and Botany

Rhubarb is a native of temperate Asia, probably Siberia, introduced in Europe probably in 1608. It was first grown in Italy. During late 18th century it was introduce in USA. The genus Rheum contains about 25 species. Small greenish-white flowers are borne in panicles, which emerge successively. Since they are protandrous, self-pollination within a flower does not take place. Lower flowers are fertilized by pollen from upper flowers.

Varieties

Rhubarb can be grown as an outdoor plant and as a forcing plant. Cultivars of rhubarb may also be chosen according to the cooler to their petioles.

For Outdoor Production

i. *Mac Donald*: The cultivar has large red stalks. It is vigorous and upright growing.
ii. *Valentine*: another red stalked cultivar that is popular for growing in home gardens.

For forcing: Timperley, Early Victoria, Crimson Red and Sutton are used.

Green-stalked cultivar: Victoria, is a heavy producer and excellent for commercial purposes. Pink- stalked cultivar: Sutton

Soil and Climate

Rhubarb is a cold resistant plant. Under a mild winter coupled with rainless summer, the plant exhibits the habit of dormancy during summer and grows well, during winter and spring season. When the winter is severe and summer is mild, the plant enters into dormancy during freezing winter but grows during summer and spring. The critical low temperature would be 3.3^{o} below which the vegetative parts of the plants are killed. Similarly, when the temperature goes 23.9^{o} during summer and below 4.5^{o} during winter the plant does not grow well.

A well-drained loamy soil with good organic matter would be the most ideal soil for rhubarb. Though it tolerates soil-acidity to certain extant neutral soil would be the best for the growth.

Planting

Rhubarb is usually propagated by dividing the crowns formed during the previous season. Crowns are divided in late fall or early spring. Plants must be divided and reset every 4 years to keep the bed in vigorous condition. Plants not divided may become large and stalks may become more numerous than desired. Seed stalks should be removed as they appear.

Typical spacing for commercial rhubarb planting is rows 4 ft apart with plants 4 ft apart in row. Trenches are dug prior to planting, generally 6 inch deep. Crown pieces are placed 2 inches below the surface of the soil in the trench. Soil is pulled over the soil and firmed. Good drainage is essential for growing rhubarb.

Fertilizer and Manuring

Soil with low organic matter should be supplied with well rotten organic manuring @ 50 tonnes/ha before ploughing. It has to be supplemented with 100-150 kg of each NPK.

During first year the nutrients are incorporated in to the soil just before planting in the bottom of the furrows.

Irrigation

The rhubarb plant responds well to moisture, although reliable yields can be obtained with minimal watering. Irrigate prior to harvest to increase crop yield and delay irrigation after harvest until plant injuries have healed.

Mulching

Straw may be applied in late fall or during the winter as a mulch to keep down weeds and ensure a cleaner harvest environment from soil. Straw mulch may also be used to surface burn a held to control diseases and insects (especially potato stem borer).

Harvesting

Rhubarb is harvested from the second year of planting. During harvesting the stalks are pulled (they are not cut) and then leaf blades are cut off. Harvesting can be done for a period of 8-10 weeks every year. The plants can be retained in the field for about 10-12 years. When they very much crowded and the leaf stalk have become small, thee plants can be uprooted from the field. The stalks are then washed with water and then tied in bunches of 0.5kg for local market.

Storage

Store only fresh stalks in good condition. Rhubarb can be hydrocooled or forced-air cooled following harvest. Store at a temperature of 0 °C and a relative humidity of 95 to 100 per cent. Stalks can be held 2 to 4 weeks under these conditions. Provide ample air circulation on all sides to prevent heating.

Insect and Pests

Potato Stem Borer

The potato stem borer is a caterpillar, which when fully grown is about 3.5cmin length and pinkish-white in colour. The first stages of the insect attack only weeds, couch grass in particular. Later they move into plants with thicker stems, such as rhubarb. They may move from stem to stem, boring into the centre of the stalk. The adult moths lay their eggs on thestems of grasses in August. The eggs do not hatch until the following spring. Damage can be accepted in June and early July. Serious infestation can lead to an unmarketable crop.

Management

i. This pest is not a problem when couch grass and other weeds are controlled in and around the rhubarb plantation.

ii. Weeds should be controlled to make the field less attractive for egg laying by the adult moth.

iii. Early spring burning of affected fields or field margins will effectively control this pest.

Tarnished Plant Bug

Adult tarnished plant bugs are light brown to reddish brown in colour and about5-6 mm in length. They occur throughout the season. They are very active and quick moving. They can damage rhubarb by feeding on young leaves. They pierce the stalk with their mouth parts and cause wilting and distortion of the leaves. Tarnished plant bugs are mainly a pest of new plantings.

Management

Keep plantings and adjacent areas weed free. Avoid planting adjacent to legumes.

Slugs

Slugs may be a problem in plantings with heavy soils, poor drainage and in weedy situations. Slugs fed at night, by rasping the surface of stems, leaving unsightly scars, which reduce the sale ability of the stem.

Management

i. Provide good soil drainage. Keep weeds under control.

ii. Remove leaves and trash from the field when harvesting.

iii. Do not use manure and/or mulches in areas of field prone to slug damage.

Diseases

Leaf Spots (*Ramularia* and *Ascochyta*)

These fungi cause circular, or angular spots, variable in size having beige centers surrounded by arid zone. When affected tissue dies, it may drop out, leaving large ragged holes in the foliage. Fungi overwinter in infected plant debris and in infected propagation stock.

Management

i. Remove and destroy leaves following the first heavy frost. During harvest, remove stems with spotted leaves first.

ii. Apply fungicide used for Botrytis control.

Botrytis Rot

May cause a leaf, stem and crown rot of forced rhubarb. Disease intensifies where there is poorair circulation and high humidity.

Management

i. Practice strict sanitation.

ii. Apply recommended fungicide at first sign of disease and at 7day intervals.

Root and Crown Rots

Plants become unthrifty. Leaves may turn yellow to red and collapse. The crowns, when sectioned, exhibit a brown-black decay. Large roots lack small feeder roots. Larger roots may have large brown-black lesions present.

Management

i. Purchase healthy propagation stock.

ii. Select well drained fields.

iii. Remove and destroy diseased plants.

CURRY LEAF

Curry leaf is an important perennial tree vegetable cum spice crop of India. It is an under exploited crop. The leaves are widely used in Indian cookery for flavouring foodstuff. The leaves have slightly pungent, bitter and feebly acidic taste and they retain their flavour and other qualities even after drying. Ground curry leaf with mature coconut kernel and spices form an excellent preserve. Curry leaf also used in many of the Indian Ayurvedic and Unani prescription. It has many industrial values and medicinal uses.

Origin, Distribution and Botany

The curry leaf is native to India and is found nearly everywhere in the Indian subcontinent. It is also found in Srilanka and many parts of South East Asia including Indonesia, Burma, Thailand *etc.* Curry leaves are mentioned in ancient Indian text. The Tamil literature specifically mentions about their use and importance. The use of curry in Indian food has also been mentioned in Ancient Kannada text. Curry-leaf or *Murraya koenigii* (Linn) sprengel belongs to the orange family *i.e.* Rutaceae. Its vernacular names in other languages are Hindi -Kathnim, Mitha neem or Kurrypatta, Assamese -Norsingha, Bisharhari; Bengali -Bar- ganga, koria phulli; Marathi -Karhi nimb, poospale, Gandla; Gujarati -Goranimb; Kannada -Karibevu; Malayalam – Kariveppila; Oriya Barsan, Basango; Punjabi -Curry patia; Tamil -Karivempu; Telugu -Karf paku; Sanskrit -Surebi nimbu.

The shrub is more or less deciduous in nature. The height varies from 1 to 6m. A strong-smelling shrub or small tree, leaves are pinnate, pubescent, or glabrous, 9 -27 foliate. Leaflets are small, obliquely ovate, elliptic, lanceolate or rhomboid, crenulate and punetate. Flowers are white in colour and many flowered and they are pedunded corymbs. Fruits are ovoid or sub-globose, becomes black when ripe. Seeds are rugose embedded in mucilage

Nutritive Value and Uses

Curry leaves usually have moisture: 66.3 per cent; protein: 6.1 per cent; fat (ether extract) 1.0 per cent; carbohydrates: 16.0 per cent; fiber: 6.4 per cent; and iron: 3.1mg mineral matter: 4.2 per cent calcium: 810mg. phosphorus 600mg. carotene as vitamin A -12600 IU nicotinic acid -2.3mg and vitamin C 4mg per 100 gills. Thiamine and riboflavin are absent. The leaves are a fair source of vitamin A. They are also rich source of calcium, but due to presence of oxalic acid in high concentration (total oxalates 1.35 per cent, soluble extracts 1.15 per cent) its nutrient availability is affected.

The chemical composition of green (fresh) curry leaves at 3 stages of maturity namely tender, medium and mature was determined recently at CFTRI, Mysore on Moisture free basis. The composition of leaves at these three stages is as follows. Protein; 5.44, 6.44 and 7.19 per cent, fat: 3.3, 4.74 and 6.15 per cent; sugar: 14.9, 17.9 and 18.9 per cent; starch: 11.4, 14.2 and 14.6 per cent; crude fiber: 5.8, 6.2 and 6.2 per cent; volatile oil: 0.82, 0.55 and 0.48 per cent; acetone extractive (oleoresin): 1.6, 1.4 and 1.3 per cent; total ash (mineral matter): 12.54, 12.7 and 13.1 per cent and acid in soluble ash: 1.2, 1.3 and 1.35 per cent.

It will thus be seen that with advancing maturity, there was a gradual decrease in volatile oil and oleoresin (acetone extracted) while there was a progressive increase in all other items of analysis. Vacuum self-drying of curry leaves gave a better product of greenish colour than dried by any other method. The free amino acids present in the leaves are asparagine, serine, aspartic acid, glutamic acid, threonine, alanine, proline, tyrosine, tryptophan, alpha aminobutyric acid, phenylalanine, leucine, isoleucine, traces of lysine, arginine and histidine. The leaves also contain a crystalline glucoside koenigin and a resin. Twigs and leaves contain 0.8 per cent potash (on dry matter basis).

Climate and Soil

Curry leaf can be cultivated in a wide range of soils. Red sandy loam soil is ideal for its cultivation. It can tolerate temperature up to 37°C. But below 16°C, its growth is affected.

Varieties

There are 2 improved varieties of curry leaf:

i. DWD 1

ii. DWD 2.

Both of these have a good aroma. They have an oil content of 5.22 per cent and 4.09 per cent respectively. They are mainly cultivated in Karnataka. DWD 1 is sensitive to winter season. During winter its growth is poor, whereas DWD 2 is winter insensitive. It gives higher yield than DWD 1. 'Senkaampu' is a local cultivar grown in many parts of Tamil Nadu.

Propagation

Curry leaf is mainly propagated through seeds. For raising seedlings, well-ripe fruits are collected from high-yielding plants. The seeds are sown either in nursery or poly bags filled with a mixture of 1:1:1 sand, soil and farmyard manure. Seeds germinate in 3 weeks. One-year-old seedlings are planted in the main field. It can also be propagated by root suckers. There are a number of root suckers near its plants. They are separated from the main plant during rainy season and planted immediately.

Field Preparation

The field for commercial cultivation is ploughed and harrowed two or three times and is cleaned from stubbles and stones. In deep, fertile and light soil transplanting is done directly in small pits. Whereas in poor and hard soil, pits are taken at the size of at least 1.5 x 1.5 x 2 ft. length, width and depth respectively. The pits are dug about six months before planting and left open to weather for few months after which they are filled with well rotten composts and green leaves.

Planting

Planting in the main field is done during the monsoon season. The main field is ploughed thoroughly. Pits of 30cm x 30cm size are dug at a spacing of 4m x 4m. Farmyard manure @ 10kg/pit is applied.

Manuring and Fertilization

Usually curry leaf plant is not given inorganic fertilizers. But for higher yields, its plant may be given 10kg farmyard manure and NPK @ 60:80:40g/plant/year. The fertilizers may be applied at the onset of the monsoon.

Aftercare

The pit should be irrigated if there is no rain. The plant should be irrigated at 3-day intervals, if there are no rains. The field should be kept weed free. The plants should be trained and pruned to maintain a height of 1m. Their terminal buds are removed to encourage lateral branching. A minimum of 5–6 branches are kept per plant.

Irrigation

If irrigation facilities are there the plants should be regularly irrigated. However moisture conservation techniques should be adopted both to conserve rain water or irrigation water. Mulching is an advantageous practice. At the same time adequate drainage facilities are provided

Interculture

Weeding and other intercultural operations are done as and when needed. Hoeing and weeding at the middle and end of rainy season and at the end of winter season will be sufficient.

Topping

Leaves are economic product of curry leaf tree. To encourage maximum leaf production the plants are topped first at around 100 cm height. This encourages profuse branching on all sides. Allow them to grow and have leaves. Then they are again pruned to encourage further branching. After every pruning or topping of branches additional dosage of NPK and compost mixture should be applied and irrigated. This will result in profuse growth of leaves. Topping is done in such a way that each plant acquires a good shape allowing all branches and leaves to have adequate sunlight.

Harvesting

The pruning or topping is also a part of harvesting of leaves. The leaf quality will decrease if the plant is allowed to flower and fruit. So, unless seed production is not indented, pruning and harvesting of leaves should be done before flowering. Similarly, where there is winter harvesting is done before the leaves start shedding. Harvested leaves are graded, bundled and marketed or sent to processing units for extraction of oil.

Yield

Fully grown curry tree can yield nearly 100 kg of leaves each year Curry leaves are picked 15 months after planting. Commercial harvest can be started from 3-year-old plants. With good management, normal yield can be obtained up to the age of 20–25 years. The leaves can be harvested at two-and-a-half to three months intervals, the average yield being 20–25 tonnes/ha.

Diseases and Pests

Fortunately, curry leaf plant is not seriously infected by diseases and pests. If needed very mild pesticides can be used at least 15 days before harvesting of leaves. If there are chances of incidence a preventive spray of malathion or tobacco decoction, *etc.* could be sprayed. For controlling soil borne pests and diseases 1-2 kg of neem cake per plant per year is recommended.

Chapter 2

Exotic Vegetables

Introduction

Introducing new vegetable crops and their successful cultivation leads to both horizontal and vertical diversification. Exotic vegetables are good in taste and have high nutritive value. Most of the exotic vegetables can be used in salad and soups. These crops are very remunerative. Broccoli, Brussels sprout, Knol-Khol, Red cabbage, Lettuce, Asparagus, Baby Sweet Corn, Snow Peas, Chive, Garden beet, Kale, *etc*. are important exotic vegetables.

Globalization has brought many opportunities and changes in developing country like India. Some of the major changes along with the globalization are the changes in the living standards and living style among Indian people. The most visible change which we can notice is the change is the food habits among the new generations. With the introduction of new food chains like McDonald's, Mainland china, California Pizza, Pizza Hut etc., the people in India are now developing new test buds to accept new food items. Preparation of these food items need many exotic vegetables like Baby corn, Red cabbage, Broccoli, Colored bell pepper, lettuce, mushroom, Asparagus,Olives etc. some of which are imported from other countries. Due to huge supply chain, more demand and less supply these vegetables comes very costly in the Indian market.

Scope

Exotic vegetables; primarily the European types is one such large group, cultivation of which on commercial lines will not only bring much desired diversification but will also boost export. Due to increasing foreign culture and increasing living standards, the demand of exotic vegetables is continuously increasing in cosmopolitan cities and five star hotels. These are good in taste and have high nutritive value. Most of the exotic vegetables can be used in salad and soups. These crops are very remunerative. Broccoli, Brussels sprout, Knol- Khol,

Red cabbage, Lettuce, Asparagus, Baby Sweet Corn, Snow Peas, chive, Garden beet, Kale, Swiss chard, Parsley, Parsnip, Chinese cabbage and Leek are important exotic vegetables. Some parts in India have a great potential to cultivate these exotic vegetables. Baby corn cultivation has gained popularity as valued vegetable in Delhi, U.P, Haryana, Maharashtra, Karnataka, A.P. and Meghalaya. Cost of production in high technology Greenhouse will lead to again high cost of cultivation, low cost polyhouse can be a suitable alternative of it. These vegetables are highly susceptible to diseases and pest hence they needs immense care while cultivation. One of the critical challenge among the exotic vegetable cultivator will be the postharvest handling since these crops are climacteric in nature and are highly sensitive to change in temperature they need proper cold storage chain till point of sales to the end consumer. Establishing postharvest units and canning these vegetables before transportation to far places may be the solution. The vegetables are rich source of roughages and essential nutrients and vitamins and exotic vegetables are no exception to these properties. The medicinal properties of some of the important exotic vegetables are as follow:

Medicinal Properties of some Exotic Vegetables

Vegetable	*Medicinal Properties*
Broccoli	A compound called Sulphoraphane isolated from it blocks the growth of tumors in mice treated with a cancer causing toxin. It may have future applications in human cancer treatment
Asparagus	As it is rich in alkaline salts it helps in reducing acidity in blood, Asparagines extracted from it is a medicine for treatment of cardiac dropsy and chronic gout.
Lettuce	Ideal food for anaemia, No iron tonic needed if lettuce taken.
Globe artichoke	Used for treatment of gastric disorders
Parsley	Contains chemical called apiin which stops the gas formation and aids in digestion. Highly useful for blood pressure patients.
Rhubarb	Recommended for liver diseases, stomach disorders and to eradicate ringworm.
Leek	It cures coughs and bronchitis and kills germs of digestive canal.

These can be grown throughout the year in hills and during winter season in plains. These crops are being grown in Punjab, Maharashtra, Gujarat, Karnataka, Bangalore, New Delhi, Uttaranchal and Himachal Pradesh. In Himachal Pradesh, these vegetables are grown as off- season and farmers are getting remunerative returns. Such vegetables, if organically produced, fetch more prices. The method of farming and selling exotic vegetables differs from the typical farming. One major progressive farmer of respective area takes the responsibility of collection and marketing and enters into a contract with a number of smaller farmers in the same region. Multinational companies distribute the seeds of exotic vegetables among farmers and take the responsibility of buying back the entire produce at a fixed rate for a year. Few multinational companies have also started processing of few exotic vegetables and the produce is being marketed to the neighboring European countries.

Improved Varieties of some Exotic Vegetable Crops

Crop	*Varieties/Hybrids*
Asparagus	Palam Sel. 841, Perfection, Block Imperial 84
Lettuce	Great Lakes, Chinese Yellow, Slobolt, Iceberg
Chinese cabbage	Chihilli, Wongbok, Pok choi
Brussels sprout	Hilds Ideal, Catskill, Topscore, Jade Cross
Broccoli	Pusa Broccoli-1, Grand Central, Midway, Premier, Premium crop
Baby Corn	VL-42, MEH-114, ME 4-133 Gold Cup, Silver Queen
Cherry tomato	Evita, Cherita, Sun cherry, Cherry wonder
Celery	Standard Bearer, Ford Hook Emperor, Giant Pascal, Wright Globe Giant
Leek	London Flag, American Flag, Conqueror, Musselburg
Parsley	Moss Curled, Curled Dwarf, Hamburg

Production Technology

Seed Sowing/Planting

Asparagus grown from seeds are sown in well prepared nursery bed where it is kept through out growing season. About 2-2.5 kg of seeds is sufficient to raise crowns for planting a hectare plot. The seeds are sown in lines of 50 cm apart in nursery bed at 2.5-5 cm deep during mild climatic conditions when the temperature is 20° C (in March or July). Before sowing, seeds should be soaked in water for few hours at 26-30° C for better germination. Well grown one year old crowns (under ground roots) are ideal for commercial planting. Since asparagus is dioecious, male and female flowers are produced separately on different plants. Male plants bear more spears than the female plants. It is not possible to recognise sex of plants in nursery but the plants are selected according to their root growth. The crown having good growth and branching are male plants and these should be selected. The

crowns are dug out from the nursery bed and planted at 50 cm apart in rows and 1 m spacing is kept between the rows. The crowns are planted in furrow-ridge system.

For **Broccoli, Brussels sprouts, celery, Chinese cabbage, leek, lettuce and parsley**, raised nursery bed is prepared during August-September in northern plains and the seeds are sown in September and October. The seeds are sown in 1-2 cm depth and covered with grasses followed by sprinkler irrigation. After germination, the grass cover is removed. Regular inspection and care should be taken up for raising healthy seedlings. The seed rate of 750g per hectare is recommended for growing of broccoli and Brussels sprouts. The seedlings of one month old are used for transplanting in prepared field in September-November. The seedlings are normally transplanted with a spacing of 60 cm between rows and 45 cm between plants. In lettuce, the spacing of 30 cm between plants and 30-45 cm between rows is maintained in the field and seedlings of 5-6 weeks old are transplanted in the well prepared field. For planting one hectare, 500 g seeds is sufficient for raising the seedlings of lettuce. In celery, planting one hectare of land requires 150-200 g of seeds and two months old seedlings of 10-15 cm height are transplanted in well manured plots at a spacing of 60 cm between rows and 15 cm between plants. In leek, 5-6 kg of seed is required to raise the seedlings for one hectare and one to one and a half months old seedlings are transplanted at a spacing of 30 x 15 cm in the prepared field. In parsley, about 200-250 g of seeds is required to raise the seedlings for one hectare. Its seeds are very small and slow to germinate and soaking the seeds for few hours helps in quick germination. Two months old are transplanted in the field during October-November at a spacing of 30 cm within rows and 15 cm within plants for proper crop growth.

Cherry tomato can be raised twice in a year under northern Indian plains. For raising spring-summer crop, the seeds are sown in nursery beds during November and December and seedlings are transplanted from mid January to early February when the danger of frost is over. The seedlings should be protected from frost in the nursery by covering the beds with polythene sheets and sirkies. The raised nursery beds are prepared and they should be drenched with 0.2 per cent captan and sterilised with 40 per cent formalin and half litre of formalin is sufficient for one square metre bed. Sometimes 10 per cent formaldehyde is used for fumigating the nursery beds and the beds are covered with polythene for 24 hours soon after fumigation. The late *kharif* or early autumn-winter crop is raised by growing the nursery in July. The seeds are sown @ 400-500g/ha after 5-6 days of fumigation and covered with grasses. The grasses are removed soon after the germination of seeds which normally takes 5 to 7 days. One or two months old seedlings depending on the season (*kharif* or winter) are transplanted in the main field at 75 x 60 cm or 60 x 60 cm spacing. Planting is done normally in raised beds of 60 cm width and seedlings are placed on one side of the beds. This provides proper moisture for the plants to stand and survive.

Baby corn is raised in monsoon season in northern plains. The seeds are directly sown in first week of July in the rows of 75-90 cm apart at 2.5-5 cm deep. Plant to plant distance is maintained at 20-30 cm. Seed rate varies from 12-14 kg per hectare depending on the seed size and plant population desired. Seed soaking with bavistin @ 3 g/kg of seeds is required before sowing.

Manures and Fertilizers

Asparagus needs FYM @ 20 tonnes/ha and NPK 120 kg, 120 kg and 100 kg per hectare per year in two split doses. First dose is applied when growth starts and second when harvesting is completed.

Broccoli, Brussels sprouts and Chinese cabbage require plenty of manure and fertilizers like cauliflower but they need more nitrogen especially in late growing season. For the better crop yield, 15-20 tonnes of FYM, 80 kg of nitrogen, 80 kg of phosphate and 40 kg of potash per hectare should be applied just before transplanting. Full dose of phosphorus and potassium and half of nitrogen are applied during soil preparation and another half of nitrogen is applied in two split doses as top dressing after 30 days and 45 days of transplanting. Boron and molybdenum deficiency can be overcome by applying borax @ 10-12 kg/ha and sodium molybdate @ 4-6 kg/ha in the soil.

Celery being exhaustive and shallow rooted crop, it requires a fertiliser dose of 140 kg nitrogen, 60 kg phosphorus and 60 kg potassium per hectare to raise a successful crop. Well rotten FYM @ 20 tonnes per hectare is mixed in the soil during soil preparation. A heavy dose of nitrogen and potassium fertilization appears to favour boron deficiency. Hence, application of 10-20 kg borax per hectare has been recommended. Plants sprayed thoroughly with 1.5 per cent boric acid solution reduced the incidence of cracked stem.

Cherry tomato requires 20-25 tonnes of well rotten farm yard manure, 200 kg of single super phosphate, 100 kg of ammonium sulpahte and 75 kg of potash per hectare. These are incorporated during soil preparation. Another dose of urea @ 100 kg/ha is applied as top dressing in two split doses after 30 and 45 days of transplanting.

In **leek**, during soil preparation the use of 25 tonnes of FYM, 75 kg of nitrogen, 100 kg phosphorous and 100 kg potassium is recommended per hectare for successful crop. Another 75 kg of nitrogen is applied in two split doses after 30 days and 45 days of transplanting for better crop yield.

In **lettuce and parsley**, well rotten FYM @ 10 tonnes per hectare and fertiliser dose of 100 kg N, 60 kg P_2O_5 and 60 kg K_2O is recommended for commercial growing of lettuce in one hectare of land. On sandy and sandy loam soil, 40-50 kg of N and 75 –100 kg each of P and K per hectare should be applied as basal dose and one third to half of the nitrogen should be applied in two doses as top dressing after 30 and 45 days of planting the seedling.

Baby corn requires 20 tonnes of FYM, 100 kg nitrogen, 50 kg phosphorus and 60 kg potash per hectare for successful growth and yield. During sowing fertilizer is applied in split bands 5 cm below the seeds.

Intercultural Operation and Irrigation

In **asparagus**, hoeing and weeding should be done carefully in the crop to avoid any injury to the roots of the plants. The crop should be watered frequently or whenever required. Blanching is major operation which is carried out by moulding the soil over the rows in order to blanch the young plants.

Broccoli, Brussels sprouts, celery, Chinese cabbage, lettuce and parsley should be irrigated frequently at least once in a week or 10 days interval, if there is no rain in the season. A short period of dry weather reduces the yield markedly and these crops have responded well to supplemental irrigation. Green manuring crops are to be preceded which increase the water holding capacity and improve the soil fertility. Early season crop needs earthing up at least once when the crop is 30-45 days old for better plant growth and also to check the weeds.

In **cherry tomato**, frequent shallow cultivation should be done to control weeds. Hand weeding is best method to control weeds. Training and pruning are important operations in this crop as it has indeterminate vine growth habit. The plants may be trained on stakes, trellies or suspended on overhead wires. Trained plant gives maximum fruits per plant and easier to pick up fruits with less damage due to rot. For early market, the cherry tomato plants are pruned to single stem and tied to a stake.

Leek being shallow rooted crop, light hoeing and weeding is necessary for better growth of the plants. Two to three hoeing and hand weeding are beneficial to this crop. The plants are blanched by banking with soil. The soil is covered up to a certain plant height. Frequent light irrigations are required for growing of this crop.

Baby corn requires regular weeding and hoeing at different stages of plant growth. It requires 15-25 acre inch of water through out growing season. The critical periods of water requirement are at tasseling and silking stages. Furrow method of irrigation is generally practiced in this crop.

Harvesting and Storage

In **asparagus** green spears are harvested after third year onwards during spring, summer and again in autumn seasons. The spears are cut by a knife 3.5 cm below the soil surface. The spears of 20-25 cm length are sent to market as early as possible. They can be stored at 0-2° C and 95 per cent relative humidity for 2-3 weeks. The yield of spears varies from 4-5 tonnes/ha after fourth year of planting.

In **broccoli**, cluster of green flower buds 7-15 cm diameter which develops in the centre are cut leaving 20-25 cm of stem from the top. The flower buds are harvested before they open. Lateral shoots develop in the axil of the leaves and produce marketable heads of 3-7 cm diameter and are harvested continuously for several weeks. The harvested broccolis heads are further trimmed to a length of approximately 15 cm and bunch are made. At room temperature, broccoli heads become yellow in about 3 days.

Brussels sprouts plant takes 120 days for sprout production in north India. The sprouts should be harvested when they reach the maximum size and are firm.

Delay in harvesting leads to bursting of the sprouts. The optimum storage condition for brussels sprouts are 0° C and 95-98 per cent relative humidity to keep them marketable for 3-5 weeks.

In **celery**, each plant is harvested by cutting just below the surface. It takes 100-120 days to become ready for harvesting after transplanting the seedlings. Plants should not be allowed to become over mature as they will develop pithy petioles which will be unmarketable. The celery can be stored in trenches or in cold storage. In cold storage they are kept at 0°C and 95-98 per cent relative humidity.

Harvesting of **cherry tomato** fruits starts from 90 days after transplanting. The optimum storage condition of 12° C temperatures and 86-90 per cent relative humidity is required in cherry tomato.

Chinese cabbage becomes ready for harvest after 80-90 days of planting. At maturity the whole plant is cut from the base. The main criteria for judging the harvesting stage of heading type is that the heads must be fully developed and firm and leafy types should develop proper size and should be tender. The heads can be kept for 1 to 2 weeks in cold storage at 0°C and relative humidity of about 95 per cent.

Leeks are harvested at green stage when the stalks reach a size of 2 to 2.5 cm in diameter and are marketed in bunches like green onions. The green plants are cut by hand and they are washed and trimmed properly before marketing. The average yield of 30 tonnes/ha can be obtained from a well managed crop.

Leaf lettuce leaves are cut at tender and succulent stage. Head lettuce should be harvested while they are in firm and compact stage. Lettuce can be stored for 2-3 weeks at 0° C temperature and 90-95 per cent relative humidity.

Parsley requires 90-100 days from planting to first harvesting. The green and tender leaves are harvested and tied in bunches for market. The leaves can be stored for 2 months under refrigeration *i.e.* at 0°C with high humidity.

Baby corn should be harvested at the milk stage, which is considered to be best edible stage. In this stage the taste is sweet but the kernels are bigger in size and juice is milky in appearance. Browning of silk also indicates the harvesting of ears.

REFERENCES

Ellison J H. (1986). In: Breeding Vegetable Crops (Ed. M.J. Bassett), pp. 521 69.

D.Kumar, R.K.Bhardwaj, M.Kumar and A.Vikram (2011). Off-season vegetable production technologies, CAFT, Dr. Y.S. Parmar UHF, Nauni, Solan.pp.181-183

Moon, S.S., Munshi, A.D., Verma, V.K. and Sureja, A.K. (2006) Heterosis for biochemical traits in muskmelon (*Cucumis melo* L. *SABRAO J. Genet. Breed*. 38: 53-57.

Pritam Kalia (2011). Off-season vegetable production technologies, CAFT, Dr. Y.S. Parmar UHF, Nauni, Solan.pp.119-128

Rubatzky V E and Yamaguchi M. (1997). World Vegetables, ITP, Singapore.

Shanmugavelu K G. (1989). Production Technology of Vegetable Crops, Oxford and IBH Publishing Co. Pvt. Ltd., New Delhi.

Shukla Y R, Jain Y C and Sharma O P (eds.) (1992). Cultural Practices for Vegetable Crops in Himachal Pradesh, Directorate of Extension Education, Dr. Y.S. Parmar UHF, Nauni, Solan.

Sirohi, P.S. and Behera, T.K. (2000). Unusual exotic vegetables for higher profit. Bulletin, IARI, New Delhi, 37 p.

Thompson H C and Kelly W C. (1972). Vegetable crops, Tata McGraw Hill Publishing Co. Ltd., New Delhi.

Chapter 3

Onion Cultivation

Onion (*Allium cepa*) is an important vegetable crop and has its importance in our diets beyond doubt. It is the also world famous spice commodity, used for flavouring the dishes. Besides culinary purposes, onion is considered as valuable medicinal items. Dehydrated powder and flakes and paste prepared out of onion provide rich agro-industrial base for these commodities. India ranks second in area (13.20 lakh ha) and production (209.31 lakh tonnes) of onion next to China. Besides meeting domestic requirements, India exported 34.92 lakh tonnes of onion worth Rs. 4651.72 crores during 2016-17 (DGCIS, 2017). In past 20 years, production of onion in India has increased more than four times. The horizontal growth in area has contributed to total production rather than vertical growth per unit area. The productivity of onion (17.32 t/ha) is far low as compared to Netherlands, USA and China. Poor yielding short day genotypes, susceptibility of all available genotypes to major pests and diseases and improper or inadequate use of production technologies lower down the productivity.

Area, Production and Productivity of Onion in India (2015-2016)

State	*Area ('000 ha)*	*Production (in '000 MT)*	*Yield (Ton/ha)*
Maharashtra	522.35	6529.34	12.50
Madhya Pradesh	118.20	2848.00	24.09
Karnataka	190.21	2695.99	14.17
Rajasthan	86.31	1435.11	16.63
Gujarat	53.20	1355.78	25.48
Bihar	54.03	1247.34	23.09
Andhra Pradesh	45.02	885.42	19.67
Haryana	30.65	705.80	23.03
West Bengal	33.98	544.55	16.03

State	Area ('000 ha)	Production (in '000 MT)	Yield (Ton/ha)
Uttar Pradesh	24.96	422.75	16.94
Telangana	20.87	395.96	18.97
Tamil Nadu	36.73	380.95	10.37
Odisha	33.45	378.58	11.32
Chhattisgarh	23.49	375.99	16.01
Jharkhand	14.86	254.63	17.14
Punjab	8.50	193.71	22.79
Assam	8.47	80.31	9.48
Jammu and Kashmir	2.85	65.27	22.90
Himachal Pradesh	2.53	47.96	18.96
Uttarakhand	4.07	41.59	10.22
Others	0.87	17.49	20.10
Mizoram	2.22	8.43	3.80
Nagaland	0.68	7.14	10.50
Manipur	0.42	5.17	12.31
Meghalaya	0.52	4.60	8.85
Sikkim	0.32	1.73	5.41
Tripura	0.23	1.38	6.00
Kerala	0.14	0.28	2.00
	1320.13	**20931.25**	**15.86**

Source: NHRDF, Nashik.

Area, Production and Productivity of Garlic in India (2015-2016)

State	Area ('000 ha)	Production (in '000 MT)	Yield (Ton/ha)
Madhya Pradesh	81.17	424.50	5.23
Rajasthan	69.10	377.49	5.46
Gujarat	40.60	318.20	7.84
Uttar Pradesh	33.60	193.62	5.76
Assam	10.39	76.95	7.41
Punjab	6.46	73.74	11.41
West Bengal	3.73	36.07	9.67
Haryana	4.44	35.83	8.07
Odisha	10.90	35.50	3.26
Maharashtra	2.05	12.69	6.19
Himachal Pradesh	4.57	9.35	2.05
Karnataka	4.73	5.19	1.10
Bihar	4.25	4.00	0.94
Chhattisgarh	1.34	3.60	2.69

State	*Area ('000 ha)*	*Production (in '000 MT)*	*Yield (Ton/ha)*
Nagaland	0.29	2.89	9.97
Tamil Nadu	0.48	2.72	5.67
Uttarakhand	1.29	1.93	1.50
Meghalaya	0.28	1.11	3.96
Telangana	0.29	1.01	3.48
Jammu and Kashmir	0.71	0.56	0.79
Kerala	0.06	0.37	6.17
Arunachal Pradesh	0.03	0.01	0.33
Mizoram	0.02	0.01	0.50
Manipur	0.17	0.00	0.00
	280.95	**1617.34**	**5.76**

Source: NHRDF, Nashik.

Major Onion Producing Countries (2014)

Area Name	*(Lakh Ha)*	*Production (Lakh Ton)*	*Productivity (T/ha)*
China	10.33	225.46	22.05
India	12.03	194.01	17.01
U.S.A.	0.56	31.66	54.62
Iran (Islamic Republic of)	0.57	21.09	31.83
Russian Federation	0.85	19.94	22.59
Egypt	0.68	25.05	33.75
Turkey	0.58	17.90	28.87
Pakistan	1.33	17.40	13.05
Brazil	0.59	16.46	24.93
Netherlands	0.30	13.79	49.68
Nigeria	4.87	9.85	6.92
Mexico	0.47	13.68	29.08
Republic of Korea	0.23	15.89	57.03
Spain	0.24	13.64	52.07
Algeria	0.47	13.40	25.57
Bangladesh	1.50	13.87	8.54
Ukraine	0.58	11.08	17.80
Myanmar	0.77	12.44	15.83
Japan	0.25	11.69	44.06

Source: FAO Website.

Major Garlic Producing Countries (2012)

Area Name	*Area (Lakh Ha)*	*Production (Lakh Ton)*	*Productivity (T/ha)*
China	7.85	19.98	23.53
India	2.31	12.52	5.69
Republic of Korea	0.25	3.37	11.99
Egypt	0.10	2.63	24.34
Russian Federation	0.28	2.56	8.64
Bangladesh	0.53	3.12	5.28
Ethiopia	0.92	9.34	10.47
Myanmar	0.28	2.08	7.27
U.S.A.	0.96	1.75	18.66
Ukraine	0.21	1.91	7.62
Spain	0.20	1.77	8.99
Argentina	0.15	1.48	8.44
Brazil	0.96	0.93	10.63
Iran (Islamic Republic of)	0.82	0.74	9.00
Peru	0.75	0.81	10.73

Source: FAO Website.

Year	*Quantity (MT)*	*Value (Rs. Lakhs)*
2001-2002	506924.00	41140.53
2002-2003	545211.00	38718.70
2003-2004	840717.00	82122.59
2004-2005	941448.00	81749.13
2005-2006	778134.00	71596.71
2006-2007	1161062.00	113542.76
2007-2008	1101401.00	128582.29
2008-2009	1783280.00	224312.25
2009-2010	1873002.00	283428.18
2010-2011	1340772.00	215905.56
2011-2012	1552904.00	214142.93
2012-2013	1822760.00	229490.94
2013-2014	1358193.00	287713.03
2014-2015	1086071.85	200994.53
2015-2016	695231.32	196160.33
2016-2017	3492718.25	465172.64
2017-2018	2135421.57	438436.00

Source: NHRDF, Nashik (www.nhrdf.com).

Export of Garlic from India

Year	Quantity (MT)	Value (Rs. Lakhs)
2001-2002	657.48	159.94
2002-2003	567.39	127.21
2003-2004	1567.23	166.07
2004-2005	2236.47	387.78
2005-2006	32495.24	3741.61
2006-2007	12210.79	1930.57
2007-2008	182.47	42.40
2008-2009	858.69	209.80
2009-2010	19767.32	4452.04
2010-2011	21827.16	7731.52
2011-2012	2126.11	748.53
2012-2013	29046.86	4898.93
2013-2014	23869.27	6352.08
2014-2015	12550.56	3357.64
2015-2016	4804.47	1651.81
2016-17	18910.01	11789.76
2017-18	26527.72	11858.11

Source: NHRDF, Nashik (www.nhrdf.com).

Major Onion Exporting Countries : China, India, Netherlands, Egypt, Iran, Turkey, USA, Brazil.

Major Onion Importing Countries : Sri Lanka, Malaysia, Maldives, Nepal, Dubai, Kuwait, Indonesia, UAE, Singapore, Seychelles, Pakistan, Saudi Arabia, Qatar, Bangladesh.

Major Garlic Exporting Countries : China, France, Spain, Egypt.

Major Garlic Importing Countries : Bangladesh, Philippines, Singapore, UK, USA.

Onion Varieties

Onion Varieties Developed by different Organizations

Sl.No.	Onion Varieties	Organization	Colour of Bulb	Suitable Season
1.	N-2-4-1	Agril. Dept., MS	Red	Rabi and LK
2.	N-53	-do-	Red	Kharif
3.	N-257-9-1	-do-	White	Rabi
4.	Baswant-780	MPKV, Rahuri	Red	Kharif
5.	Phule Safed	-do-	White	Rabi
6.	Phule Suvarna (RHR-87015)	-do-	Yellow	Rabi and LK

Sl.No.	*Onion Varieties*	*Organization*	*Colour of Bulb*	*Suitable Season*
7.	Phule Samarth (S-1)	-do-	Red	LK
8.	Pusa Red	IARI, New Delhi	Red	Rabi and LK
9.	Pusa White Flat	-do-	White	Rabi
10.	Pusa White Round	-do-	White	Rabi
11.	Pusa Ratnar	-do-	Red	Rabi
12.	Pusa Madhavi (Line-120)	-do-	Red	Rabi
13.	Early Grano	-do-	Yellow	Rabi and LK
14.	Brown Spanish (Long day)	-do-	Brown	In hills
15.	Arka Niketan	IIHR, Bangalore	Red	Rabi and LK
16.	Arka Kalyan	-do-	Red	Kharif
17.	Arka Bindu	-do-	Red	All 3 seasons in Krt.
18.	Arka Pragati	-do-	Red	Rabi
19.	Arka Pitambar	-do-	Yellow	Rabi
20.	Arka Lalima (F_1 hybrid)	-do-	Red	Kharif and Rabi
21.	Arka Kirtiman (F_1 hybrid)	-do-	Red	Kharif and Rabi
22.	Hissar-2	HAU, Hissar	Red	Rabi
23.	HOS-1	-do-	Red	Rabi
24.	Agrifound Dark Red	NHRDF, Nashik	Red	Kharif
25.	Agrifound Light Red	-do-	Red	Rabi and LK
26.	Agrifound White	-do-	White	Rabi
27.	Agrifound Rose	-do-	Red	Kh in AP/all 3 Krt.
28.	Agrifound Red (Multiplier)	-do-	Red	Kharif and Rabi
29.	NHRDF Red (L-28)	-do-	Red	Rabi
30.	NHRDF Red-2 (Line-355)	-do-	Red	Rabi
31.	VL Piaz-1 (Long day)	VPKAS, Almora	Red	Rabi
32.	VLPiaz-3 (Long day)	-do-	Red	Rabi
33.	Udaipur 101	RAU, Rajesthan	Red	Rabi
34.	Udaipur 102	-do-	White	Rabi
35.	Udaipur 103	-do-	Red	Rabi
36.	Kalyanpur Red Round	CSAUAT, Kanpur	Red	Rabi
37.	Punjab Selection	PAU, Ludhiana	Red	Rabi
38.	Punjab Red Round	-do-	Red	Rabi
39.	Punjab Naroya (PBR-5)	-do-	Red	Rabi
40.	Punjab-48 (S-48)	-do-	White	Rabi
41.	Punjab White	-do-	White	Rabi
42.	CO-1 (Multiplier)	TNAU, Coimbatore	Red	Kharif and Rabi
43.	CO-2	-do-	Red	Kharif and Rabi
44.	CO-3	-do-	Red	Kharif and Rabi
45.	CO-4	-do-	Red	Kharif and Rabi

Sl.No.	Onion Varieties	Organization	Colour of Bulb	Suitable Season
46.	CO No-5 (Mutlore type)	-do-		Kharif and Rabi
47.	MDU-1	-do-	Red	Rabi
48.	Rajasthan Onion -1(RO-1)	RARS, Durgapura	Red	Rabi
49.	Aprita (RO-59)	-do-	Red	Rabi
50.	Akola Safed	PDKV, Akola	White	Rabi
51.	GWO-1	GAU, Junagarh	White	Rabi
52.	Bhima Raj	DOGR, Rajgurunagar	Red	Rabi/Kh and LK
53.	Bhima Super	-do-	Red	Kharif and LK
54.	Bhima Red	-do-	Red	Kharif and LK
55.	Bhima Kiran	-do-	Red	Rabi
56.	Bhima Shakti	-do-	Red	Rabi and LK
57.	Bhima Shubra	-do-	White	Kharif and LK
58.	Bhima Shweta	-do-	White	Rabi
59.	Bhima Dark Red	-do-	Red	Kharif

Climate

Onion is a temperate crop but can be grown under a wide range of climatic conditions such as temperate, tropical and subtropical climate. The best performance can be obtained in a mild weather without the extremes of cold and heat and excessive rainfall. However, onion plant is hardy and in the young stage can withstand freezing temperature also. In India, short-day onion is grown in plains and requires 10-12 hours day length. The long-day type onion varieties are grown in hills requiring 13-14 hours day length. For vegetative growth, lower temperature combined with short photoperiod is required and relatively higher temperature along with longer photoperiod is required for bulb development and maturity. The optimum temperature for vegetative phase and bulb development is 13-24°C and 16-25°C, respectively.

It requires about 70 per cent relative humidity for good growth. It can grow well in places where the average annual rainfall is 650-750 mm with good distribution during monsoon period. Areas with low (< 650 mm) or heavy rainfall (>750 mm) are not suitable particularly for rainfed crop.

Soil

Onion can be grown in all types of soils such as sandy loam, clay loam, silt loam and heavy soils. However, the best soil for successful onion cultivation is deep, friable loam and alluvial soils with good drainage, moisture holding capacity and sufficient organic matter. In heavy soils, the bulbs produced may be deformed. Onion crop can be grown successfully on heavy soil with application of organic manure prior to planting and preparation of the field for onion cultivation should be very good. The optimum pH range, regardless of soil type, is 6.0 - 7.5, but onion can also be grown in mild alkaline soils. Onion crop is very sensitive to highly acidic soil and water logging condition. Onions do not thrive in soils having pH below 6.0 because of trace element deficiencies, or occasionally, Al or Mn toxicity. Low lying (water logged) marshy lands, highly alkaline and saline soils are not suitable for onion cultivation. Threshold electrical conductivity of a saturation extract (ECe) for onion crop is 4.0 dS/m. When the ECe level exceeds this, crop yield starts declining.

Nursery Raising

Proper nursery management and transplanting are important operations in the onion crop. About 0.05 hectare nursery bed area is enough for getting seedlings to transplant in one hectare. Field should be ploughed 5-6 times to break clods and well pulverized to hold water. The debris of previous crops, weeds and stones should be removed before bed preparation. Apply half tone of well decomposed farmyard manure (FYM) at the time of last ploughing in 0.05 ha and mix well with soil. For raising nursery, raised bed of 10-15 cm height, width of 1m and length as per our convenience may be prepared. The distance between beds should be at least 30 cm, so that water movements are uniform and drainage of excess water is possible. Raised beds are recommended for nursery because in the case of flat bed, water moves from one end to the other and there is possibility of washing away of seeds. Drainage of excess water is also a major problem in flat bed method of raising seedlings. Pre emergence herbicide pendimethalin @ 0.2 per cent is recommended to control weeds in nursery. About 5-7 kg seeds arerequired to raise seedlings for one hectare. Before sowing, seeds should be treated with thiram @ 2 g/kg of seed to avoid damage from damping off disease. Application of *Trichoderma viride* @ 1,250 g/ha is also recommended to manage damping off and raise healthy seedlings. Seeds should be sown in lines 50 mm to 75 mm apart to facilitate the removal of seedlings for transplanting, quick weeding, spray of pesticides *etc.* The seeds after sowing should be covered with fine powdered farmyard manure or compost followed by light watering. After sowing, water can be applied through drip or micro sprinkler irrigation. Foliar spray of Metalaxyl @ 0.2 per cent is recommended to control soil borne diseases in nursery. When the severity of thrips infestation is high, foliar application of Fipronil @ 0.1 per cent is recommended. Seedlings are available for transplanting in 35-40 days after sowing for *Kharif* and 45-50 days after sowing for late *Kharif* and *Rabi* seasons.

Land Preparation for Main Field

Prior to transplanting, field should be ploughed and disked properly to eliminate debris and soil clods. Organic manures (approximately FYM 15 t/ha or poultry manure 7.5 t/ha or vermicompost 7.5 t/ha) equivalent to 75 kg N/ha should be incorporated at the time of last ploughing and beds with appropriate size should be prepared after leveling. Mostly, flat beds of the size 1.5-2.0 m width and 4-6m length are formed. However, flat bed should be avoided to prevent water logging during *Kharif* or rainy season.Water logging favours *Anthracnose* disease which is most devastating during *Kharif* season. Broad bed furrow (BBF) is the best method for *Kharif* onion production because the excess water can be drained out through the furrow. This improves the aeration and helps in reducing the incidence of *Anthracnose* disease. BBF of 15 cm height and 120 cm top width with 45 cm furrow are formed to achieve proper spacing and population density. It is suitable for drip and sprinkler irrigation as well.

Transplanting

Proper care should be taken while selecting seedlings for transplanting. Over and under aged seedlings should be avoided for better establishment. At the time of transplanting, one third of the seedling top should be cut to get good establishment. The onion seedling should be transplanted after dipping roots in carbendazim solution (0.1 per cent) to reduce the incidence of fungal diseases during the establishment. The optimum spacing is 15 cm between the rows and 10 cm between plants.

Nutrient Management

The nutrient removal by onion crop mainly depends upon bulb yield, variety, soil condition, quantity of fertilizers applied, season and bulb yield. The results of the experiment carried out at DOGR, Rajgurunagar showed that onion crop removes about 90-95 kg of N, 30-35 kg of P_2O_5, and 50-55 kg of K_2O to produce 40 t onion bulbs/ha. Therefore, it is necessary to apply plant nutrients in balanced manner externally through different sources of plant nutrients for sustainable crop production and soil health. Based on the results of field experiments conducted at DOGR recommended doses of organic manures and fertilizers have been standardized and presented in Table given on next page. Fertilizer requirement of long day onion (grown in hills) is higher than the short day onion crop due to its larger crop production and higher yield potential.

One third of recommended N and full dose of P_2O_5 and K_2O are applied at the time of planting while remaining two third N is applied in two equal splits at 30 and 45 days after planting. In addition to NPK, sulphur is also an essential plant nutrient important for onion crop for improving yield and pungency of onion bulbs. Application of 15 kg S/ha is sufficient for growing onion crops in soils having sulphur level above 25 kg/ha while 30 kg S/ha is needed for soils having sulphur level below 25 kg/ha for optimum production of onion. Soil application of 50 kg

Fertilizer Schedule for Onion (per ha)

Schedule	*N*	*P_2O_5*	*K_2O*	*Organic Manures*
***Kharif* onion (Yield potential – 25-30 t/ha)**				
Basal	25 kg	40 kg	40 kg	Organic manures equivalent to 75 kg N (FYM – Approx. 15 t/ha or Poultry manure- Approx. 7.5 t/ha or Vermicompost – Approx. 7.5 t/ha)
30 DAT	25 kg	-	-	-
45 DAT	25 kg	-	-	-
Total	**75 kg**	**40 kg**	**40 kg**	**-**
Late *Kharif* and *Rabi* onion (Yield potential- 40-50 t/ha)				
Basal	40 kg	40 kg	60 kg	Organic manures equivalent to 75 kg N (FYM – Approx. 15 t/ha or Poultry manure- Approx. 7.5 t/ha or Vermicompost – Approx. 7.5 t/ha)
30 DAT	35 kg	-	-	-
45 DAT	35 kg	-	-	-
Total	**110 kg**	**40 kg**	**60 kg**	**-**
Long day onion (Yield potential-100 t/ha)				
Basal	60 kg	60 kg	70 kg	Organic manures equivalent to 75 kg N (FYM – Approx. 15 t/ha or Poultry manure- Approx. 7.5 t/ha or Vermicompost – Approx. 7.5 t/ha)
30 DAT	60 kg	-	-	-
60 DAT	60 kg	-	-	-
Total	**180 kg**	**60 kg**	**70 kg**	**-**

S/ha is recommended for long day onion crops. Sulphur is applied as basal dose at the time of transplanting. Foliar application of Zn @ 0.5 per cent at 45 and 60 days after transplanting improves nutritional quality of onion bulbs. If the soil test shows deficiency of any micronutrients, besides NPKS, the deficient micronutrient should also be applied to correct the deficiency. If the plant is diagnosed with micronutrient deficiency during growth stages, the deficiency should be corrected by either foliar or soil application of concerned nutrients, immediately.

Biofertilizer

Biofertilizer is a substance which contains living microorganisms. The biofertilizers can be used either for seed treatment or soil application. When applied to seed or soil, the microbe colonizes the rhizosphere or the interior of the plant and promotes growth by increasing availability of primary nutrients to the host plant by biological nitrogen fixation, phosphorus solubilization and stimulating plant growth through the synthesis of growth-promoting substances. Based on the experiment carried out at DOGR, biofertilizers @ 5 kg/ha each *Azospirillum* and phosphorus solubilizing bacteria are recommended for onion crop. Addition of *Azospirillum* improves soil nitrogen through biological nitrogen fixation while application of phosphorus solubilizing bacteria solubilizes unavailable phosphorus present in soil and makes them available to plants and improves the efficiency of applied P fertilizer.

Weed Management

Frequent irrigation and fertilizer application to onion crop favour severe crop-weed competition. Weeds compete with onion crop for water, soil nutrients, light and space. Onion crop exhibits greater susceptibility to weed competition than most other crops, mainly due to its slow growth at initial growth stages and inherent characteristics such as short stature, non-branching, sparse foliage and shallow root system. Control of weeds at the initial growth stages is essential for getting high marketable bulb yield. Because of labour scarcity, chemical control of weeds along with cultural methods is inevitable. Application of Oxyflurofen @ 23.5 per cent EC (1.5 -2.0 ml/L)/Pendimethalin @ 30 per cent EC (3.5-4ml/L) before transplanting or at the time of transplanting followed by one hand weeding at 40-60 days after transplanting is recommended for efficient weed control.

Irrigation Management

Irrigation requirement of onion depends upon the season, soil type, method of irrigation and age of the crop. In general, onion needs irrigation at the time of transplanting, three days after transplanting and subsequently at 7-10 days interval depending upon the soil moisture. In general, *Kharif* crop needs 5-8 irrigations, late *Kharif* crop requires 10-12 and *Rabi* crop needs 12-15 irrigations. Onion being a shallow rooted crop, needs frequent light irrigation to maintain optimum soil moisture for proper growth and bulb development. Irrigation needs to be stopped when the crop attains maturity (10-15 days before harvest) and top starts falling which helps in reducing the rotting during storage. Excess irrigation is always harmful and dry spell followed by irrigation will result in splitting of the outer scales and also formation of bolters. Water loss with flood irrigation is too high due to conveyance, seepage and percolation losses. Modern irrigation techniques such as drip and micro sprinkler irrigation help in saving irrigation water and improve the marketable bulb yield significantly. In case of drip irrigation, seedlings need to be planted at a spacing of 10 x 15 cm in a broad bed furrow (BBF) of 15 cm height and 120 cm top width with 45 cm furrow. Each BBF should have two drip laterals at (16 mm size) 60 cm distance with inbuilt emitters. The distance between two inbuilt emitters should be around 30-50 cm and the discharge flow rate is 4 l/hr. In case of micro-sprinkler, the distance between two laterals (20 mm) of micro-sprinkler should be 6m and with a discharge rate of 135 l/hr. The research outcome indicated that the drip irrigation at 100 per cent Pan Evaporation (PE) significantly improved the marketable bulb yield (15-25 per cent) with higher per cent A grade bulbs, water saving of about 35-40 per cent and labour saving of 25-30 per cent as compared to flood irrigation.

Fertigation

Fetigation is an effective and efficient method of applying fertilizers through drip irrigation which is used as the carrier and distributor of irrigation water and crop nutrients. Application of 40 kg nitrogen as basal dose at the time transplanting and remaining nitrogen in seven splits at weekly interval from transplanting to 60 DAT through drip irrigation is recommended for achieving higher marketable bulb yield and profit. Drip irrigation system not only helps in water saving but also reduces nitrogen losses by leaching into ground water, as in fertigation, fertilizer nutrients are applied in root zone only.

Kharif Onion Production Technology

Kharif season is characterized by heavy rain fall which leads to poor drainage and diseases like anthracnose, purple blotch and *Stemphylium* blight. The technology includes combination of following practices to reduce the drainage and disease problem and raise healthy crop.

- ☆ Raising nursery in summer on broad bed furrow with drip or sprinkler irrigation under shade nets and keeping the seedlings ready for transplanting in the first week of June.
- ☆ Transplanting of seedlings on broad bed furrow with drip or sprinkler irrigation. The raised bed in broad bed furrow facilitates quick and efficient drainage of rainwater, which minimizes the incidence of soil borne and foliar diseases.
- ☆ Application of 75:40:40:20 kg NPKS/ha + organic manure equivalent to 75kg N/ha is recommended for *Kharif*.
- ☆ Application of Azospirillum and phosphorus solublizing bacteria at 5kg each per ha is recommended.
- ☆ Full of PKS and 1/3 of N need to be applied at the time of transplanting and remaining 2/3 of N in two equal splits at 30 and 45 DAT.
- ☆ Application of FYM or Vermicompost pre-mixed with *Trichoderma viride* before bed preparation; It helps in reducing the incidence of soil borne diseases.
- ☆ Fertigation through drip avoids leaching losses of nutrients, which is common in high rainfall conditions: 2/3 of top dressing N needs to be applied in seven splits at weekly interval from transplanting to 60 DAT.
- ☆ Application of pre-emergence herbicide pendimethalin @0.2 per cent.
- ☆ This technology ensures 25 tons of yields per hectare without compromise in quality of bulbs.

Maturity

Onions are ready for harvest when the necks are reasonably dry and the tops have fallen over. As onions mature, their dry matter content and pungency increase, with a resulting increase in storage potential.

Harvesting, Handling and Storage

Harvest onions when the weather is dry; harvesting after a rainfall, or when the humidity is high increases susceptibility to postharvest disease. At harvest, bulbs must be firm, with mature necks and scales, and must be a good size. Defective onions (i.e. sprouted, insect damaged, sun scalded, green, bruised) should be discarded. For optimum storage quality, onions must be cured soon after harvest by placing them in a drying room at 20-30°C and 70 per cent relative humidity for 12 to 24 h. Curing decreases the incidence of neck rot, reduces water loss during storage, prevents microbial infection, and is desirable for development of good scale colour. The optimum temperature for long-term storage of onions is 0°C with 65-70 per cent relative humidity. To ensure a storage life of up to 8 months, onions must be promptly stored after curing. Exposure to light after curing will induce greening of the outer scales. Pre-mature sprouting in onions reduces marketing potential. Preharvest application of a sprout suppressant, such as maleic hydrazide, retards sprouting and prolongs storage life. Different onion types have different storage potentials. The storage potential of onions follows the order: yellow>red>white>Spanish and sweet. Within each colour group there are significant differences between cultivars in their storage potential. For further information on the storage potential of various cultivars, consult the annual vegetable trial results published by Dr. Doug Waterer, Department of Plant Sciences, University of Saskatchewan. Onions are susceptible to a number of physiological disorders during storage such as, watery scales, translucent scales and freezing injury. Symptoms of watery scales include a thick leathery skin with watery glassy scales below; freezing injury resembles watery scales and is characterized by soft watersoaked scales.Translucent scales are characterized by a water-soaked translucent appearance. These physiological disorders often become entry points for fungal and bacterial rots. For control of these problems, effective curing and prompt storage are critical.

Diseases

1. Purple Blotch (*Alternaria porri*)

Symptoms: On leaves eye shaped, purple colour spots develop which are surrounded by a broad chlorotic margin. These spots are very prominent on the flower stalk. Lesions may girdle leaves and stalks, which drop after 2-3 weeks.

Management: Follow clean cultivation, good drainage and use drip irrigation. Foliar sprays of Mancozeb @ 0.25 per cent, Tricyclazole @ 0.1 per cent and Hexaconazole @ 0.1 per cent at 30, 45 and 60 days resp. after transplanting helps in checking disease incidence.

2. Stemphylium Leaf Blight (*Stemphylium vesicarium*)

Symptoms: Small yellow to orange flecks or streaks develop in the middle of the leaf which soon develop into elongated, spindle shaped to ovate elongate diffused spots surrounded by characteristic pinkish margin. The spots progress from the tip to the base of the leaves. The spots coalesce into extended patches, blighting the leaves and gradually the entire foliage.

Management: Follow crop rotation and clean cultivation. Three sprays of Mancozeb @ 0.25 per cent, Tricyclazole @ 0.1 per cent and Hexaconazole @ 0.1 per cent at 30, 45 and 60 days resp. after transplanting helps in checking disease incidence.

3. Anthracnose/Twister Disease (*Colletotrichum gleosporioides*)

Symptoms: The characteristic symptoms are curling, twisting, chlorosis of the leaves, and abnormal elongation of neck (false stem). Initially pale yellow water soaked oval sunken lesions appears on leaf blades. Numerous black coloured slightly raised structures (acervuli) are produced in the central portion, which may be arranged in concentric rings. The affected leaves shrivel, droop down and finally wither.

Management: Since this disease is prevalent in Kharif season, growing of onion should be done on raised beds, which assures good drainage. Clean cultivation, removal of debris from previous crop with longer crop rotation helps to minimize inoculums load in soil. Application of benomyl @ 0.2 per cent as soil treatment is recommended. Foliar sprays as mentioned under purple blotch.

4. Fusarium or Basal Plate Rot (*Fusarium oxysporum* f. sp. *cepae*)

Symptoms: The roots may turn pink and gradually decay until the entire root disappears. A semi watery decay affecting the fleshy scales starts from the base and progresses upward and with early infection and may be almost complete by harvest time. White mycelium appears on the stem plate. Infected stem plate may show a brown discoloration.

Management: Good drainage, deep ploughing in hot summer, avoiding injury during cultural practices reduces the disease incidence. Crop rotation of 4-5 years with non-host crop has been found effective in eliminating the disease. Mixed cropping with tobacco and sorghum is effective. Seed treatment with *Trichoderma viride* and *Pseudomonas fluorescence* reduced onion basal rot incidence. Dipping onion sets in Carbendazim @ 0.2 per cent provide protection to basal rot. Spraying of Carbendazim @ 0.1 per cent before harvest minimizes the storage loss due to this disease.

5. Pink Root (*Pyrenochaeta terrestris*)

Symptoms: The affected roots turn yellow, shrivel and die, meanwhile taking on a distinct pink colour. The affected plants are commonly not killed but development of bulbs retarded.

Management: Soil solarization reduce pink root incidence. Long rotations with non-host crop should be followed.

6. Damping Off

Symptoms: Seedlings topple over after they emerge from the soil. It usually occurs at or below the ground level and infected tissues appears soft and water soaked.

Management: Seed treatment with Thiram or Captan @ 0.3 per cent. Drenching the nursery beds by captan or thiram @ 0.2 per cent or carbendazim @ 0.1 per cent or copper oxychloride @ 0.3 per cent.

7. White Rot or Sclerotial Rot (*Sclerotium cepivorum*)

Symptoms: Yellowing and dying back of leaf tips. Roots are normally destroyed. Superficial white fluffy mycelium may present on decaying scales. Brown or black sclerotia develop on surface or within tissue.

Management: Crop rotation should be followed, infected plant may be destroyed and the soil around these plant spot should be treated. Solarization of soil at high temperature reduces the disease incidence. Carbendazim @ 0.1 per cent may be applied for controlling the disease.

8. Black Mould (*Aspergillus* spp.)

Symptoms: Bulbs show black discoloration at the neck and streaks of black mycelium and conidia beneath the outer dry scales. In advanced stages all scales are infected and the onion shrivels.

Management: After proper drying onion should be stored at 1-15°C. Bruising should be avoided when bulbs are harvested, stored or transported.

9. Iris Yellow Spot Virus

Symptoms: Iris yellow spot symptoms first appear as straw-coloured, dry, tan, spindle or diamond-shaped lesions, with or without distinct green centers with yellow or tan borders on leaves. The symptoms are more pronounced on flower stalks. Infected leaves and stalks lodge during the latter part of the growing season.

Management: Plant high quality transplants free from thrips and Iris yellow spot virus. Practice three year or longer rotation between onion crops. Eliminate volunteers, culls, and weeds in and around onion fields. Avoid crop stress. Thrips control may provide some reduction in iris yellow spot, but thrips control alone is not sufficient to economically control the disease.

10. Onion Yellow Dwarf Virus

Symptoms: Onion yellow dwarf virus (OYDV) is the major viral pathogen of garlic crop and is reported to occur worldwide. OYDV is a member of family Potyviridae, genus potyvirus, characterized by monopartile, single-strang positive sense RNA genome encapsulated in flexuous filamentous particle. OYDV transmitted by Myzes persicae in a non-persistent manner or mechanically to garlic. It produces symptoms of mold chlorotic stripes to bright yellow stripes depending on the virus isolates and cultivars.

Management: Use of virus-free planting material is only viable solution available at present.

Pests

1. Thrips (*Thrips tabaci*)

Symptoms: If infestation is in the early stages of the growth, plants show curling and twisting of leaves. Small white silvery patches are seen all over the leaves which shine in the sun. In severe infestation, whole plant looks blemished and turns white

Management: Plant barrier of 2 rows of maize or inner row of wheat and outer row of maize atleast 30days before onion planting. Spray insecticides like profenofos, carbosulfan, cypermethrin, lamda cyhalothrin, dimethoate, monocrotophos and methomyl.

2. Eriophyid Mites

Symptoms: Leaves do not open completely. Whole plant shoe curling. Yellow mottling is seen mostly on the edges of the leaves.

Management: Spray dicofol (2 ml/l) as soon as the symptoms appear in the field. Repeat the spray if necessary after 15 days.

3. Red Spider Mites

Symptoms: In garlic webbing on leaves is seen. Small patches along with faeces, eggs, larvae and adults are seen. Webbing encircles onion umbels.

Management: Spray dicofol (2 ml/l) as soon as the symptoms are noticed.

Integrated Pest and Disease Management

- Follow crop rotation by non host crops and clean cultivation by destroying plant debris of previous season.
- Use of drip irrigation over conventional irrigation to avoid disease outbreaks.
- Application of high rates of calcium superphosphates and potassium fertilizers increases endurance in plants, while lower or higher rates of nitrogen increases disease/pest occurrence.
- Provide good drainage through raised beds in Kharif to minimize soil borne diseases.
- Seed treatment with Thiram + Carbendazim (2:1) @ 3g/kg seed or*Trichoderma* spp. @ 4-6 g/kg seed
- Multiply 2 kg of *Trichoderma* spp. in 1 quintal of FYM and apply in one hectare.
- Dip the seedlings in 0.025 per cent carbosulfan + 0.1 per cent carbendazim solution for 2h before transplanting in the main field.
- Plant 2 rows of maize or outer row of maize and inner row of wheat surrounding onion crop (250sq.m) at least 30 days prior to transplanting to block adult thrips.
- Initiate foliar sprays of pesticides from 30 days after transplanting or as soon as the pest/disease appears in the field.

- Spray insecticides when thrips population crosses economic threshold level (ETL) *i.e.*, 30/plant.
- Spray fungicides and pesticide in combination for effective management of pest and diseases.

  Mancozeb @ 0.25 per cent with Methomyl @ 0.8 g/l at 30 days after transplanting,

  Tricyclazole @ 0.1 per cent with Carbosulphan @ 2 ml/l at 45 days after transplanting

  Hexaconazole @ 0.1 per cent with profenofos @ 1 ml/l at 60 days after transplanting.

  However if disease/pest incidence is higher, then one additional spray of any of the above combination should be taken.
- Spray at 10-15 days interval depending on insect pest/disease intensity.
- Always add spreader @ 0.5-1.0 per cent
- Avoid repeated application of pesticide belonging to same class.

REFERENCES

Government of India, Ministry of Commerce and Industry, Directorate General of Commercial Intelligence and Statistics.

ICAR - Directorate of Onion and Garlic Research, Rajgurunagar, Pune.

Chapter 4

True Potato Seed (TPS)

Potato (*Solanum tuberosum* L.) is one of the most important food crops after wheat, maize and rice, contributing to food and nutritional security in the world. This tuber crop of the family solanaceae has about 200 wild species. It originated in the high Andean hills of South America, from where it was first introduced into Europe towards the end of 16th century through Spanish conquerors. There the potato developed as a temperate crop and was later distributed throughout the world largely as a consequence of the colonial expansion of European countries. It was introduced to India by early 17th century probably through British missionaries or Portuguese traders.Potato is a highly nutritious, easily digestible, wholesome food containing carbohydrates, proteins, minerals, vitamins and high quality dietary fibre. A potato tuber contains 80 per cent water and 20 per cent dry matter consisting of 14 per cent starch, 2 per cent sugar, 2 per cent protein, 1 per cent minerals, 0.6 per cent fibre, 0.1 per cent fat, and vitamins B and C in adequate amount. Thus, potato provides more nutrition than cereals and vegetables. Keeping in view the shrinking cultivable land and burgeoning population in India, potato is a better alternative to deal with the situation. According to NHB database, 2013, in India potato having area, Production and productivity are 1.99 million ha, 45.34 million MT, 22.8 MT/ha respectively. Uttar Pradesh is the leading state in area and production, while Gujarat leads in productivity. India is largest producer of potato in the world after China.

True Potato Seed (TPS) is the actual botanical seed produced by the potato plant (*Solanum tuberosum*). Found in tiny seed balls resembling tomatoes, TPS is occasionally formed after the potato has finished flowering (Figure 4.1). Potato crops are usually planted from the potato (or tuber) itself, but planting from TPS has several advantages. Firstly, while TPS can be challenging to obtain, it is far less likely to harbour disease. In fact, only one disease (Spindle Tuber Virus) has been found in TPS, while tubers can host bacterial wilt, late blight, and many other diseases affecting the commercial potato industry. More importantly, the peculiarities of potato genetics cause plants grown from TPS to be markedly different from the parent plant and from each other. This diversity helps ward off incidences of plant disease while offering gardeners an opportunity to develop their own varieties. The potato plant contains a wealth of genetic resources. While containing only 12 chromosomes, potato varieties can have multiple copies of these chromosomes. Cultivated varieties, for example, have four copies, for a total of 48 chromosomes. When the potato plant reproduces, usually though self-pollination, the chromosomes (along with the genes they carry) are reshuffled, distributing themselves randomly to the seeds. Each seed will develop into a plant with unique characteristics. Some will have red tubers, others will demonstrate excellent disease resistance. Some will be worth growing out for generations, while others will grow poorly and have to be discarded.

Figure 4.1

TPS is collected and saved in a manner similar to that used to save tomato seeds. When the seed balls are green and soft to the touch, they are removed and cut in half. The seeds are then squeezed out into a shallow container, covered with water, and allowed to ferment for three days. They are then removed, washed using a sieve, and allowed to air dry. TPS is usually stored in a cool, dry place for about eight months before planting them indoors into trays and transplanted out to the field (Figure 4.2). Before planting out, the seeds are usually treated with plant growth hormone. This, along with the fermentation process, helps to ensure proper germination.

What is TPS?

1. TPS is a botanically seed developed by sexual reproduction and it is enclosed in berry (100-200 seeds/berry).
2. TPS is used as seed material for potato cultivation and in plant breeding trials.
3. The progeny plants obtained are genetically heterogeneous.
4. The synonyms of TPS are true seed, potato seed, botanical seed and sexual seed.

Figure 4.2

5. This is an alternative method for production of seed tubers and ware tubers.

Main Characteristics of TPS

1. 100 seed weight (mg): 75
2. No. of seeds per berry (No. per berry): 200
3. Flower production (Number per stem): 50-100
4. TPS production (kg/hav200
5. TPS weight sown per 1 m^2 nursery bed in mg (50-100) stems/m^2: 50-75
6. TPS weight sown per ha in mg (20 stems/m^2): 150-200
7. Seedling tuber weight (kg/ha;14 stems/m^2, 5-10 g tubers): 700
8. Seed tuber weight (kg/ha; 14 stems/m^2, 40-60 g tubers): 200

History

1. The idea of using TPS is not new as South American farmers have been using TPS since the time immemorial to rejuvenate their seed stocks.
2. In India, the idea of utilizing TPS for commercial potato production was conceived as early as 1949 by **Dr. S. Ramanujam.**
3. Dr. Ramanujam conducted an experiments at Patna in the early 50's, mainly using open pollinated (OP) seeds of **Phulwa,** (andigena group) that flowers and sets seed even under the short day conditions of the plains.
4. The work on TPS was restarted in 1976.
5. Since 1985 AICPIP has been involved in testing various aspects of this technology by conducting trails in different parts of the country.
6. Standardization of this technique for large scale TPS production was given attention in the later period.

Why TPS?

TPS in place of traditional seed tubers offers several advantages:

1. TPS is a low-cost planting material and is quite useful to small and subsistence farmers providing them a viable option to overcome weaknesses of clonally propagated tuber seed.
2. Only 100 g TPS are needed for one hectare as compared to nearly 3 tonnes of seed tubers required to plant the same area. The seed tubers thus replaced could be saved for table purpose.
3. Problems associated with tuber-transmitted diseases especially viruses, are minimized considerably as TPS carries fewer pathogens except potato virus T (PVT) and potato spindle tuber viroid (PSTVd) no other potato diseases are transmitted through TPS.
4. TPS derived seedling tubers cost approximately one-tenth the cost of quality seed tubers (Rs. 25,000-30,000) needed for planting one hectare.
5. TPS is convenient and inexpensive to store from one planting season to another and can be stored even for several years under ambient conditions by maintaining seed moisture content between 3-5 per cent during storage.
6. Easy transportation, as only 100g TPS are needed for planting one hectare area instead of nearly 3t seed tubers.
7. TPS provides an opportunity to fit potato into different cropping systems as tuber seed of correct physiological age cannot be available to the farmers as and when required. TPS would also help in expanding potato cultivation into farming areas previously unable to produce potatoes due to lack of good quality seed tubers or into warm humid tropical areas where seed tubers could not be produced or stored.
8. Multiplication of healthy/quality planting material through TPS is much faster than the traditional process of certified seed production. Utilization of TPS can eliminate the production of foundation and basic seed required in the formal tuber seed production system.

TPS families from

1. **CIP hybrids:** HPS I/13, HPS II/13, HPS 7/13, HPS II/67, HPS 7/67
2. **CPRI Regional Station, Patna:** TPS C 3, 92-PT-27

Production of Hybrid TPS

Selection of Parent

The programme of developing high yielding TPS progenies in India consists of production of biparental crosses, preferably involving one of the parents in the cross which is a good general combiner for yield. Studies on TPS quality parameters and factors affecting them have shown that genetic constitution of male and female parental lines determine the TPS quality and quantity. Upadhya *et al.*

(1984) suggested that the selection of parental lines should be made on the basis of their yield potential, resistance to major diseases, ability to bloom under long and short day conditions, and set berries containing a number of bold A type seed. Their progeny should have attributes of high germination percentages, seedling vigour, withstanding transplanting shock, early maturity, high yield potential and homogeneity for plant and tuber characteristics.

Hybridization Block/Crossing Block

The Crossing block area is divided into two separate blocks for planting male and female parental lines. The area marked for planting male parents is nearly $1/4^{th}$ - $1/6^{th}$ of the area reserved for planting female parents. During layout, the quantity of hybrid TPS to be produced is fixed for individual cross combination to avoid a shortage of pollen. There are 2 male and 3 female parents are now utilised for production of different hybrid populations. Male parents are planted one week before female parents, preferably in the fourth week of October whereas the female parents are planted during the first week of November. Well sprouted treated tubers are planted in raised beds of 1m width on which in furrows at a 10 cm depth, 10cm apart (from tuber to tuber), with a liner to line distance of 35 cm.

Flowering

The flowering in potato depends on species, cultivar and environmental conditions. In general, *S. tuberosum* ssp. *andigena* flowers more frequently under short day condition than ssp. *tuberosum*. It is known that photoperiods of 18-19 hours are optimal for maximizing flowering and berry set. Such conditions are available in the hills of our country where the crop is during summers. In the hills, however, the cloudy weather and frequent rainfall during hybridization period and subsequent attack of late blight affect berry and seed set. In contrast, during the crop season in the plains, the days are bright and sunny and there is low or infrequent incidence of late blight. Hence, the hybridization for large scale TPS production can be better managed in the plains than in the hills.

Light Arrangement for Artificial Illumination

Sodium vapour lamps are arranged over the crossing block area in such a way that the extra illumination can be provided so as to have more than 14 hours light period in a day cycle with a minimum light intensity 150 W, which is essential to bring all the plants to come to flowering.

Irrigation

A drip irrigation system is being used in the TPS programme. The flow of drip irrigation and the time schedule are maintained as per optimum requirement of soil moisture and crop growth. Two laterals are drawn in between three rows on a bed and apertures are at 60cm apart.

Staking

Since, in long day situation the plants become taller, therefore, to provide necessary support to plant, half – split 1m long bamboo sticks are fixed 1.5 m apart and tied with 3 –tier longitudinal bamboo splits at 25, 50, and 75 cm height along the side of plant lines. This keeps the plants erect and in line, also and to facilitates pollination work. It also prevents the flowers and berries from touching the soil.

Trimming

After emergence, the plants in the female block are trimmed to retain only 30 stems per Sq.mt. In addition side branches of individual plants are trimmed regularly. Trimming of flower bunches is done to retain 8 -10 large sized buds per bunch.

Pollen Collection and Pollination

Flowers from the male parents are harvested in the morning and spread over blotting paper in shed house for drying. Other lobes are separated from the flowers and again spread over blotting paper. The dried anther lobes are sieved through specialized sieves to collect the pollen grains in clean glass petri dishes. Immediately after extraction the pollen grains are dried sufficiently at room temperature and stored in small air – tight plastic vials placed in desiccators in refrigerated condition. On the day of pollination the desiccators are brought to room temperature and taken out for pollination. At the time of pollination the vials containing the pollen grains are taken to the concerned flowers of the parents and the stigma of the flowers are dipped into the vials, so that the pollen grains get adhered to the stigmatic surface. This is continued for at least three days to each flower. Small berries are formed and are visually noticed within seven days of pollination. The optimum time for pollination is from 8am to 10am. Pollination technique adopted is simple and the emasculation process is avoided. The berries can be observed within a week of pollination.

Harvesting, Seed Extraction and Store

After about 45- 50 days of pollination, the berries turn dull green. The well matured berries are harvested, collected in plastic trays and stored in shed for softening. The berries are allowed to ripen at room temperature for about 10 -12 days. Soft, ripe berries are crushed with the help of a berry pulper. A manual reverse screw type fruit juice extractor can serve the purpose of a berry pulper. The pulper with seeds and the juice with same seeds come out from the berry pulper, and collected separately in plastic troughs. The pulper with seeds is kept at room temperature for 24 hours. The juice with seeds collected separately is also washed the same day. The seeds were treated with 10 per cent HCL for 20 minutes with continuous stirring, with the help of wooden rod and washed with fresh water repeatedly. The seeds are then soaked in 0.5 per cent sodium hypochloride solution for 10 min. To remove any surface seeds contaminants and later washed several times with clean water to make sure the no sodium hypochloride residue remains on the seed. Excess water from the seeds lot is squeezed out by wrapping and pressing in a nylon net.

Use of TPS

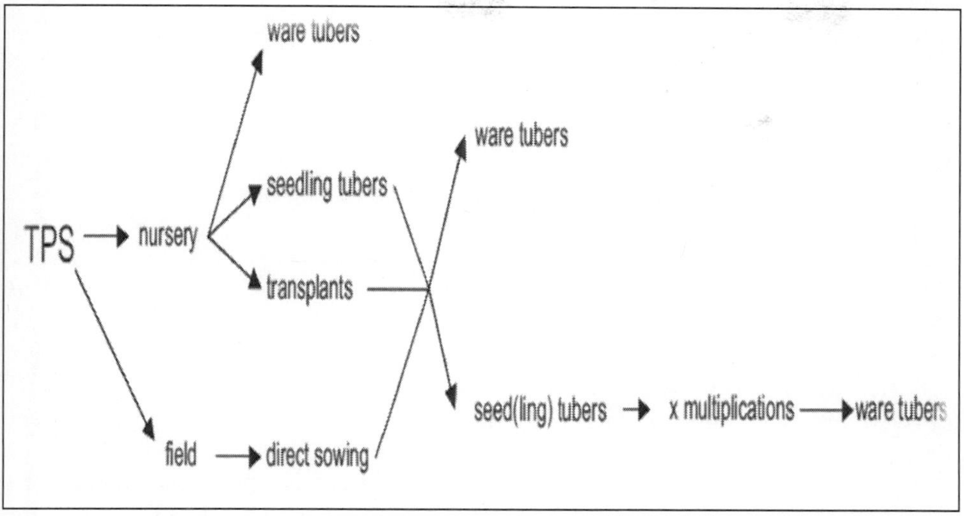

Schematic Presentation of Possible TPS Utilisation Systems.

1. Direct Seeding

Potato true seeds are small and seedlings rather delicate, and as such make severe demands on horticultural skills. Thus, raising the crop from direct seeding is prone to risks involving failure due to poor germination and mortality of seedlings. This method is thus rarely recommended for raising a commercial potato crop. However, under experimental conditions direct sowing of 200 g TPS per ha and an emergence of 75 per cent in well-controlled field conditions was reported to produce a yield of 28-30 tons of seedling tubers with an average weight of 25-30 g (Renia, 1995).

2. Seedling Transplanting Method

Preparation of Nursery Bed

Nursery beds are made 1 m wide and the length as per convenience with a 10 cm, high border made of bricks or any suitable material available locally. The soil of the nursery is ploughed thoroughly to bring the soil to fine tilth. The substrate for the seed is prepared by mixing sterilized soil and well rotten FYM or bio-gas slurry in 1:1 ratio. The lower 7-8 cm depth of the bed is filled with the substrate and 2-3 cm at the top with a layer of sieved FYM. In areas where brown rot is endemic, the seed bed should be raised 25-30 cm above ground level so that the seedling do not rot in the native infested soil. Higher production of FYM is used for heavy soil. Fertilizer is added @ 4-5 g N, 6-8 g P_2O_5 and K_2O per M^2.

Sowing of TPS

The optimum date of sowing TPS in nursery beds varies from region to region depending on its agroclimate. Nankar and Deshpande (1989) reported that sowing on 12 and 27 October, and 10 November were at par and better than later dates of sowings in Maharashtra. Singh (1990) reported the optimum time of sowing TPS in nursery beds in eastern Indo- Gangetic plains to be last week of October. The nursery beds are lightly irrigated a day before sowing of TPS. Following day, the bed is hoed and levelled for breaking the crust and getting proper texture. Furrows of 0.5 cm depth and drawn 10 cm apart are made across the width of the bed. The TPS is sown in these furrows thinly and covered with the same substrate. Grewal (1990) Singh (1990) advocated pre- germination of TPS before sowing by soaking them in water for 24 h and mixing it with sieved FYM (1:2 ratio), and keeping the mixture moist for next 4-5 days to a stage when the radical just starts coming out. About 100 gm TPS is required to be thinly sown in 50 m^2 nursery bed area at 10cm inter- row distance for raising and transplanting seedlings in one hectare area. After seed sowing, the irrigation is provided to the nursery beds 4-5 times a day for a week. The moisture content of the seed bed is to be maintained at field capacity. If necessary, the seed beds are shaded during day time to reduce the inhibitory effect of high temperatures on seed germination and seedling growth. The areas where day temperatures are above 25°C, the nursery beds are to be shaded from 10 AM to 5 PM for the following 15 days after TPS sowing. IT has been observed that covering of the seed beds with rice straw or wet gunny bags for 5-7 days after sowing helps in better emergence of seedling are given 0.1 percent urea as spray on alternate days till they are ready for transplanting. Seedlings are ready for transplanting (4-5 leaf stage) after about 20-30 days of sowing depending upon the area and climate. Small quantity of BHC dust/thimet should be applied around the beds to discourage ants and other from taking away the seeds.

Influence of Temperature and Photoperiod on TPS Germination and Seedling Growth

TPS germination and seedling establishment is very poor if seeds are not sown under proper environmental conditions. To find out the optimum environmental conditions for true potato seed (TPS) germination and seedling growth, a series of experiments were conducted in growth chambers at 20, 22, 24, 26, 28 and 30°C in combination with 12, 14 and 16 h photoperiod. Temperature had the major effect on seed germination and seedling growth followed by interaction of temperature with photoperiod and photoperiod alone. The optimum photoperiod for seed germination and seedling growth was 12 h. The optimum temperature for seed germination was found to be 24-26°C, whereas optimum root and shoot growth occurred at 28-30°C. (Minhas *et al.*, 2007)

Transplanting of Seedlings

The field is prepared traditionally; however, it is advantageous to practise pre sowing irrigation. Fertilization is done in split doses as per usual practise for potato crop in the region. Singh (1985) reported that yield from the seedling transplanted at close spacing (60 x 10 cm^2) was significantly higher than that for wider spacing (60 x 20 cm^2). In subsequent study, Singh (1990) suggested drawing of furrows in East-West direction 40 cm apart if seed tubers are to be produced, and 45 cm apart if ware crop is to be produced, and 45 cm apart if ware crop is to be produced. The

Effect of Day Length and Temperature on Seed Germination and Seedling Characteristics

Temperature (°C)	*Photo-period (h)*	*Root Length (mm)*	*Shoot Length (mm)*	*Germi-nation (Per cent)*	*Shoot Dry Weight (mg)*	*Leaf Formation (per cent)*
20	12	12.45	3.04	50	16.00	0.00
20	14	10.99	3.02	29	9.80	0.00
20	16	10.95	3.11	45	15.00	0.00
22	12	14.49	3.48	49	15.00	49.07
22	14	13.74	3.32	45	13.50	39.88
22	16	16.63	3.86	66	18.50	46.88
24	12	15.35	3.88	87	40.00	18.83
24	14	17.22	4.24	93	41.00	49.40
24	16	14.29	3.48	64	25.00	18.77
26	12	18.75	4.40	94	43.50	52.04
26	14	16.26	4.06	86	29.50	32.56
26	16	18.46	4.23	89	47.00	47.05
28	12	24.72	5.95	70	32.00	73.53
28	14	16.49	4.24	32	14.00	29.41
28	16	18.67	5.06	44	16.50	20.83
30	12	24.72	6.20	45	17.80	11.11
30	14	16.49	6.04	82	29.00	5.88
30	16	18.67	4.44	39	14.00	0.00
Grand Mean		16.74	4.23	61.61	24.28	27.51
CD ($P \leq 0.05$) Temp (T)	3.52	0.91	7.69	3.01	3.23	
CD ($P \leq 0.05$) Photoperiod (P)	2.49	0.65	5.43	2.13	2.28	
CD ($P \leq 0.05$) T x P	6.09	1.58	13.31	5.21	5.59	

Minhas *et al.*, 2007.

furrows are lightly irrigated and the seedlings are transplanted (one seedling per hill) at the water mark alongside the northern phase of the ridges. Upadhya *et al.* (1990) recommended drawing of half ridges after light irrigation in furrows. The furrows are irrigated every second or third day till seedlings get established. The remaining dose of fertilizers is applied at time of earthing up when seedling attain a height of 30-40 cm. All other operations including plant protection measures are followed as per standard cultivation practices of the region. Singh (1990) estimated that 15 gm TPS, 6 m^2 nursery bed area and 500 m^2 field area would be sufficient to produce seedling tubers to plant one hectare area next year.

Other Management

1. Earthing up is done 30-35 days after transplanting.
2. The haulm of the crops are cut on the date of recommended for dehaulming.
3. Irrigation should be stopped 10-15 days before dehaulming.
4. 10-15 days after dehaulming digging of tuber should be done.
5. Curing of the seed tuber for longer storage.
6. After harvesting tubers are graded according to size and shape.

Control of Diseases and Pests

The seedlings, because of their tenderness, are more likely to be injured by insects and diseases of potato crop. Cutworms, leaf beetles, potato tuber moth and leaf eating caterpillars are important pest under Indian conditions. These can, however, be controlled using foliar insecticidal sprays. Similarly, soil borne pathogens, *viz., Rhizoctonia solani, Sclerotium rolfsii* and *Pythium* spp., causing damage during seedling emergence and after transplanting in the field, can be controlled by fungicides applied as seed dressing at sowing time.

Method Using Seedling Tubers

Seedling tubers can be produced in nursery beds and these can be used as seed tubers to produce a commercial crop. This method is more suited to areas like the North Western plains where the season is very short and the extra time required to raise seedlings is not available.

This method is divided into two stages as follows:

1. First Stage.
2. Second Stage.

First Stage

1. In this method, the seedlings are raised in primary nursery bed and subsequently transplanted in secondary (production) nursery bed for tuberization.
2. Here the soils are removed from nursery bed to a depth of 20-25 cm and the bed is filled with FYM- soil mixture containing the initial dose of fertilizers, to a height of 10 cm above the ground level.
3. The seeds are sown further apart, usually in ½ cm depth holes (2 seeds per hole) spaced at 10x10 cm and thinning is done subsequently to retain one seedling per hole.
4. The other cultural method is same as described in seedling transplanting method.
5. The seedling tubers produced in this manner are relatively free from tuber borne disease.
6. About 60 g of TPS and 450 m^2 of nursery bed are sufficient for producing seedling tubers for planting one hectare.

Second Stage

1. Seedling tubers larger than 5 g can be used for planting the field crop in the next season.
2. Seedling tubers are generally smaller than conventional seed tubers.
3. So it is important to adjust the spacing for obtaining high yields from the crop grown in field.

Use of Tissue Culture in TPS Technology

Steps Followed for Production of Tissue Cultured Potato Parental Lines:

1. Selection of healthy, disease free tubers of known parental lines.
2. Treatment of the selected tubers with fungicides like carbendazim *etc.*
3. Selection of explants: Primary buds are used as explants, which are collected from the selected and pre-treated sprouted potato tubers (healthy and disease free tubers of known parental lines).
4. Explants are surface sterilised with sodium hypo-chloride solution or with mercuric chloride solution for specific period.
5. After surface sterilisation explants are washed thoroughly 4 to 5 times with sterile distilled water to free the explants from any surface sterillent chemicals.
6. Transfer of the explants into the culture media Inoculation of the surface sterilized explants has been carried out into the 25 X 150 mm size test tubes having suitable nutrient media under aseptic condition in laminar air flow inside the inoculation room. The inoculation room environment should always be free of any contaminants (germ free).
7. Incubation Inoculated explants are then kept in the incubation room on the illumination racks, where artificial controlled atmospheric condition are maintained like 16 hours photoperiod and 8 hour dark periods, room temperature being 25°C (± 2°C), RH at 60-70 per cent.
8. Multiplication of plantlets through sub culturing within one week after inoculation explants shoe visible growth. The growth of the culture can be observed first a leafy structure along with few roots, after which shoot growth is noticed. After every four weeks the plantlets are sub cultured by taking nodal segments from each plantlet which inoculated in fresh media. Sub culturing may continue as per requirement of plantlets.
9. Transfer of tissue cultured plantlets to soil media from test tubes in net houses. In the month of November four week's old TC plantlets are planted in well prepared sterilized soil of the net house under shed net condition.

Net House for Production of Pre-basic Seed Tubers of Parental Lines

Net house for production of pre- basic seed tuber: Transfer of the regenerated plants to net house is followed only when freely grown plants are obtained. The test tube rooted plantlets are first subjected to acclimatization during which they were kept in outside the incubation room for at least 12 hrs. Before transferring plantlets from the test tube, the roots were washed thoroughly with tap water to remove any trace of the medium. Then plantlets with sufficed leaves were transferred to greenhouse for better growth. Plantlets are washed free of sugar and planted in the net house (a house like structure size of which is 4mt X 25mt., covered with 35 mesh nylon nets to prevent aphids infestation which act as vector to different potato viruses). Spacing followed is 10cm X 35cm in raised beds. Initially the plantlets are provided with 50 per cent shed net for establishment. Once established the shed net is removed and hereafter no one is allowed to enter or touch the plantlets. An absolute hygiene and sanitation is maintained. Even watering is done through drip lines. Plant prophylactic measures and nutrient management *etc.* are taken up as per schedule. These plantlets become full grown plants within a short period and give rise to tubers. These tubers are called pre-basic seed tuber. These are harvested after skin hardening and stored in the cold store with many precautions for the next year planting materials for basic seed production.

Basic Seed Tuber Production in Open

The pre basic seed tubers are taken out from the cold store in the next season before the planting time and are put into condition for sprouting. Based upon the experiments conducted earlier and following the aphid population monitoring system the pre basic seed tubers are planted in the open field for bulking in such a way that the tuber production takes place avoiding/escaping the aphid population reaching critical level. The technique followed here is the "Seed Plot Technique", through which good quality seed tubers could be produced in the plains. Proper management with regards to plant prophylactic and nutrition *etc.* are taken up to maintain the health standard. The main theme is to produce good quality seed tubers at any cost so that no degeneration of tubers takes place due to aphid infestation and virus load. The tuber, thus obtained are graded and kept in cold store after necessary actions as required.

Yield Performance of True Potato Seeds (TPS) Hybrids under Climatic Conditons of Northern Areas

Four true potato seed (TPS) hybrids were evaluated for tuber yield with a standard variety (Diamont) at Naltar Seed Valley Northern Areas, Gilgit during the 2005 crop season. Various agronomic parameters like number of stems per plant, seedling vigor, number of tubers per m^2, yield of tubers per hectare and grading weight percentage were assessed. The TPS hybrids Atzimba x TPS-67 and LT-8 x TPS-67 gave greater tuber yield (43 tons/ha) than the standard variety Diamont. Diamont and the TPS hybrid MF-I x TPS-67 did not significantly differ for tuber yield per hectare whereas the TPS hybrid MF-II x TPS produced the lowest number of tubers per m^2, number of tubers per plant, number of tubers per m2 and yield per hectare (29.2 ton). On the basis of this study, it is concluded that TPS parent TPS-67 (male parent) has a better combining ability with TPS parents LT-8 and Atzimba, hence true potato seed (TPS) of these hybrids are recommended for general cultivation in Northern Areas of Pakistan (Nizamuddin *et al.*, 2010).

Performance Evaluation of TPS Hybrids for Grading by Weight Yield

Genotypes	*Grading by Weight (Per cent)*			
	1-25 g	*25-50 g*	*50-100 g*	*100 g and above*
Diamont	0.00	0.00	45.00	55.00
Atzimba x TPS-67	45.00	37.66	10.00	7.33
LT-8 x TPS-67	37.66	41.33	13.33	7.66
MF-1 x TPS-67	48.33	28.33	15.66	7.33
MF-II x TPS-67	40.00	33.33	20.00	6.33
LSD 0.05	18.38	14.00	17.37	14.34

Nizamuddin *et al.*, 2010.

Minimum Field and Seed Standard for TPS

Field Standard

Minimum	Land requirement	
	Isolation (m)	50
	No. of field inspection	4
Maximum (per cent)	Off type	0.10
	Plants/heads affected by designated disease	3.0

Seed Standard

Minimum	Germination (per cent)		80
	Pure seed (per cent)		98
	Inert matter (per cent)		2
Maximum (per cent)	Weed seed (No./Kg)		10
	Moisture (per cent)	Ordinary pack	8
		Vapour proof	6

TPS Populations Recommended for Commercial Production

TPS-C3 (JTH/C 107 x EXIA680-16)

Recommended for commercial cultivation in 1991 AICPIP workshop.

1. Medium maturing with yield-350-400 q/ha in 90-100 days, crop raised from seedling tubers.
2. Tubers are white-yellow, round-oval with fleet to medium deep eyes.
3. Produces medium size tubers.
4. Highly resistant to Phoma leaf spot and both early and late blights.

HPS-1/13 (MF-1 x TPS-13)

1. This was also recommended in 1991.
2. Medium to late maturing, yield- 350-400 q/ha in 90-100 days
3. Tubers are yellow and oval-round in shape.
4. Highly resistant to Phoma leaf spot and both early and late blights.

92-PT-27 (83-P-47 x TPS/D-150)

1. Recommended in 2001.
2. Higher potential than TPS-C3 and HPS-1/13.
3. Medium to late maturing but has high tuber bulking habit so high yield-10 per cent higher over the above varieties.
4. Tubers are generally yellow-white, oval, fleet and large.
5. Highly resistant to Phoma leaf spot and both early and late blights.
6. Can flower naturally under short day conditions of plains that would reduce cost of TPS production.

Agencies Involved in TPS

The ***Central Potato Research Institute, Shimla*** and ***International Potato Centre, Region SWA, IARI Campus, New Delhi 110 012***, produce TPS mainly for experimental purpose.

The names of some organizations involved in TPS production are as follows:

1. Director of Horticulture and Conservation, Agarthala - 799 001, Tripura.
2. Joint Director of Horticulture, (Development), Department of Horticulture, Govt. of Karnataka, Lalbagh Bengaluru - 560 003
3. Sr. Technical Officer, West Bengal Comprehensive Area Development Corporation, 6-A, Raja Subodh Mullick Sq., 9th Floor, Kolkotta -700 013.
4. Centre for Technology Development, Po. Box No.1209, CSIC Complex, IISC Campus, Bengaluru - 560 612.
5. Economic Botanist-III, West Bengal, Directorate of Agriculture, Govt. of West Bengal, Mission Compound, Midnapore - 721 101.

Constraints

1. TPS has a dormancy of 6 months.
2. Low quality and dormant seeds usually do not germinate and produces slow-growing seedlings that are vulnerable to transplanting shock.
3. TPS produced crop takes 15-20 days more for maturity than that from seeds tubers.

Future Strategies

The following traits need to be incorporated in TPS parental lines, either by conventional breeding or through transferring desired genes with help of biotechnology:

1. Synchrony in tuber formation together with desirable size of tuber.
2. Capacity of seedlings to withstand transplantation shock.
3. Early bulking (75-90 days).
4. Higher yields (> 25 t/ha).
5. Higher dry matter and Better keeping quality.
6. Resistance to diseases.

Conclusion

The True Potato Seeds are cheap, easy to carry and store for long and do not transmit most diseases. The technology needs to be given serious thought and should be promoted in most developing countries so as to increase potato yields. It is evident that the technology of raising a commercial crop from true hybrid seeds holds great promise especially for developing countries. If adapted, it is not only going to increase the total production in the countries but also promises to generate more jobs, income and low-cost nutrition.

REFERENCES

Adhikari, R.C. 2005. Performance of different size true potato seed seedling tubers at Khumaltar. *Nepal Agric. Res. J.*, 6: 28-34.

Agrawal, R.L. 1980. Seed Technology. New Delhi, Oxford and IBH, pp. 664-692.

Almekinders, C.J.M.; Chujoy, E. and Thiele, G. 2009. The use of true potato seed as pro-poor technology: The efforts of an International Agricultural Research Institute to innovating potato production. *Potato Research*, 52: 275-293.

Chujoy, E. and Cabello, R. 2007. The canon of potato science: true potato seed (TPS). *Potato Research*, 50: 323-325.

Das, P.C. 2000. Potato in India. New Delhi, India, Kalyani Publishers. pp. 120-126.

Deb, S.; Kumar, S. and Chowdhary, A.P. 2013. Production technology of hybrid true potato seed. *CIB Tech Journal of Biotechnology*, 3.**3**: 10-19.

Dubey, S.K.; Sah, U. and Gupta, V.K. 2010. True potato seed (TPS) vis-a-vis seed potato: A study from the North Eastern region of India. *Journal of Community Mobilization and Sustainable Development*, 5.**2**: 002-006

Gaur, P.C.; Ilangantileke, S.G. and Thakur, K.C. 1999. True Potato Seed: Asian scenario (ed. Khurana, S.M.P.; Shekhawat,G.S.; Singh, B.P. and Pandey, S.K.). Potato, Global Research and Development. Vol.1, New Delhi, India. Malhotra Publishing House. pp. 656-667.

Gaur, P.C. and Pandey, S.K. 1993. True Potato Seed (TPS) Technology (ed. Chadha, K.L. and Grewal, J.S.). Advances in Horticulture, Vol. 7. New Delhi, India. Malhotra Publishing House. pp. 85-111.

Gopal, J.; Kumar, V. and Thakur, S.S. 2004. Hybrid and open-pollinated true potato seed production: Some considerations particularly for developing short duration families. *Journal Indian Potato Association*, 31: 13-20.

Kadian, M.S.; Pandey, P.C. and Upadhaya, M.D. 1990. TPS as a propagating material for north-western indo-gangetic plains. In: Commercial Adoption of TPS Technology: Prospects and Problems. Report of Group Meeting, Delhi, India.pp.40-48.

Kumar, R.; Kang, G.S. and Pandey, S.K. 2008. Estimation of genetic parameters and combining ability for characters related to potato propagation by true potato seed. *Potato J.*, 35.**1-2**: 12-18.

Kumar, S.; Pandey, S.K. and Prasad, B. 2005. Evaluation of some TPS progenies as transplanted and seedling tuber crops. *Potato J.*, 32.**3-4**: 143-144.

Mihaela, C.; Anca, B.; Andreea, N. and Monica, P. 2012. Production of seedling tubers from true potato seed (TPS) in protected area. *Journal of Horticulture, Forestry and Biotechnology. 16.**4**: 136-141.*

Muthoni, J.; Kabira, J.; Shimelis, H. and Melis, R. 2014. Producing potato crop from true potato seed (TPS): A comparative study. *Australian Journal of Crop Science*, 8.**8**: 1147-1151.

Muthoni, J.; Shimelis, H. and Melis, R. 2013. Alleviating potato seed tuber shortage in developing countries: Potential of true potato seeds. *Australian Journal of Crop Science*, 7.**12**: 1946-1954.

Renia, H. 1995. True seed is a commercial reality in USA. *Potato Review*, **5**: 48-51.

Rojoni, R.N.; Islam, N.; Roy, T.S.; Sarkar, M.D. and Kabir, K. 2014. Yield potentiality of true potato seed seedling tubers as influenced by its size and clump planting. *App. Sci. Report.*, 2.**2**: 41-46.

Swaminathan, M.S. and Sawyer, R.L. 1983. The potential of the potato as a world food. In Research for the potato in the year 2000. Lima, Peru. International Potato Center. pp. 1-10.

Upadhya, M.D.; Cabello, R.; Falcon, R. and Chujoy.; E. 2003. Effects of location and year of production on hybrid true potato seed quality and performance. *Acta Hort.*, 619: 371-374.

Upadhya, M.D. 1994. Potato: Present and Future. (Ed. Shekhawat,G.S.; Khurana, S.M.P., Pandey, S.K. and Chandla, V.K.). Shimla, H.P., India, Indian Potato Association, CPRI.16p.

Vaghela, K.O.; Patel, N.H.; Patel, R.N. and Patel, C.K. 2007. Performance of parents for true potato seed attributes at Dessa (Gujarat). *Potato J.*, 34.**1-2**: 53-54.

Verma, V. and Sarnaik, D.A. 2007. Comparison of different transplanted true potato seed populations. *Agric. Sci. Digest*, 27.**4**: 243-246.

Wiersema, S.G. 1986. A method of producing seed tubers from true potato seed. *Potato Research*, 29: 225-237.

Chapter 5

Vegetable Hybrid Seed Production

Vegetables consist of many species and cultivars, and can be classified in many ways such as by botanical family and species, cultivar group, the edible part, climatic region, user ethnic origin, life cycle and nutrition. In seed production they can be categorized into open-pollinated, F_1 hybrid and clonally propagated cultivars. The trend of F_1 hybrid seed usage in vegetable crops is increasing globally in term of species, cultivars and volume of seed used. Most of the seed of our main vegetables including tomato, sweet pepper, eggplant, cucumber, squash, pumpkin, melon, watermelon, brassicas such as cabbage, cauliflower, broccoli, Chinese cabbage and radish, and onion in developed countries are of F_1 hybrid cultivars. The popularity of F_1 hybrid cultivars is due to their vigor, uniformity, disease resistance, stress tolerance and good horticultural traits including earliness and long shelf-life expressed and therefore giving consistent stable high yield. From the breeder point of view, it is a fast and convenient way to combine desirable characters of a vegetable together, for example fruit size and colour, plant type and disease resistance, and as a mean to control intellectual property rights through control and protection of the parental lines by the breeders.

Seed, the basic and primary requisite is most critical input for successful crop production. In most of the vegetable crops, the seed is an insignificant item in the total cost of production India has emerged as the second largest producer of vegetables (125mt), after China (147mt) in the world and is gradually striding towards achieving food and nutritional security at national level. The average productivity of vegetable crops is 16.13t/ha (NHB, 2008) which is comparatively lower than the productivity of China (17.06t/ha), Korea (41.80t/ha) and USA (79.38t/ha). The lower productivity could be attributed to limited use of quality seeds, inefficient production management, impact biotic stress and climatic factors during crop production. Among the limiting factors limited availability of quality seed is one of the important factors. Since the performance of other inputs is also depend on the quality of seed. At present the seed replacement rate among vegetable crops is around 25 per cent, whereas highest in cabbage (>90 per cent) followed by tomato, capsicum, bitter gourd, muskmelon, bottle gourd *etc.* The use of hybrid seed is in increasing due to higher productivity, tolerance to biotic and a biotic stresses and better market value than the open pollinated varieties but the higher price of the hybrid and their availability is still a constraint in popularizing the use of hybrid seeds among small and marginal farmers.

Role of Hybrids in Vegetable Productivity

The average productivity of vegetable during 1991-92 was 10.46t/ha which has increased to 17.61t/ha (Table 5.1). The tremendous improvement in vegetable productivity was realized after the introduction of new seed policy, 1988 which came into operation 1989 and has allowed the import of hybrids under OGL from different counties. As a result the hybrids in number of crops were introduced by NSC (cabbage; Green Boy and Green Express) and by private sector companies (tomato, sweet pepper, summer squash and parthenocarpic cucumber).

Table 5.1: Vegetable Productivity at a Glance

Year	*Area (000ha)*	*Production (000MT)*	*Productivity (t/ha)*
1991-92	5593	58532	10.46
2001-02	6265	88622	14.39
2005-06	7213	111399	15.44
2012-13	9205	162186	17.61

The impact of the use of hybrids in improving the crop productivity especially cabbage, tomato, brinjal and onion has been realized in many vegetable crops (Table 5.2). This steady increase in productivity has been achieved mainly by the use of quality seeds with built in inbred and hybrid vigor, coupled with the application of modern technology and sound government policies.

Table 5.2: Increased Productivity of some Vegetable Crops (2001-02 to 2012-13)

Crop	*2001-02*	*2012-13*
Brinjal	16.6	18.6
Cabbage	15.6	22.9
Cauliflower	14.8	19.6
Okra	8.5	12.0
Onion	14.2	16.0
Tomato	14.7	20.7

Development of Hybrids in Vegetable Crops

Vegetable seed industry in India with a history of more than 80 years was quite slow to pick up the potential of hybrid seeds. Wide range of skepticism pertaining to the cost of hybrid seeds prevailed in the country up to 1973. The NARS also laid major emphasis to exploit inbred vigor rather than hybrid vigor in vegetables. It was in 1973 when Bangalore based Indo-American Hybrid Seed Company from the private sector launched its first successful hybrid in tomato and capsicum in India, amply demonstrating to the Indian farmers, good returns possible for the money invested in hybrid seeds.

The emphasis has been laid out in the development of hybrids and testing under the All India Coordinated Improvement Project on vegetable during mid 1980's and has resulted the identification and release of large number of F_1 hybrids in various vegetable crops. There are number of F_1 hybrids developed by public sector organization which are popular and multiplied by national and state level seed corporations (Table 5.3) and many private sector companies.

Table 5.3: Popular Public Sector Seeds Hybrids under Seed Production in India

Crop	*Hybrids*
Bitter gourd	Pusa hybrid 1, Pusa hybrid-2, Summer Green
Bottle gourd	Pusa hybrid-3, Pant Shankar Lauki-1,Pusa Meghdoot
Brinjal	Pant hybrid baigan-1, Pusa hybrid-5, Pusa hybrid-6, Pusa hybrid-9, Arka Navneet, Arka Anand
Cauliflower	Pusa hybrid-2, Pusa Kartik Shankar, Pusa Synthetic
Cucumber	Pant sanker khira-1, Pusa Sanyog, Solan hybrid-1
Hot pepper	CH-1,Ch-3, Arka Meghna, Arka Harit, Arka Sweta
Musk melon	Punjab hybrid-1
Okra	CO-3 (hybrid-8), Shitla Uphar, Shitla Jyoti, Phule Kirti
Onion	Arka Kritiman, Arka lalima
Pumpkin	Punjab hybrid-1, Pusa Rasraj, NDPH-1
Summer squash	Pusa Alankar
Sweet pepper	Arka Meghna, Arka Harit
Tomato	Pusa hybrid-1, Pusa hybrid-2, Pusa hybrid-4, Arka vishal, Arka Sheshta, Arka Abhijit, Kashi Amrit
Water melon	Arka Jyoti

Areas Suitable for Hybrid Seed Production

The temperature, photoperiod, rainfall pattern, amount and distribution greatly affect flowering, seed set, seed development and maturation, therefore due consideration should be given at the time of selection of site for hybrid seed production to the above factors. Besides the climatic factors the availability of skilled labour, irrigation facility, mode of transport and security should be considered. Thus the various locations in northern Karnataka (Ranebannur, Haveri, Dharwad, Koppal, Belgum), southern Karnataka (Bangalore rural, Ramnagar, Chikkaballapur),

Andra Pradesh (Vijaywada, Guntur, Karimnagar, Anantpur), Maharashtra (Jalna, Aurangabad), Gujarat (Rajkot, Jamnagar) have been commercially exploited for hybrid seed production of tomato, brinjal, chilli, cucumber, pumpkin, capsicum, okra, gourds, melons and onion. The hybrid seed production of tropical carrot, radish and cauliflower is produced in south-west irrigated and northern part of Haryana. There are various locations (Sproon valley, Kullu valley, Kalpa valley, Kashmir valley) which are suitable for hybrid seed production of temperate vegetable hybrids. However the temperate locations are not being exploited due to shift in commercial vegetable production or security reasons.

Method of Hybrid Seed Production

The hybrid seed of vegetable crops are being produced by different methods and systems commercially in different vegetable crops (Table 5.4). Hybrid seed in tomato, brinjal, capsicum and chilli are produced through hand emasculation and pollination, bottle gourd, bitter gourd and pumpkin through protection of female flower and hand pollination in case of gynoceious seed parent, onion, cabbage and cauliflower hybrid seed are being produced through the use of ethephon for inducing the pistilate flower and natural pollination. The functional male sterility (Psaij) has been exploited for hybrid seed production of tomato cv Pusa Divya under poly house condition by Manjunath (2009).

Table 5.4: Method of Hybrid Seed Production

Hybrid Seed Production Methods	*Crop*
Hand emasculation and manual pollination	Tomato, Brinjal, Sweet pepper, Okra, Hot pepper
Pinching of staminate flowers and hand pollination	Bitter gourd, Bottle gourd, pumpkin
Removal of staminate flower + emasculation + hand pollination	Watermelon and muskmelon
Functional male sterility and hand pollination	Tomato, Brinjal
GMS + bee pollination	Chilli
CMS + natural pollination	Capsicum, onion, cabbage, carrot, radish
Self Incompatibility and natural pollination	Cauliflower, broccoli
Gynocecism and natural pollination	Cucumber
PGR and natural pollination	Squash's
Detasseling + wind pollination	Sweet corn, baby corn

Development and Maintenance of Parental Lines

High yielding plants are selected from varietal population for hybrid seed production. Population of breeder seed may be for this purpose. After selection of plants may be raised in single plane rows. Further, selected lines are produced by selfing either naturally or artificially to attain homozygocity, fixation of desired characters and uniformity. The degree of selfing or inbreeding depends on the response of parental lines to selfing, and degree of uniformity required in hybrids. Phenotypic uniformity of an F1 hybrid depends upon genetic homozygocity in the inbred parental lines. In cross pollinated vegetables like carrot, cabbage, cauliflower and onion which exhibits severe reduction of vigor upon selfing, inbreeding is restricted to three to four generations only. In cucurbitaceous vegetables inbreeding can be practiced to attain homozygous breeding lines without significant loss in vigor. Self pollinated vegetables like brinjal tomato, pea and beans do not loss vigor upon selfing. Cole crops permit inbreeding to fifth generation with low seed production, but onion and carrot scarcely be taken to third cycle of selfing and in leek inbreeding depression may be as high as 35 per cent at a single cycle of selfing. This loss of vigor results in low yield of hybrid seed and difficulties in maintaining the inbred. In this kind of crops some variation in hybrid (early generation inbred) and as well as in the development of hybrids by three way or double cross. In case of diseases resistant hybrid, heterogeneity offer greater insurance against new pathogen or physiological races, therefore little variability is allowed in the parental lines.

Maintenance of Male Sterile and Gynoceious Parental Line

The genetic male sterility has been reported and commercially exploited for hybrid seed production of muskmelon cv Punjab Hybrid 1 (MS-1 x Hara Madhu). The male sterile line is maintained by sib pollination from the fertile counterpart and seed is collected from the sterile plant only. The CMS line is maintained by crossing with isogenic line which is having recessive genes in nucleus and fertile cytoplasm. This system of maintenance is applied in cabbage, onion and broccoli. In case of cole crop the SI system is also utilized and maintained through bud pollination or enhanced level of CO_2 (500ppm for 18-24 hours depending upon the level of SI) for temporary induction of self compatibility. Similarly the gynoceious line of cucumber could be maintained with three application of GA_3 (1000ppm) at fortnight interval from true leaf stage or by single spray of silver nitrate solution (600mg/l) before first flower opening or silver thio-sulphate (25-50ppm) at 2-3 leaf stage to produce staminate flower (*Gautam et.al. 2006*).

Isolation Distance for Multiplication of Parental Lines and Hybrid Seed Production

In order to produce genetically pure seed of parental lines and to achieve high genetic purity during field production/multiplication plot should strictly adhered to the prescribed isolation distance (Table 5.5) with the isolation distance no other varieties of same crop and wild relative should not be present.

Table 5.5: Isolation Distance for Multiplication of Parental Lines and Hybrid Seed Production

Sl.No.	*Crop*	*Maintenance for Parental Lines (m)*	*For Hybrid Seed Production (m)*
1	Brinjal	`200	100
2	Cabbage, Cauliflower	1600	1000
3	Carrot	1000	800
4	Melons and gourds	1500	1000
5	Okra	400	200

Sl.No.	*Crop*	*Maintenance for Parental Lines (m)*	*For Hybrid Seed Production (m)*
6	Onion	1000	500
7	Pepper (hot/sweet)	400	200
8	Tomato	200	100

Planting Ratio and Methods of Planting

The planting ratio is determined by the mode of pollination and system of hybrid seed production. The planting ratio between female and male is higher when pollination is arranged by hand or by wind. Generally, the planting ratio in case of cauliflower is determined weather the one of the parent or both the parental line containing SI system. If seed parent is SI and pollen parent is self compatible than planting ratio kept 2:1 and in the event that both seed and pollen parent is SI than planting ratio is advice to kept 1:1 for harvesting higher seed yield. In case of hand pollination block planting (tomato, brinjal, chilli, capsicum, bitter gourd, bottle gorud and pumpkin) is advised where as regular planting of female and male is practiced when pollination is carried out by natural. Augmented population of honey bee (cabbage, cauliflower, carrot, cucumber, summer squash and onion) or by wind (sweet corn, baby corn and spinach). The planting ratio and method of planting generally followed in hybrid seed production is presented (Table 5.6).

Table 5.6: Planting Ratio and Methods of Planting

Sl No.	*Crop*	*Planting Ratio (M:F)*	*Method of Planting*
1	Bottle gourd, Bitter gourd	1:4	Block planting or continuous/Regular planting
2	Brinjal	1:5	Block Planting
3	Carrot	1:2 or 1:4	Continuous/Regular planting
4	Cauliflower, Cabbage	1:1 or 1:2	Continuous/Regular planting
5	Cucumber	1:2 or 1:3	Continuous/Regular planting
6	Hot pepper	1:2	Block planting or continuous/Regular planting
7	Muskmelon	1:2	Block planting or continuous/Regular planting
8	Okra	1:4 or 1:5	Block planting
9	Onion	1:4 or 1:8	Continuous/Regular planting
10	Pumpkin	1:3	Continuous/Regular planting
11	Radish	1:1	Block planting
12	Summer squash	1:5	Continuous/Regular planting
13	Sweet pepper	1:4	Block planting
14	Watermelon	1:1 or 1:2	Block planting

Pollination Management

Pollination management refers to optimum time of emasculation (bisexual flower), time of pollination, collection of pollens from anther, method of pollination and repeated pollination. The emasculation is generally done day before the anthesis preferably in afternoon (3-5PM) followed by protection from chance pollination by covering with white butter paper bag/non moisture absorbent cotton swab. On the same day the male flower is also protected to avoid genetic contamination from unwanted source and robbing of pollen. The time of pollination is affected by season, location and very crop to crop. The optimum time of pollination in different vegetable crop is presented in Table 5.7.

Table 5.7: Optimum Time and Method of Pollination

Crop	*Time of Pollination*	*Method of Pollination*
Bitter gourd	7-9 AM	Hand pollination
Bottle gourd	1-3 AM	Hand pollination
Brinjal	9-11AM	Hand pollination
Cabbage, cauliflower	9-11 AM	Insect pollination
Carrot	9-11 AM	Insect pollination
Cucumber	7-9 AM	Hand pollination/Insect pollination
Muskmelon and watermelon	7-9 AM	Hand pollination/Insect pollination
Okra	7-9 AM	Hand pollination
Onion	8-11 AM	Insect pollination
Pepper (hot/sweet)	9-10 AM	Hand pollination
Pumpkin	5-7 AM	Hand pollination
Summer Squash	7-9 AM	Hand pollination/Insect pollination
Tomato	7-11 AM	Hand pollination

Hand pollination is most common method of pollination employed for hybrid seed production of many vegetable crops. Hand pollination method is recommended for higher number of fruit set, higher number of seed per fruit and seed yield per plant by Pham Duc tuan (2006) and Vishwanath (2007) in bottle gourd and pumpkin respectively. Repeated pollination which involves removal and putting of covering bags increase the chance of damage to the gynaceium and some of the flower withered next day hence have limited scope of application but contrary to the above Manjunath (2009) has suggested the repeated pollination in hybrid seed production of tomato and recorded higher fruit set (78 per cent), increased fruit weight (36.8g), higher seed yield per fruit (102mg) in polyhouse under Delhi condition.

Hybrid Seed Production under Protected Structures

High value low volume vegetable hybrid seed can be produced successfully under insect proof nets and naturally ventilated polyhouse condition. In hybrid seed production genetic purity and seed health of parental line is a matter of concern because of non availability of adequate isolation and attack of various diseases and viruses. Singh *et al.* (2009) has reported the production of high quality seed of the parental lines of pumpkin Pusa Hybrid-1 under insect proof net house condition and compared with open field condition and observed significant difference for fruit development attributes (Table 5.8), seed yield attributes (Table 5.9) and seed quality attributes (Table 5.10) in female and male parental lines under insect proof net house conditions.

Sujata (2008) has standardized the hybrid seed production technology of tomato cv. Pusa hybrid-4 in polyhouse under Delhi conditions and also compared the seed yield and quality attributes with open field conditions.

Table 5.8: Effect of Growing Conditions on Fruit Development Characters in Parental Lines of Pumpking Pusa Hybrid-1

Character/Parental line	*Growing Condition*	
Female	*Open Field*	*Insect Proof Net House*
Fruit weight (g)	2.80	5.31*
Fruit length (cm)	20.67	24.49*
Fruit width (cm)	18.37	23.70*
Fruit Thickness (cm)	3.12	3.30
Cavity size (LxW) cm^2	179.83	306.44*
Male		
Fruit weight (g)	1.46	3.27*
Fruit length (cm)	10.18	11.64*
Fruit width (cm)	17.89	22.75*
Fruit thickness (cm)	2.4	2.93*
Cavity size (LxW) cm^2	90.26	126.91*

* Significant at 5 per cent level.

Table 5.9: Effect of Growing Conditions on Seed Yield Attributes in Parental Lines of Pumpkin Pusa Hybrid-1

Character/Parental line	*Growing Condition*	
Female	*Open Field*	*Insect Proof Net House*
Total seed(g)	376.40	389.83*
Un-filled seed	16.80	6.83*
Filled seed	359.60	382.75*
Seed yield (g)	61.88	78.98*
100 seed wt. (g)	14.19	15.28*
Male		
Total seed(g)	304.35	387.20*
Un-filled seed	10.57	18.06*
Filled seed	293.78	368.46*
Seed yield (g)	42.20	65.03*
100 seed wt. (g)	13.36	17.79*

* Significant at 5 per cent level.

Table 5.10: Effect of Growing Conditions on Seed Quality Attributes in Parental Lines of Pumpking Pusa Hybrid-1

Character/Parental line	*Growing Condition*	
Female	*Open Field*	*Insect proof net house*
Germination (per cent)	99.30	100
Root length (cm)	18.84	20.71*
Shoot length (cm)	17.13	21.17*
Fresh Weight (cm)	9.42	15.65*
Dry weight (cm)	0.78	0.84*
Seed vigour Index (I)	3571.82	4188
Male		
Germination (per cent)	99.78	100
Root length (cm)	17.53	21.90*
Shoot length (cm)	16.79	20.04*
Fresh Weight (cm)	10.08	18.12*
Dry weight (cm)	0.76	1.00*
Seed vigour Index (I)	3424.44	4203*

* Significant at 5 per cent level.

Future Thrust

Since the demand of vegetable is bound to increase with the increase in the population and to overcome the problem of malnutrition among the Indian population especially in children's and women the vegetables can play an important role being majority of Indian population is vegetarian in diet. There is an urgent need to developed to develop high yielding F1 hybrids coupled with biotic resistance and standardization of hybrid seed production technology of various hybrids in vegetable crops. Secondly the new locations for hybrid seed production of vegetables should be searched since the existing locations is over exploitation and built up of soil borne pathogens are posing serious problem in successful hybrid seed production. Thirdly the change in environment behavior is also a matter of concern thus to ensure higher yield and better quality of hybrid seed there is a need of explore the possibility of low cost insect proof net house and naturally ventilated polyhouse.

REFERENCES

Gautam, P.L., Hari Har Ram and Singh, H.P. (2006). Cucurbits breeding and production technology, *Proceedings of national seminar on cucurbits*, 22-23 Sept, 2005, Pantnagar.

Manjunath, C (2009). Studies on functional mal sterility in Tomato (*Lycopersicon esculentum* Mill.) and its application in hybrid seed production. PhD Thesis submitted to PG School, IARI, New Delhi-110012.

National Horticulture Board (2013). *Indian Horticulture Database*. Ministry of Agriculture, government of India.

Pham Duc Tuan (2006). Study on hybrid seed production in bottle gourd (*Lagenaria siceraria*) Thesis submitted to PG School, IARI, New Delhi-110012

Singh, Balraj, Tomar, B.S. and Shailija Thakur (2009). Quality seed production of parental lines of pumpkin (*Cucrubita moschata* L.). Paper presented in 4th International cucurbitaceous Symposium held at HAU, Changla (Human), China during September 20-24, 2009.

Sujata Patta (2008). Studies on standardization of hybrid seed production technology in tomato (*Lycopersicon esculentum* Mill. PhD Thesis submitted to PG School, IARI, New Delhi-110012

Vishwanath (2007). Studes on floral attributes and methods of pollination on seed yield and quality in pumpkin (*Cucurbita moschata* L.).cv. Pusa Hybrid-1.M.Sc. Thesis submitted to PG School, IARI, New Delhi-110012.

Chapter 6

Hybrid Seed Production in Cole Crops

Introduction

Cole crops are an important group of cool season vegetables. Hybrids are known to surpass the open-pollinated varieties in plant vigour, tolerance to biotic and abiotic stresses, morphological uniformity, quality of economic product, early and total yield thereby leading to their acceptability by the growers all over the world. In general, these are highly cross-pollinated crops and show preponderance of non-additive gene action for most of the economic traits. Hence, heterosis breeding is desirable. Hybrid seed production can not be economical in the absence of genetic mechanisms. Fortunately, the genetic phenomena of sporophytic self incompatibility and male sterility (particularly cytoplasmic male sterility) have proved instrumental in commercialization of hybrid seed production.

Self Incompatibility

The term self-incompatibility refers to the partial or complete incapacity of a plant, producing functional gametes, to set viable seed on self pollination. Alternatively, it is the failure of the genetically identical gametes to unite in fertilization. In cole crops, the sporophytic self-incompatibility (SSI) exists wherein the incompatibility reaction is governed by the genotype of the pollen producing plant and it is controlled by a series of alleles at a single locus 'S'. SSI system was confirmed in kale (Thompson, 1957), sprouting broccoli (Sampson, 1957), cabbage (Adamson, 1965) and cauliflower (Hoser-Krauze, 1979). However, its use in cabbage hybrid seed production had been demonstrated much earlier (Odland and Noll, 1950).

Basic Steps in the Use of SSI

a) Identification of self-incompatible plants in diverse population/genotypes.
b) Development of homozygous self-incompatible lines.
c) Identification of S-alleles in the homozygous self-incompatible lines.
d) Establishment of inter-allelic relationships among the S-alleles.
e) Identifying the best combining lines.
f) Maintenance of parental self-incompatible lines.
g) Commercial hybrid seed production.

Identification of self-incompatible plants is carried out by making different types of pollination *viz.*, self pollination in freshly opened flowers (OP), compatible pollination with unrelated S-allele pollen (CP) and bud pollination to ascertain whether the plant in question is male and female fertile and also to get selfed seeds to raise its progeny. The plants are categorized as self-incompatible/compatible based on seed set in OP in relation to CP (Watts, 1963). For quicker (within 24-48 hours of pollination) identification of self-incompatible plants, fluorescence microscopy can be used (du Crehu, 1968; Vidyasagar and Chatterjee, 1984). Wallace (1979) suggested the use of seed set as well as pollen tube penetration (fluorescence microscopy) data.

Homozygous self-incompatible lines are developed by making intra-progeny crossings/pollinations in freshly opened flowers in the progeny of a self-incompatible plant in full diallel by utilizing at least 7 progeny plants (Mackay, 1977). The intra-progeny crossings/pollinations reveal heterozygous nature of the original self-incompatible plant. After grouping the progeny plants on the basis of compatible/incompatible reaction, we get at least two (one homozygous and one heterozygous) or all the three (both homozygous and one heterozygous) phenotypic groups. By selecting plants from the homozygous groups, homozygous lines could be developed in the next 2-3 generations.

Information about the inter-allelic relationships among the S-alleles is important to ascertain their level of dominance and S-allele interactions. The S-alleles high in the dominance series are likely to give minimum selfs and sibs in hybrid seed. S-allele interactions (in pollen and stigma) are worked out by using the data (seed set as well as pollen tube penetration) obtained from the pollinations carried out in freshly opened flowers reciprocally between a heterozygote (SxSy) and its two corresponding homozygotes (SxSx and SySy). Four types of S-allele interactions *viz.*, type I (same S-allele dominant over the other in both pollen and stigma), type-II (one S-allele dominant over the other in pollen but codominant in stigma), type-III (one S-allele dominant over the other in stigma but codominant in pollen) and type-IV (both S-alleles codominant in pollen as well as stigma) have been reported.

In order to have heterotic hybrids, it is essential to identify the best specific combining S-allele lines. This can be ascertained from the SCA studies and *per se* performance. Self-incompatible lines can also be combined with self-compatible lines but the hybrid seed quantities shall be lesser since the hybrid seed will be harvestable on the plants of self-incompatible lines only.

Maintenance of self-incompatible lines is a costly affair. The various methods being followed are large scale seed production through manual sib mating in bud stage, carbon dioxide gas treatment (3-5 per cent conc.) for 8-24 hours at 100 per cent relative humidity in air-tight growth chambers and tissue culture by using meristem as explant. Of late, sprays of sodium chloride (3-5 per cent) have been reported to be effective in temporary breakdown of self-incompatibility (Kucera, 1990; Yang *et al.*, 1995 and Kucera *et al.*, 2006). This method is being followed at IARI to produce the seeds of the parental self-incompatible line ScSc which is one of the parents of Pusa Hybrid -2 of cauliflower (personal communication).

Commercial hybrid seed production is done by way of developing single cross, three-way cross or double cross. In single cross, two self-incompatible but cross-compatible best combiners are planted in alternate rows in isolated plots. The hybrid seed is harvested on both the lines. In three ways cross, one single cross and a self-incompatible line are planted in alternate rows. Similarly in double cross, two single crosses are used. In USA, for hybrid seed production of cabbage, top cross is being used. For every 2 or 3 rows of a self incompatible line, one row of a good open pollinated (OP) cultivar as a pollen parent is provided. However, the hybrid seed is harvested from the self incompatible plants only.

The main problems being faced in hybrid seed production are depression in S-allele lines by continuous inbreeding, pseudo-compatibility, the effect of environmental factors on the level of self-incompatibility and higher proportion of selfs/sibs in hybrid seed due to lack in proper synchronization of flowering. These could be managed by resorting to vegetative propagation, using the S-allele lines which behave stable under diverse environments and selecting the parental lines which have perfect synchronization in flowering.

Male Sterility

Male sterility is defined as the deviant condition in normally bisexual plants (monoecious as well as hermaphrodite) when no viable pollen is formed. Genic male sterility which is governed by recessive nuclear genes has been reported in cabbage (Rundfeldt, 1960), cauliflower (Nieuwhof, 1961) and other members of the cole group as well. In view of the problems associated with the maintenance of genic male sterile lines, its commercial use has been rather limited. In cauliflower, it has been utilized for hybrid production by maintaining the male sterile lines clonally (Grout, 1988).

Pearson (1972) reported male sterility controlled by *Brassica nigra* nuclear-cytoplasm interaction but this could not be used on commercial scale due to partial opening of petals and less developed nectar glands leading to poor bee-activity. Ogura male sterility (Ogura, 1968) was reported in Japanese radish. No restorer nuclear genes could be found in Japanese genotypes but the same could be obtained in European radish. Bannerot *et al.* (1974) could introduce cabbage nucleus into the cytoplasm of Ogura male sterile radish (R-cytoplasm) by repeated back crossing. This CMS in cabbage had the problem of chlorosis at low temperature (below 12°C). This drawback was overcome by replacing radish chloroplasts with *Brassica oleracea* chloroplasts through protoplast fusion by Robertson *et al.* (1987). Sigareva and Earle

(1997) standardized the protoplast fusion procedure to transfer desirable male sterility cytoplasm from broccoli into cabbage much more rapidly than conventional back cross method. No fertility restorer genes have been found for R-cytoplasm (Ogura) induced male sterility in cole crops (*Brassica oleracea*). Ogura-CMS is stated to be a mitochondrial DNA encoded male sterility. This implies that all *Brassica* spp. including cole crops act as maintainers of R-cytoplasm (Ogura) induced male sterility. Fang *et al.* (1997) have also reported the presence of dominant male sterile gene in cabbage. Its usage may not be preferred over R-cytoplasm (Ogura) induced male sterility because of the possible problems associated in maintaining the male sterile lines in homozygous dominant condition. R-cytoplasm (Ogura) induced male sterility already present/introduced in any genotype of a cole crop can be transferred into the desired genetic background through back cross method.

Basic Steps in the Use of CMS

1. A-line (female parent) of desired genetic background. (genetically S-msms).
2. B-line (maintainer): This is an isogenic line in the genetic background as that of A line and its function is in the maintenance of A-line (genetically N-msms).
3. C-line (male parent): This is a male parental line and also the best specific combiner with A line. Genetically this could be N/S-Ms/- (fertility restoration) or N-msms since the economic product in cabbage and cauliflower is not the true seed.
4. Maintenance of A, B and C lines.
5. Hybrid seed production.

The first increase of the seeds of the lines A, B and C must be in insect proof cages/structures followed by an increase in the open but not more than twice to obtain a high degree of purity in the stock seeds of the parental lines used for the production of F_1 hybrid seeds. The seeds of lines A and B can be produced in the same cage while the line C must be grown separately.

Hybrid seed production on commercial scale is carried out in the open by providing recommended isolation distance of at least 1000m. Usually for every 2 or 3 rows of A-line, one row of C-line is planted. The lines A and C must have perfect synchrony in flowering for good pollination and seed set. The hybrid seed is harvested from the plants of A-line only.

The main problem being faced is the lower quantity of hybrid seed on account of honey-bees preference for the pollen fertile C-line. This could be overcome to a certain extent with appropriate flower morphology and manipulating the ratio of plants of A and C lines, spacing and planting design. Inbreeding depression is another problem which results in low seed production of inbred parental lines and also that of single cross hybrids. Three-and four way (double cross) crosses may prove economic.

Self-Incompatibility versus Cytoplasmic Male Sterility

Both the genetic phenomena have their own merits and demerits. The use of self-incompatible lines ensures the harvest of hybrid seed on all the plants in the hybrid seed production block. In CMS system, the hybrid seed will be harvested only from 67-75 per cent of the plants in the hybrid seed production block. The latter phenomenon (CMS) has been considered better in avoiding selfs in the hybrid seed. However, in CMS lines also, some pollen production has been noticed especially at relatively higher temperatures nearing end of flowering stage thereby creating conditions for the possible selfs in the ultimate hybrid seed in this system as well. In my opinion, both the genetic systems (SSI and R/Ogura-CMS) will prove equally good provided the S-allele and CMS lines are tested over space and time in variable weather conditions for their stability and consequent use in the hybrid seed production programme.

REFERENCES

Adamson, R.M. 1965. Self-and cross-incompatibility in early round-headed cabbage. *Canadian Journal of Plant Science*, 45: 493-497.

Bannerot, H.O., Boulidard, L., Cauderon, Y. and Tempe, T. 1974. Cytoplasmic male sterility (CMS) transfer from *Raphanus* to *Brassica*. Cruciferae conference, Scottish Horticultural Research Institute, Dundee, Scotland, pp52.

Chiang, M.S., Chong, C., Landry, B.S. and Crete, R. 1993. Cabbage pp113-155 In: G. Kalloo and B.O. Bergh (Edited) *'Genetic Improvement of Vegetable Crops'* Pergamon Press, Oxford, UK.

Crehu, G. du 1968. Early testing of pollen-stigma compatibility relationships in *Brassica oleracea* by fluorescence. *Proceedings Brassica Meeting of Eucarpia*, Dixon, G.E. (ed.): 34-36.

Dickson, M.H. and Wallace, D.H. 1986. Cabbage Breeding pp. 395-432, In: Bassett, M. J. (Edited) 'Breeding Vegetable Crops' AVI Publishing Company Inc. Connecticut (USA).

Fang, Z., Liu, Y., Lou, P. and Liu, G. 2004. Current Trends in Cabbage Breeding pp75-107, In: P.K. Singh, S. K. Dasgupta and S. K. Tripathi (Edited) 'Hybrid Vegetable Development'. The Haworth Press Inc. NewYork, USA.

Fang, Z., Sun, P., Liu, Y., Yang, L., Wang, X., Hou, A. And Bian, C. 1997. A male sterile line with dominant gene (Ms) in cabbage and its utilization for hybrid seed production. *Euphytica*, 97: 265-268.

Gill, H. S. and Sharma, S.R. 1996. "Cole-Crops" in 50 Years of Crop Science Research in India by R. S. Paroda and K. L. Chadha (Technical Editors), ICAR, New Delhi. pp. 635-47.

Grout, B.W.W. 1998. Cauliflower: in Biotechnology in Agriculture and Forestry, Volume 6, Crops-II, Y.S.P. Bajaj (Ed), Springer-Verlag, Berlin, pp.211.

Hoser-Krauze, J. 1979. Inheritance of self-incompatibility and the use of it in the production of F_1 hybrids of cauliflower. *Genetica Polonica*, 20: 341-367.

Kucera, V 1990. Overcoming self incompatibility in *Brassica oleracea* with a sodium chloride solution. Sbornik-UVTIZ, Zahradnictvi, 17: 13-16.

Kucera, V., Chytilova, V., Vyvadilova, M and Klima, M. 2006. Hybrid breeding of cauliflowers using self incompatibility and cytoplasmic male sterility. *Horticultural Science* (Prague) 33: 148-152.

Mackay, C.R.1977. A diallel cross method for the recognition of S-allele homozygotes in turnip (*Brassica campestris L.* ssp. *rapifera*). *Heredity*, 38: 201-208.

Nieuwhof, M. 1961. Male sterility in Brussels sprouts, cauliflower and cabbage. *Euphytica*, 10: 351-356.

Odland, M.L. and Noll, C.J. 1950. The utilization of cross compatibility and self incompatibility in the production of F_1 hybrid cabbage. *Proceedings of American Society for Horticultural Science*, 55: 391-402.

Ogura, H. 1968. Studies of the male sterility in Japanese radish with special reference to the utilization of this sterility towards the practical raising of hybrid seeds. Memoirs of the Faculty of Agriculture, Kagoshima University, 6: 39-78.

Pearson, O.H. 1972. Cytoplasmically inherited male sterility characters and lavor components from the species *Brassica nigra* (L.) Koch x *B. oleracea* L. Journal of the American Society for Horticultural Science, 97: 397-402.

Riggs, T.J. 1988. Breeding F_1 hybrid varieties of vegetables. *Journal of Horticultural Science*, 63: 369-382.

Robertson, D., Palmer, J.D., Earle, E.D. and Mutschler, M.A. (1987). Analysis of organelle genomes in somatic hybrids derived from cytoplasmic male sterile (CMS) *Brassica oleracea* and atrazine resistant *Brassica campestris. Theoretical and Applied Genetics*, 74: 303.

Rundfeldt, H. 1960. Untersuchungen zur zuchtung des koptkohls (*B. oleracea* L.var. *capitata*). Z. Pflanzenz, 44: 30-62.

Sampson, D.R. 1957. The genetics of self-and cross-compatibility in *Brassica oleracea*. Genetics, 42: 253-263.

Sigareva, M.A. and Earle, E.D. 1997. Direct transfer of a cold tolerant Ogura male sterile cytoplasm into cabbage via protoplast fusion. *Theoretical and Applied Genetics*, 94: 213-220.

Swarup, V. 2006. Vegetable Science and Technology in India. Kalyani Publishers, Ludhiana, 656p.

Thompson, K.F. (1957). Self-incompatibility in marrow stem kale *Brassica oleracea* var. *acephala*. I. Demonstration of sporophytic system. *Journal of Genetics*, 55: 45-60.

Vidyasaar, 2011. Department of Vegetable Science, CSKHPKV, Palampur – 176 062

Vidyasagar and Chatterjee S.S. 1984) Early testing of pollen-stigma compatibility in Indian cauliflower by fluorescence microscopy. *Vegetable Science* 11: 113-117.

Wallace, D.H. 1979. Procedures for identifying S-allele genotypes of *Brassica*. *Theoretical and Applied Genetics*, 54: 249-265.

Watts, L.E. 1963. Investigations into the breeding system of cauliflower I. Studies on self-incompatibility. *Euphytica*, 12: 323-340.

Yang, R., Yu, Y.J., Xu, J.B., Chen G. and Zhang, F.L. 1995. Studies on techniques of spraying NaCl solution on flowers combined with honeybee pollination to overcome self-incompatibility of Chinese cabbage. *Acta Agriculturae Boreali Sinica*, 10: 77-81.

Chapter 7

Hybrid Seed Production in Solanaceous Fruit Vegetable

Historical Background

At the national level first report of hybrid vigour appeared during 1993 in chilli at Indian Agricultural Research Institute (I.A.R.I), New Delhi. However, first F1 hybrid "Pusa Meghdoot" of bottle gourd was developed at I.A.R.I Regional Station, Katrain and released in 1971. Immediately after two years F1 hybrids of summer squash "Pusa Alankar" and cucumber "Pusa Sanyog" were also developed. From the beginning of vegetable hybrid research, private sector undertakings were actively associated with the development of hybrid varieties. Indo-American Hybrid Seed Company, Bangalore, took the lead in the development of first tomato hybrid "Karantaka" and first capsicum hybrid "Bharat" in 1973 for commercial cultivation. Subsequently during mid eighties intensive work started by private sector and exporters of fresh fruits and vegetables availed license for import of hybrid seed. Growing of F1 hybrids become popular with the introduction of new seed policy declared in 1988 and this policy liberalized seed imports under Open General License with the objective of providing the farmers best planting material.

Current Status of Vegetable Hybrid Technology

Hybrid varieties play a vital role in increasing vegetable production due to its high yield potential, earliness, quality and resistance attributes. The cultivation of hybrid varieties in India is of recent origin whereas in many countries hybrids were largely grown much earlier. Tomato, eggplant, pepper, cucumber, muskmelon, watermelon, cabbage, cauliflower, carrot, onion *etc.* are important crops in which hybrid varieties are largely available and farmers are adopting such varieties to a considerable extent. Ten F_1 hybrid varieties have been identified/released by All India Coordinated Vegetable Improvement Project (Table 7.1). Besides several private companies have introduced and are testing/distributing the seed to the farmers (Table 7.2).

Table 7.1: Tomato Hybrids Identified/Released for Cultivation through AICVIP

Tomato

1.	ARTH-4	Ankur	IV,VII	Indeterminate
2.	MTH-6	MAHYCO	VII,VIII	-do-
3.	ARTH-3	Ankur	II,VII,VIII	Determinate
4.	Arka Vardhan	IIHR	I,IV,VII	Indeterminate
5.	Pusa Hybrid-2	IARI	I,IV,VI,VII	Determinate
6.	KT-4	Katrain	IV	Indeterminate
7.	NA-601	Nath Seeds	VI,VII	-do-
8.	FMH-1	IIHR	IV	-do-
9.	NA-501	Nath Seeds	IV,VII	Determinate
10.	DTH-4	IARI	VII	-do-

Table 7.2: Tomato Hybrids of Private Companies

Tomato Rupali, Vaishali, Mangla, Karnataka Indo-American Hybrid seeds
Naveen, MTH-1, MTH-2, MTH-6 MAHYCO, Jalna
MTH-15, MTH-16
Larica, Avinash-2 Sandoz

Realising potential of hybrid technology in India, Indian Council of Agricultural Research (I.C.A.R) initiated a research network project on "Promotion of Hybrid Research in Vegetable Crops" during 1995-96. Scheme works were initiated in nine vegetable crops *viz.* tomato, brinjal, chilli, capsicum, okra, onion, cabbage, cucumber and bitter gourd with the objectives (i) to promote hybrid research in order to increase productivity per se of selected vegetable crops in the country (ii) to incorporate biotic stress resistance in the hybrids (iii) to strengthen hybrid seed research and hybrid seed production technology. This project has been completed recently with considerable amount of achievements. Several hybrids have been found promising at various locations (Table 7.3).

Table 7.3: List of Promising Hybrids an Achievement of Promotion of Hybrid Project

Crop	*Location*	*Promising Hybrid*
Tomato	Varanasi	Avinsah-2, Hemlata, TH-2312 and Ratna
	Banagalore	TH-2312 and ARTH-13, Avinash-2 and DTH-6
	Hisar	ARTH-3
	Coimbatore	Avinash-2

Based on critical review of these achievements a mission mode project has been formulated under National Agricultural Technology Project (NATP) funded by World Bank. This project is aimed at hybrid research especially on development of specific quality hybrids in tomato, brinjal, chilli and onion at twelve centres. Presently, only about 10 per cent are of vegetable cultivation is under the hybrids of which 36 per cent and 30 per cent area is covered by tomato and cabbage hybrids respectively. These two crops are very important in which hybrids have tremendous advantages. Tomato (*Lycopersicon esculentum* Mill.) is a self- pollinated crop. The varieties developed in the past were true breeding. However, later some workers carried out genetic studies on the extent of heterosis. Variable responses were observed ranging from high degree of heterosis to nearly absence of it for various characters depending on the parental material. Hybrid cultivars were developed that possessed earliness, uniformity of plants and fruits and resistance to diseases. Punjab Agricultural University (PAU) has released three hybrids namely TH-2312, TH-802 and TH-1. The commercial production of F1 seed in Punjab may not be very economical due to a very short span of environmental conditions conducive to fruit set and high cost of labour for emasculation and hand pollination. However, the production of hybrid seed to meet one's own requirement is a fruitful proposition when compared with the retail market prices.

Characteristics of the Hybrids and their Parents

Hybrid: TH-2312

This hybrid is a cross between VFN-8 and Punjab Chhuhara. The plants are dwarf and spreading. The foliage is dense and protects the fruits from sun-scalding. Fruits are medium sized, oval round, thick skinned, medium firm, free from cracking and deep red on maturity. It is resistant to root knot nematode (*Meloidogyne incognita*). First picking is possible after 180 days after nursery sowing when sown during the last week of October. The average yield is 260q per acre.

Female Parent: VFN-8

VFN-8 (Accession No. 23) is an introduction from the USA. The plants are determinate and foliage is medium dense. Fruits are large, round, multi-locular and juicy. It is resistant to root knot nematode. The fruit is ready for first picking 190 days after nursery sowing. The average yield is 200 quintals per acre. The average seed yield is 200 g per quintal of fruits.

Male Parent : Punjab Chhuhara

Punjab Chhuhara (Accession No.12) is a variety developed at PAU. The plants are determinate with dense foliage. Fruits are pear shaped, bilocular, fleshy with thick pericarp. It has high level of productivity. First picking can be carried out 190 days after nursery sowing. The average yield is 320 q per acre. The average seed yield is 100 g per q of fruits.

Hybrid : TH-802

This hybrid is a cross between Healani and Castle Rock.The plants are determinate and spreading. The foliage is dark green and leaflets are broad. The fruits are smooth, round, firm, uniformly red and average fruit weight is 75 g. It is resistant to root knot nematode. It takes 170 days from nursery sowing to first picking when sown during the last week of October. The average yield is 260 quintals per acre.

Female Parent: Healani

Healani (Accession No.8) is an introduction from the USA. The plants are determinate and compact, foliage is dark green, leaflets are broad with serrated margin and show slight rolling. Fruits are flat and round with conspicuous ribbing at the shoulder. The colour of the fruit is uniform. It is resistant to root knot nematode. It matures for first picking in about 180 days after nursery sowing. The average yield is 220 q per acre and seed yield is 350 g per q of fruits.

Male Parent : Castle Rock

Castle Rock (Accession No.2) is an introduction from the USA. The plants are determinate, foliage is compact, very dense and dark green, leaflets are broad and deeply lobed. Fruits are oval, symmetrically round and very firm. The fruits mature for first picking in 183 days after nursery sowing. The average yield is 220 q per acre and seed yield is350 g per q of fruits.

Hybrid TH-1

It has determinate growth habit, plant height 70 cm, foliage cover is dense. Fruits are deep red, firm and round. Its average yield is 613 qtl. per acre.

Female Parent : W 321

Determinate growth habit, plant height 8 cm. Foliage cover medium, fruits flat round, medium firm.

Male Parent : I 181

Determinate growth habit, plant height 50 cm. foliage cover dense, compact, fruits oval, deep red and very firm.

System of Pollination Control

Tomato is a self-pollinated crop but it shows some natural cross-pollination (less than 5 per cent). Flowers are hermaphrodite. There is varietal variation for length and thickness of the style which is surrounded by the anthercone. Stigmatic disc maybe present inside the sterile tips of anthers or maybe exserted. The stigmatic position is also known to be affected by environments. Dehiscence is through the longitunal slits on the sides of anthers. Dehiscence normally takes place in the morning hours. Stigma stays receptive for 3-4 hr depending upon the temperature. Hand emasculation and hand pollination are done for the production on hybrid seed. Male sterility has also been reported in tomato.

Use of Male Sterility

The genic male sterile lines and functional male sterile lines are freely available.

In genic male sterility more than 50 loci have been reported of which ms 1035 line is very useful. It has been developed in Bulgaria and is of great value for the production of hybrid seeds. The line is maintained under heterozygous condition by back cross method. For seed production the back cross progenies (ms ms x Ms ms) seeds are closely sown/planted which segregate 50 per cent male sterile (ms ms) and 50 per cent male fertile (Ms ms). The fertile plants are uprooted at the initial flowering and only male sterile plants are used as seed parent. In this case emasculation is not required and if emasculation is done it is much easier than usual fertile lines. This male sterility is linked with character anthocyaninless (aa) marker which helps in identification of male sterile plants and purity of hybrid seeds. Functional male sterility is characterized by viable pollen which include positional sterility (ps, non-opening of anther (ps2) and short style st st). The p2 is non-opening anther and has good potential for hybrid seed production. The ex type controlled by recessive factor has a great advantage because F1 hybrids will produce normal style flower without any problem of fruit set. Since it is easy to maintain functional male sterile lines, breeders and seed producers may uses such types for commercial hybrid seed production which will be much advantageous to the farmers as the cost of seeds will be low.

Hybrid Seed Production

Agronomic Practices

Selection of field: The soil should be loamy, fertile and well drained. The pH should range from 6 to 7. To avoid volunteer plants in the seed crop, the field should not have been under tomato crop in the previous season. The tomato crop should also not follow potato and brinjal, to minimize risk from diseases and nematodes. The minimum isolation distance required for seed production is 100 m.

Seed rate and seed treatment : The seed rate is 100g per acre. As the required ratio of female and male plants is 4:1, 80 g seed of female parent and 20g seed of male parent are required. Procure the seed from authenitc sources.

The sowing is done in the second fortnight of October and in November. The seeds are sown about 1.5 cm deep in lines at a spacing of 5 cm. The seed beds are regularly irrigated with sprinkler to keep them moist. To protect the seedlings form damping-off, the nursery beds are drenched with 0.4 per cent Captan after 5 to 7 days of germination and the process is repeated after 7 to 1o days. Care should be taken to sow the nursery when the population of white fly (*Bemisia* spp.) has reduced so as to minimize the transmissions of various viruses. Further, nursery should not be thick sown so as to obtain study seedlings.

Nursery raising: The land should be prepared will by ploughing/digging thoroughly. Prepare 1.5 m wide and 15 to 20 cm raised beds in an area of about 50 m2 to raise seedlings for 1 acre. Mix 10q of well rotten FYM in the soil at the time of bed making and irrigate the beds at last 10 days before sowing. Drench the beds with 1.0 to 1.5 per cent solution of Formalin by applying 4 to 5 litres of solution per m2 to check pre-emergence and post-emergence death of seedlings. Cover the beds immediately with a plastic sheet for 24 hours. Turn the soil thoroughly in beds once a day for 5 days to eliminate Formalin so that there is no adverse effect of Formalin on germinating seeds. To avoid there infection of treated beds, the entry into the beds should be restricted and no material should be added after the treatment. The beds should be properly levelled for sowing of nursery. All operations should be carried out with clean tools.

Field preparation and fertilization : Good preparatory tillage is recommended to get the line levelled field. Apply 10 tonnes of well rotten FYM and plough it into the soil Add 20 kg N along with 25 kg P_2O_5 and 25 kg, K_2O per cent in bands, 15 cm in side of the edge of bed mark and prepare the channels and beds. Another dose of 35 kg N per acre is applied in the rows by mid-February after removing the frost protection (sarkanda/polyethylene bags) used to protect seedlings from frost.

Transplanting : The seedlings are ready for transplanting after 3 to 4 weeks, that is by the end of November, when they are 15 to 20 cm tall. The seedlings should be transplanted in the middle of the bed keeping a distance of 1.35 m between rows and 45 cm between plants with a row. Transplanting should preferably be done in the evening for proper establishment of the seedlings. The plants are protected by the use of sarkanda or polyethlene bags of 35 x 25 cms size and of 100 gauge thickness. Both the female and male parents are transplanted in the adjacent blocks.

Weed control : To control weeds,apply1 litre of Stomp 30 EC (pendimethaline) per acre using 150 to 200 litres of water or 750 ml of Stomp per acre followed by one hoeing. The weedicide should be sprayed 3 to 4 days before transplanting.

Irrigation: The first irrigation is applied immediately after transplanting. The subsequent irrigations are dependent on the weather conditions. During the winter months, the crop maybe irrigated twice a week. At the time of flowering the frequency of irrigation is increased as it influences the fruit set and fruit size. Irrigation frequency maybe slightly reduced when fruits start ripening, to reduce fruit rot.

Harvesting : The healthy fruits are harvested at red ripe maturity from the female parent. The fruits should be carefully harvested after checking the cross-pollination identification mark (clipped sepals or jewel tag).Depending on the efficiency of a person, precision and weather conditions the seed yield per acre varies from 15 to 25kg.

Plant Protection

Diseases and their Control

Damping-off (*Pythium* spp., *Rhizoctonia* spp. and *Fusarium* spp.) : Damping-off causes both pre and post-emergence death of seedlings in nursery beds. The seed should be treated with Captan at the rate of 3 g per kg of seed. Drench the nursery beds with 0.5 per cent of Captan 5 to 7 days after germination. The drenching maybe repeated after 7to10 days, if necessary.

Early blight (*Alternaria solan*): Concentric, dark brown spots appear on leaves and induce yellowing and shedding of leaves. The fruits are also affected. Such fruits show dark circular area which is followed by rotting. The control this disease treat the seed before sowing with Captan at the rate of 3 g per kg of seed. Spray the crop after transplanting with Indofil M-45 75 WP (mancozeb) at the rate of 500 to 700 g per acre at an interval of 10 to15 days.

Late blight: (*Phytophthora infestans*): Dark water soaked patches appear on the leaves and stem. The fruit is also affected. The crops rapidly destroyed if rains occur during February. Late blight is controlled by spraying the crop as recommended under early blight especially during February and March just after the rains.

Insect-Pests and their Control

Aphid : (Aphis gossypii) Aphid may attack the crop during January and February. To control aphid, spray 250 to 500 ml of Malathion50 EC or 100 to 350 ml of Thiodan (*endosulfan*) in 80 to 100 litres of water per acre. Repeat the spray after 10 days if necessary.

Fruit borer : (*Helicoverpa armigera*) : The damage starts right from the flowering stage. The larvae damage ovaries of the flowers and thus impair fruit setting. Holes are bored into developing fruits which eventually rot. Fruit borer maybe controlled by giving three or more sprays at 2- week intervals starting from the initiation of flowering with any of the following insecticides using 100 litres of water per acre. The insecticides and the doses are :800 ml of Thiodan 35 EC, 800 g of Sevin/Hexavin 50 WP (*carbaryl*), 100 g of Sumicidin 20 EC (*fenvelerate*), 200 ml of Ripcord 10 EC (*cypermethrin*) or 160 ml of Decis 2.8 (*decamethrin*).

Seed Production Technology

Field Inspection : A minimum of four inspections are required. The first inspection shall be made before flowering in order to check isolation, volunteer plants, outcrosses, demarcation between female and male parent blocks *etc.* The second and third inspections are made during flowering and fruiting stages to check isolation, off- types, accuracy in emasculation *etc.* The fourth inspection is made prior4 to harvesting at mature fruit stage in order to check the true characteristics of the fruits.

Crossing procedure: The crossing operation should be undertaken when the minimum temperature is 18°C and the optimum temperature around 25°C. However, to train the workers, this operation should be initiated when the temperature is 2 to 3°C lower than the optimum.

Emasculation : Flowers should be emasculated by use of forceps in the evening. Only those buds which are expected to open next morning should be emasculated. Emasculation should be done carefully to avoid injury to style or ovary. Emasculate only three buds per cluster. The remaining buds should be removed.

Pollen collection :Pollen maybe collected in bulk by plucking freshly opened flowers of the male parent and taking out anther cones. These cones should be desiccated in a desiccator or by placing these on unslaked lime overnight. The desiccated cones should be shaken vigorously between two layers of fine cloth placed in a box with lid. Small iron balls maybe put along with the anther cones to give them a beating effect. The pollen can be collected from the box and kept in refrigerator for 3 to 4 days for pollinating emasculated flowers.

Cross-pollination : Pollination maybe undertaken around 9 a.m. in the beginning of the season and maybe advanced to 7 a.m. or so as the season warms up, and may be continued till noon. The pollination should be done by placing the pollen on the stigma with camel hair brush. The pollinated flowers should be left with an identification mark either by clipping-off two adjacent sepals or by tying a jewel tag.

Field Standards

General Requirements

Contaminant Minimum distance (m) for certified seed

Fields of other varieties including hybrids 100

Between blocks of the parental lines, in case 5 seed parent and pollinator are planted in separate blocks.

Specific Requirements

Maximum permitted for

Factor* certified seed (per cent)

Off-types in seed parent 0.05

Off-types in pollinator 0.05

CAS Hort (Veg.) Seed and Planting Material

Plants affected by seed borne diseases** 0.05

* Standards for off-types shall be met with at, after flowering, and for seed borne diseases at final inspection.

** Seed borne diseases are early blight (*Alternaria solani*), leaf spot (*Stemphylium solani*) and tobacco mosaic virus (TMV).

Seed extraction: The seed is extracted from the fruit by hand or machine. The mucilaginous material from the seed is removed by fermentation of fruit juice or acid treatment. This is generally done by putting the pulped fruits in wooden or earthenware vats and fermentation is allowed for about 2 days. The seed is then washed after straining off the clear juice. For acid treatment, 50 ml of hydrochloric acid (commercial) is added to 1 kg of tomato pulp. The mixture is stirred regularly for 30 minutes. The seed and pulp are separated through a sieve. The seed is cleaned by winnowing and graded to separate light and small seed to improve the germination and appearance.

Seed standards: All certified seed lots which have been produced by doing hand emasculation and hand pollination shall be subjected to grow-out test and shall conform to the following minimum genetic purity requirements:

Factor Seed Standards for Certified Seed

Pure seed (minimum) 98 per cent

Inert matter (maximum) 2 per cent

Other crop seeds (maximum) 10/kg

Weed seeds (maximum) None

Germination (minimum) 70 per cent

Moisture (maximum) 8 per cent

Moisture (maximum for vapour proof containers) 6 per cent

The minimum genetic purity of certified seed is 90 per cent. During grow-out test, the off type plants (other than selfed plants) such as segregants, outcrosses and plants of other varieties should not exceed more than 1.5 per cent out of the 10 per cent plants, earmarked for selfed plants. In grow-out test, the minimum population size of 400 plants shall be maintained in two replicates of 200 plants each or four replications of 100 plants each and all plants shall be examined individually.

Chapter 8

Drought Resistance Breeding in Vegetable Crops

Drought stress is one of the most significant environmental stress causing huge loss to the agriculture worldwide. It is a natural feature of climate variability throughout the world. It is a phenomenon that is linked to a sustained lack of precipitation and in certain cases, excess evapo-transpiration. It is difficult to precisely define drought because meteorological drought results from precipitation deficits, agricultural drought is identified based on total soil moisture deficits and hydrological drought is related to a shortage of stream-flow (Keyantash and Dracup, 2002).

Drought stress is the major abiotic stress for many Indian states *viz.*, Rajasthan, parts of Gujarat, Haryana and Andhra Pradesh (Mitra, 2001). Out of net sown area of 140 million hectares about 68 per cent is reported to be vulnerable to drought conditions and about 50 per cent of such vulnerable area is classified as 'severe', where frequency of drought is almost regular. Statistical data suggested that percentage of drought affected land area has doubled from the 1970 to the early 2000 worldwide (Isendahl and Schmidt, 2006).

In combination with elevated temperatures, decreased precipitation could cause reduction of irrigation water availability and increase in evapo-transpiration, leading to severe crop water-stress conditions, which affects photosynthetic kinetics, thus intensifying the effects of drought and further reducing crop yields (Pena and Hughes, 2007). Vegetables, being succulent products by definition (generally consist of greater than 90 per cent water), are sensitive to drought stress, particularly during flowering to seed development stage. Moreover, the legume vegetables, for instance cowpea, vegetable pea, Indian beans *etc.*, grown in arid and semi-arid regions are generally affected by drought at the reproductive stage (Kumar *et al.*, 2012).

Drought is generally defined as an extended period - a season, a year, or several years - of deficient precipitation compared to the statistical multi-year average for a region that results in water shortage for some activity, group, or environmental sector.

Types of Drought

Meteorological Drought

It is generally defined by comparing the rainfall in a particular place and at a particular time with the average rainfall for that place. When we define drought this way, we only consider the reduction in rainfall amounts and don't take into account the effects of the lack of water on water resevoirs, human needs or on agriculture.

Hydrological Drought

It is associated with the effect of low rainfall on water levels in rivers, reservoirs, lakes and aquifers. Hydrological droughts usually are noticed some time after meteorological droughts. First precipitation decreases and, some time after that, water levels in rivers and lakes drops. Hydrological drought affects uses which depend on the water levels. Changes in water levels affect ecosystems, hydroelectrical power production and recreational, industrial and urban water use.

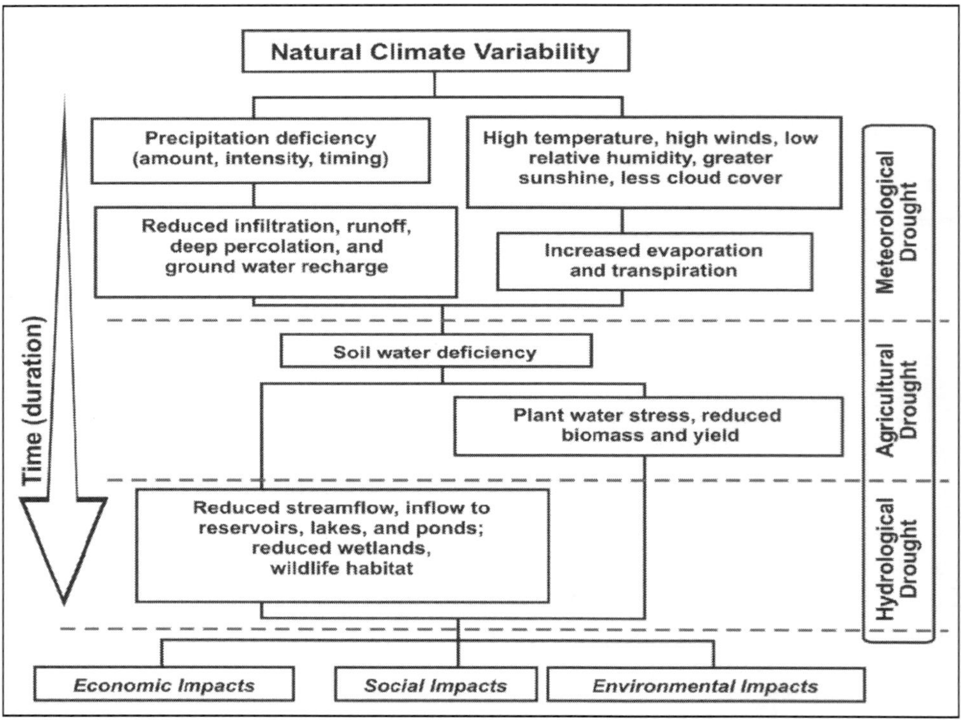

Sequence of Drought Occurrence and Impacts for Commonly Accepted Drought Types. (*Source*: National Drought Mitigation Center, U.S.A., 1985).

Agricultural Drought

It occurs when there is not enough water available for a particular crop to grow at a particular time. This drought doesn't depend only in the amount of rainfall, but also on the correct use of that water. Agricultural drought is typically seen after meteorological drought (when rainfall decreases) but before a hydrological drought (when the water level in rivers, lakes and reservoirs decreases).

Why Drought Occur in India ?

Indian agriculture is heavily dependent on the climate of India: A favorable southwest summer monsoon is critical in securing water for irrigating Indian crops. In some parts of India, the failure of the monsoons result in water shortages, resulting in below-average crop yields. This is particularly true of major drought-prone regions such as southern and eastern Maharashtra, northern Karnataka, Andhra Pradesh, Odisha, Gujarat, and Rajasthan.

All such episodes of severe drought correlate with El Nino-Southern Oscillation (ENSO) events (Kumar *et al.*, 2006). A phenomenon is that, instead of the usual high pressure air mass over the southern Indian Ocean, an ENSO-related oceanic low pressure convergence center forms; it then continually pulls dry air from Central Asia, desiccating India during what should have been the humid summer monsoon season. This reversed air flow causes India's droughts. Around 43 per cent of El Niño events are followed by drought in India (Anonymous, 2014).

Year	Occurrence	Impact	Monsoon*
2004	El Nino	Drought	88%
2005	Neutral	Normal	101%
2006	Neutral	Normal	103%
2007	La Nina	Excess	110%
2008	La Nina	Above normal	105%
2009	El Nino	Severe Drought	79%
2010	La Nina	Normal	100%
2011	La Nina	Normal	104%
2012	Mild El Nino	Below Normal	92%
2013	Neutral	Above Normal	106%

**Monsoon as percentage of 50-year average*

Impact of El Nino and La Nina Over a decade.

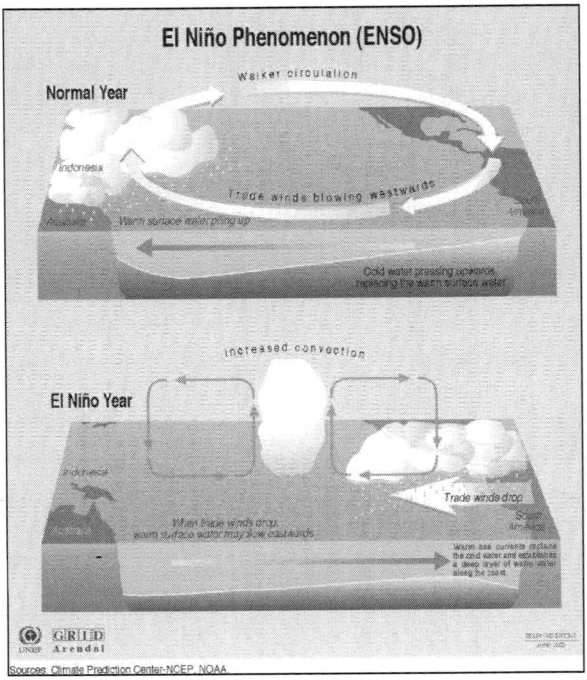

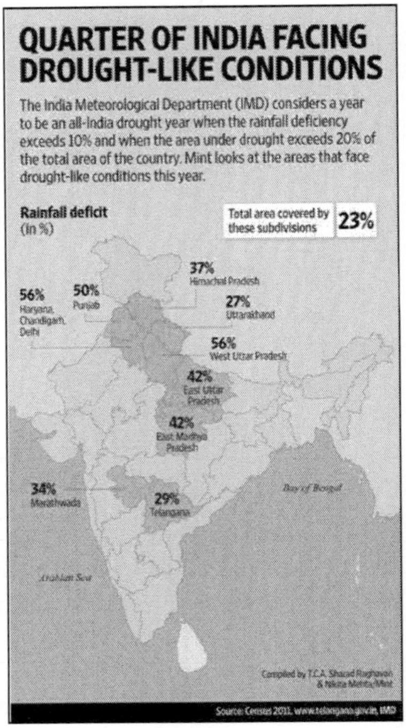

Problems of Drought Prone Area

1. Low and erratic precipitation (100-420 mm/year).
2. Extreme temperature (up to 50 °C).
3. Long sunshine duration (6.6-10 hr).
4. Low relative humidity (30-80 per cent).
5. High wind velocity (9-13km/hr).
6. High evapo-transpiration (1500-2000 mm/year).
7. Poor physical and fertility conditions of soil.

Physiological Changes during Drought

Drought is the one of the most limiting factors in vegetablte production. Understanding of physiological process that occurred during drought is necessary to ameliorate the stress effect either by management practices or by plant improvement. The responses of plants to drought stress are highly complex, involving deleterious and/or adaptive changes. Drought stress affects water status in plants. Leaf water potential and relative water content are useful means for determining the physiological water status of plants (Gonzales and Gonzales-Vilar, 2001). It is well known that leaf water status always interacts with stomatal conductance and a good correlation between leaf water potential and stomatal conductance always exists, even under drought stress (Giorio *et al.*, 1999). It is now clear that there is drought-induced root-to-leaf signalling, which is promoted by soil drying through the transpiration stream, resulting in stomatal closure, which is an important adaptation to limited water supply in the field.

The level of abscisic acid, solutes, photosynthesis, stomatal opening, protein synthesis, wall synthesis and cell expansion at deferent water regime.

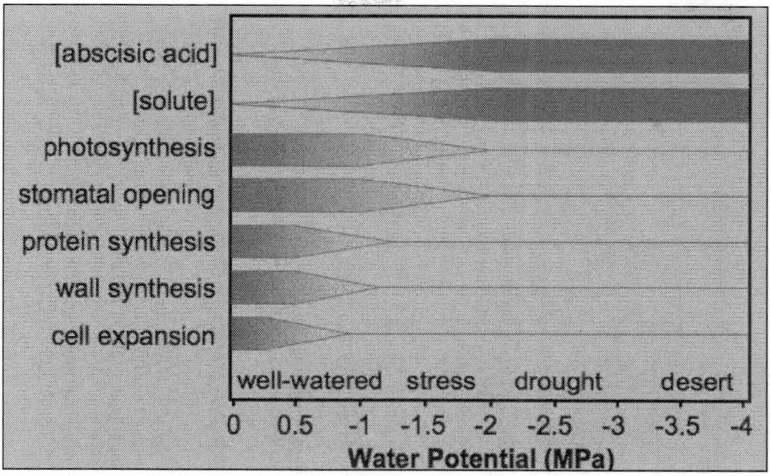

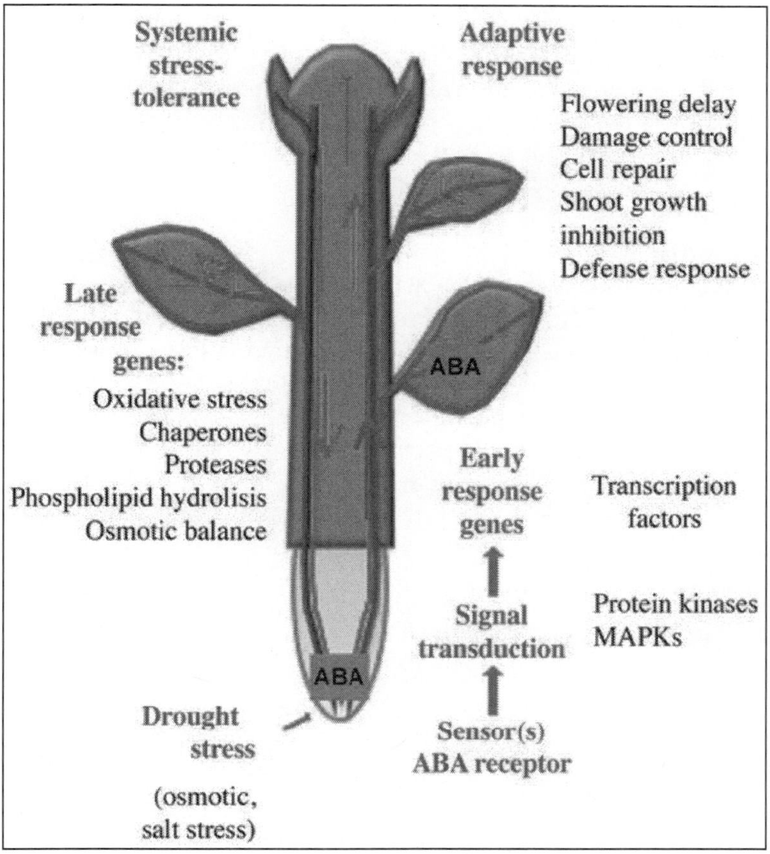

Time	Water stress effects (Observed effect on growth of a salt-tolerant plant)
Minutes	Instant reduction in leaf and root elongation rate then rapid partial recovery
Hours	Steady but reduced rate of leaf and root elongation
Days	Leaf growth more affected than root growth; Reduced rate of leaf emergence
Weeks	Reduced final leaf size and/or number of lateral shoots
Months	Altered flowering time, reduced seed production

Water Specific Effects on Plant Growth.

The Concept and Mechanism of Drought Resistance

Drought Escape

The ability of a crop plant to complete its life cycle before development of serious soil and plant water deficits is called as drought escape. This mechanism involves rapid phonological development *i.e.* early flowering and maturity, variation in duration of growth period depending on the extent of water scarcity. For instance, in cow pea early erect cultivars, such as 'Ein El Gazal' and 'Melakh', have performed well when the rainfall season was short but distinct due to their ability to escape late-season drought (Hall, 2004).

Drought Avoidance

It refers to the ability of a crop to endure periods without significant rainfall even as maintaining a high plant status at high plant water potential, *i.e.*, dehydration postponement or drought avoidance. In other way, drought avoidance is the ability of plants to maintain relatively high tissue water potential despite a shortage of soil moisture. Improving the mechanisms of water uptake, storing in plant cell and reducing water loss confer drought avoidance. Drought avoidance mechanisms are associated with physiological whole-plant mechanisms such as canopy tolerance and leaf area reduction (which decrease radiation, adsorption and transpiration),stomatal closure and cuticular wax formation, and adjustments of sink-source relationships through alteringroot depth and density, root hair development and roothydraulic conductance (Rivero *et al.*, 2007).

Drought Tolerance

The ability of a crop to enduremoisture deficits at low tissue water potential ordehydration tolerance. Under droughtcondition, plants survive through a balancing actbetween maintenance of turgor with reduction of waterloss (Begg and Turner, 1976). Drought tolerancemechanisms are balancing of turgor through osmoticadjustment (solute accumulation in cell), increase inelasticity in cell but decrease in cell size and desiccationtolerance by protoplasmic tolerance

(Ugherughe, 1986). Drought tolerance can be increasedthrough osmotic adjustment by maintaining plant turgor,but the increased solute concentration responsible forosmotic adjustment may have detrimental effect inaddition to energy requirement for osmotic regulation (Turner, 1979). Therefore, crop adaptations to droughtmay be established through a balance between escape,avoidance and tolerance while maintaining adequateproductivity.

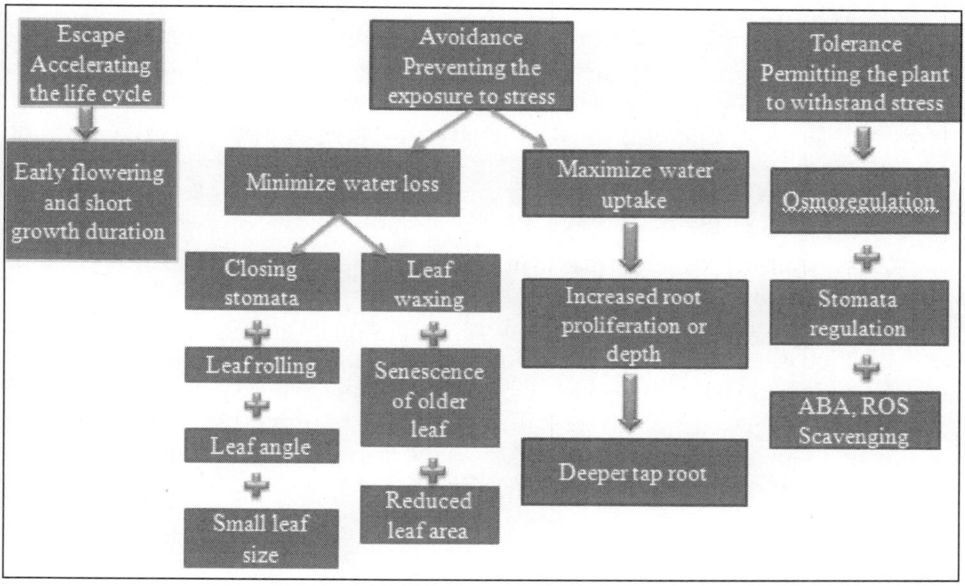

Mechanism of Drought Tolerance.

Schwarz *et al.* (2010) suggested combined use of genetic and agronomic technologies to sustain water status may maintain plant growth under water deficit conditions.

Components of Drought Tolerance

Drought tolerance is induced by:

- ☆ Adaptation of improved agronomic practices,
- ☆ Use of advance technologies in vegetable production,
- ☆ Conservation of natural energy resources,
- ☆ Use of microbes,
- ☆ Breeding for resistance,
- ☆ Improvement at molecular level of plant.

Adaptation of Improved Agronomic Practices

Selection of Suitable Crops and Varieties

In vegetable crops like dolichos bean, cowpea, cluster bean, lima bean, chilli, drumstick, brinjal, okra are suitable for rain-fed cultivation. Among these, legume vegetables can be recommended for contingency crop-planning in an eventuality of late monsoon rains. Varieties having good root system and capacity torecoup after the alleviation of stress need to be selected. Depending upon situation, it is recommended to use short duration varieties.

Adoption of Soil and Moisture Conservation Techniques

Contour cultivation, contour trip cropping, mixed Cropping, tillage, mulching, zero tillage, are some of the agronomical measures for the *in-situ* soil moisture conservation. Mechanical measures like contour bunding, graded bunding, bench terracing, vertical mulching *etc.* also need to be followed for effective soil and moisture conservation in dry lands.

Enhancing Soil Organic Matter Content

Constant efforts must be made to improve the soil organic carbon. Incorporation of crop residues and farm yard manure to soil improves the organic matter status, improves soil structure and soil moisture storage capacity. Organic matter content of the soil can also be improved by fallowing alley cropping, green manuring, crop rotation and agro forestry. Vegetable being short duration crop and having faster growth phases, the available organic matter needs to be properly composted. Vermi composting can be followed for quicker usage of available organic matter in the soil and improving the soil moisture holding capacity.

Application of Foliar Nutrition

The foliar application of nutrients during water stress conditions helps in the better growth by quick absorption of nutrients. The spraying of K and Ca induces drought tolerance in vegetable crops. Spraying of micronutrients and secondary nutrients improves crop yields and quality.

Drought Hardening

Improvement of drought tolerance ability of a genotype is referred to as drought hardening. Two type of treatments are in common use:

a. **Pre-sowing treatment**: Seeds are soaked in water for 24 hours and then sun-dried. Plant developed from such seeds exhibit improve drought tolerance.

b. **Post-sowing treatment**: The post-sowing treatment is given to the young seedling.

Use of Advanced Technologies

Improved Method of Seedling Production

Improved method of seedling production such as Protray grown seedling using coco peat, nylon net protection and bio-fertilizers/biopesticide inoculation at nursery stage has good potential for obtaining sturdy, uniform and healthy seedlings. These seedlings when transplanted in the main-field will establish better with less root damage and fare better in overcoming biotic and abiotic stresses particularly during water stress conditions.

Use of Drip Irrigation

Drip irrigation has proved its superiority over other conventional method of irrigation, in horticulture due to precise and direct application of water in root zone. A considerable saving in water, increased growth, development and yields of fruits and vegetables and control of weeds, saving in labour under drip irrigation are the added advantages. Drip irrigation can be adopted in fruit crops and also to all vegetable crops including closed spaced crops like onions and beans. The saving in water is to the tune of 30-50 per cent depending on the crop and season. Generally inline drip laterals having emitting point spaced at 30cm distance and emitting at the rate of 2LPH is selected for vegetable crops. In crops like chilli, brinjal, cauliflower and okra paired row planting is practiced and one drip lateral is used for two crop rows.

Use of Micro Sprinkler Irrigation

Depending upon situation and availability of water, this technology can be used for fruits and vegetable crops. The cost of initial establishment is lower compared to drip system. Further in summer the sprinkling of water helps in reducing the microclimate temperature and increasing the humidity, thereby improving the growth and yield of the crop. The water saved is to the tune of 20 to 30 per cent.

Moisture Saving Methods under Limited Water Resource Conditions

The following methods may be adopted under limited water conditions to save water:

Water Saving Irrigation Method

Under limited water situations, water-saving irrigation methods like alternate furrow irrigation or widely spaced furrow irrigation and drip irrigation systems can be adopted. Studies conducted on methods of irrigation in capsicum, tomato, okra and cauliflower indicated that adopting alternate-furrow irrigation and widely-spaced furrow irrigation saved 35 to 40 per cent of irrigation water without adversely affecting yield.

Critical Stages of Drought Stress and its Impact on Vegetable Crops

Sl. No.	*Vegetable Crops*	*Critical Period for Watering*	*Impact of Water Stress*
1	Tomato	Early flowering, fruit set, and enlargement	Flower shedding, lack of fertilization, reduced fruit size, fruit splitting, blossom end rot, poor seed viability
2	Brinjal	Flowering and fruit development	Reduced yield with poor colour, poor seed viability
3	Chilli and Capsicum	Flowering and fruit set	Shedding of flowers and young fruits, reduction in dry matter production and nutrient uptake, poor seed viability
4	Potato	Tuberization and tuber enlargement	Poor tuber growth and yield, splitting, internal brown spot

Sl. No.	*Vegetable Crops*	*Critical Period for Watering*	*Impact of Water Stress*
5	Cole crops	Head/curd formation and enlargement	Tip burning and splitting of head in cabbage; browning and buttoning in cauliflower
6	Root crops	Root enlargement	Distorted, rough and poor growth of roots, strong and pungent odour in carrot, accumulation of harmful nitrates in roots
8	Cucumber	Flowering as well as throughout fruit development	Deformed and non-viable pollen grains, bitterness and deformity in fruits, poor seed viability
9	Leafy vegetables	Throughout growth and development of plant	Toughness of leaves, poor foliage growth, accumulation of nitrates

Kumar *et al.,* 2012.

Mulching Practices in Vegetable Production

The technique of covering the soil with natural crop residues or plastic films for soil and water conservation is called mulching. Mulching can be practiced in fruits and vegetable crops using crop residues and other organic material available in the farm. Recently plastic mulches have come into use due to the inherent advantages of efficient moisture conservation, weed suppression and maintenance of soil structure. Wide variety of vegetables can be successfully grown using mulches. In addition to soil and water conservation, improved yield and quality, suppression of weed growth, mulches can improve the use efficiency of applied fertilizer nutrients and also use of reflective mulches are likely to minimize the incidence of virus diseases. For vegetable production generally polyethylene mulch film of 30micron thick and 1 to 1.2 m width is used. Generally raised bed with drip irrigation system is followed while laying the mulch film.

Use of Protected Cultivation of Vegetables

In peri-urban regions where climate does not favour year round production of crops in the open field, vegetable production can be taken up in protected environment. Protective structure is a facility to protect crop from biotic and abiotic constraints. Structures for protected cultivation include greenhouses, plastic/net houses and "tunnels". Commonly used protected structures are polyhouses and net or shade houses. Rain-shelter is a simple structure covered with polyethylene sheet which helps in producing the crops which are affected by excessive rainfall. The productivity of tomato, onions and melons are adversely affected in the event of high rainfall due to difficulty in managing the foliar diseases, lack of proper soil aeration and drainage and also depending on the nature of crop physical damage of the foliage and flower drop. Net house cultivation and shade net cultivation provide better microclimate especially during summer in minimizing the high temperature effect and improving the relative humidity. The productivity of tomato, French bean and capsicum can be improved during high temperature period by using net/shade net on the top.

Grafting

One way to reduce losses in production and to improve water use efficiency under drought conditions in high-yielding genotypes would be grafting them onto rootstocks capable of reducing the effect of water stress on the shoot as observed in tree crops (Satisha *et al.*, 2007).

Grafting experiments with ABA deficient mutants of tomato showed that stomata can close independently of the leaf water status suggesting that there is a chemical signal produced by the roots that controls stomatal conductance (Holbrook *et al.*, 2002).

Grafted mini-watermelons onto a commercial rootstock (PS 1313: *Cucurbita maxima* Duchesne x *Cucurbita moschata* Duchesne) revealed a more than 60 per cent higher marketable yield when grown under conditions of deficit irrigation compared with ungrafted melons (Rouphael *et al.*, 2008).The higher marketable yield recorded with grafting was mainly due to an improvement in water and nutrient uptake, indicated by a higher N, K, and Mg concentration in the leaves, and higher CO_2 assimilation.

Treatment	*Yield (t/ha)*		*Marketable Fruit*		
	Total	*Marketable*	*Mean Mass (kg/fruit)*	*Number (No./plant)*	*Dry Biomass (t/ha)*
Ungrafted	23.2	19.8	2.86	1.39	1.04
Grafted	49.9	31.9	3.21	2.00	1.70
Significance	***	***	**	**	*

Note: *, **, *** significant at $P < 0.05$, 0.01 and 0.001, respectively.

(Rouphael *et al.*, 2008).

Conservation of Natural Energy Resources

Another technology for efficient utilization of runoff is water harvesting recycling. Rainwater harvesting includes collecting runoff water into dug out ponds or tanks in small depressions, gullies and into storage dams of earth or masonry structures.Rain water harvesting is possible in areas having rainfall as little as 500 to 800 mm.Depending on the rainfall and soil characteristics, 10-50 per cent of the runoff can be collected in farm pond. Surface run off thus collected in a farm pond can be used to provide protective irrigation in the period of prolonged dry spell.

Use of Microbes

BBS inducing drought tolerance in cucumber plants: After withholding watering for 13 days, the leaves of BBS treated cucumber plants displayed much darker green and lighter wilt symptoms (*i.e.* still being able to rehydrate at night or in an early morning) than those of control plants, which were unable to rehydrate at night or in an early morning (Wang *et al.*, 2012).

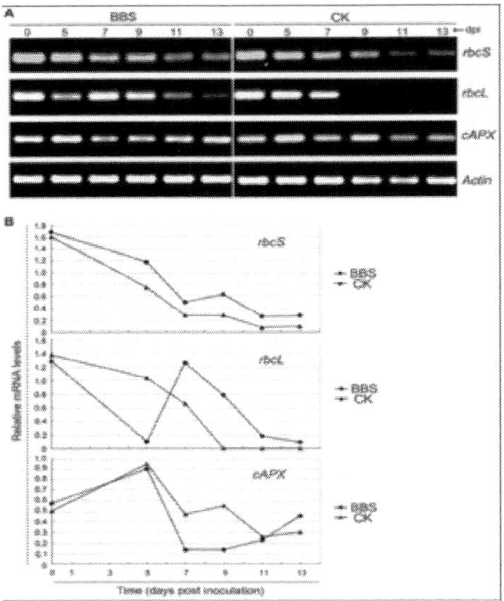

A- The expression of the genes rbcS, rbcL and cAPX was detected at 0, 5, 7, 9, 11, and 13 dpi by RT-PCR. **B**- Relative mRNA levels of genes.

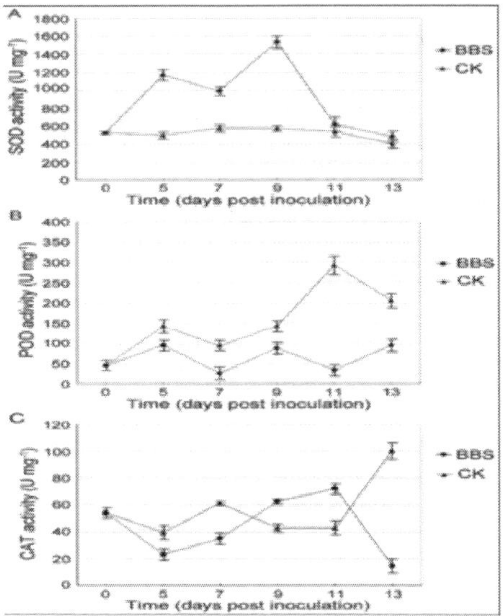

The leaf SOD, POD, and CAT activities in cucumber plants under drought stress.

(Wang *et al.*, 2012)

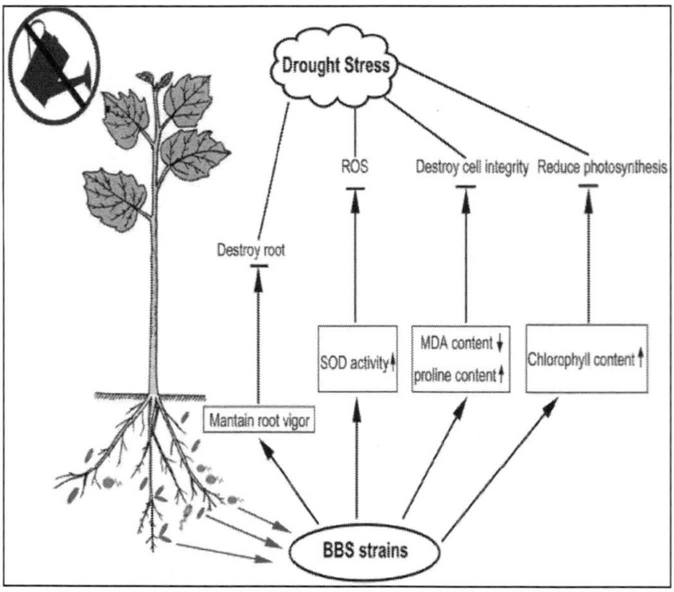

BBS Consortium Induced Systemic Tolerance to Drought Stress in Cucumber Plants.

Physiological Traits Relevant for Response to Drought Conditions

Plant Traits	*Effects Relevant for Yield*	*Modulation under Stress*
Stomatal conductance/leaf temperature	More/less rapid water consumption. Leaf temperature reflects the evaporation and hence is a function of stomatal conductance	Stomatal resistance increases under stress
Photosynthetic capacity	Modulation of concentration of Calvin cycle enzymes and elements of the light reactions	Reduction under stress
Timing of phenological phases	Early/late flowering. Maturity and growth duration, synchrony of silk emergence and anthesis, reduced grain number	Wheat and barley advanced flowering, rice delayed, maize asynchrony
Single plant leaf area	Plant size and related productivity	Reduced under stress (wilting, senescence, abscission)
Rooting depth	Higher/lower tapping of soil water resources	Reduced total mass but increased root/ shoot ratio, growth into wet soil layers, regrowth on stress release
Osmotic adjustment	Accumulation of solutes: ions, sugars, poly-sugars, amino acids, glycinebetaine	Slow response to water potential

Cattivelli *et al.*, 2008.

Drought Resistant Breeding

Breeding for drought resistance refers to breeding for yield under soil moisture stress conditions. In other words, it refers to yield improvement in environment represented by water deficit. Four breeding methods are:

1. Introduction
2. Selection
3. Hybridization
4. Mutation

Drought Tolerant Species and Genotypes of Vegetables

Sl.No.	*Vegetable Crops*	*Drought Tolerant Genotypes/Species*
1	Tomato	*S. pennelli* (IIHR 14-1, IIHR 146-2, IIHR 383, IIHR 553, IIHR 555, K-14, Sel-28), *S. pimpinellifoloium* (Pan American, LA1579), *S. esculentum* var. *cerasiforme, S. chilense,* Arka Vikas, RF- 4A, *L. pennellii* (LA0716),
2	Brinjal	*S. microcarpon, S. gilo, S. macrosperma, S. integrifolium,* Bundelkhand Deshi
3	Chilli	*C. chinense, C. baccatum var. pendulum, C. eximium,* Arka Lohit, IIHR - Sel.-132
4	Potato	*S. acaule, S. demissum and S. stenotonum,* Alpha, Bintje, *S.curtilobum,* Kufri Sheetman, *Solanum chacoense,* Kufri Sindhuri
5	Okra	*Caillei, A. rugosus, A. tuberosus*
6	Onion	*Allium fistulosum, A. munzii,* Arka Kalyan, MST 42, MST 46
7	French bean	*P. acutifolius*

Sl.No.	*Vegetable Crops*	*Drought Tolerant Genotypes/Species*
8	Water melon	*Citrullus colocynthis* (L.) *Schrad.*
9	Cucumber	INGR-98018 (AHC-13)
10	Sweet potato	VLS6, IGSP 10, IGSP 14, Sree Bhadra

Kumar *et al.*, 2012.

Limitations of Drought Resistance Breeding

1. Breeding for resistance to drought stress generally yields to reduction in yield due to strict selection pressure for resistant gene.
2. Genes for drought resistance mostly found in the germplasm line which are generally unadapted type.
3. In some cases, the drought resistant gene are available in the wild species, so transfer of resistant gene from wild sources possess several problems such as hybrid sterility and inviability.
4. Breeding for drought resistance requires co-operation among geneticist, breeder and crop physiologist.

Plant Improvement at Molecular Level of Plant

To understand water deficit stress at the molecular level, many genes have been isolated, such as *rd* (responsive todehydration), *erd* (early responsive to dehydration), and *Lea* (late embryogenesis abundant). The accumulation of LEA protein occurs during seed maturation, desiccation, and increases in vegetative tissue when plants are exposed to water deficit.Drought tolerance is a typical quantitative trait, however single genes, such as those controlling flowering time, plant height, ear type and OA, may have important roles in adaptation to drought-prone environments.

Relevant Examples of Genes Conferring Drought Tolerance

Genes	*Function*	*Mechanism of Action*
SNAC1	Stress induced transcription factor	*SNAC1* expression reduces water loss increasing stomatal sensitivity to ABA
OsCDPK7	Stress induced Ca-dependent protein kinase	Enhanced expression of stress responsive genes Conti.
HVA1	Stress induced LEA proteins	Over-accumulation of LEA increases drought tolerance also in field conditions
mtlD	Mannitol-1-phosphate dehydrogenase	Mannitol accumulation leads to increased osmotolerance
GF14λ	14-3-3 protein	Lines overexpressing *GF14λ* have a "stay green" phenotype, improved water stress tolerance and higher photosynthetic rates under water defcit conditions
NADP-Me	NADP-malic enzyme	The overexpression decreased stomatal conductance and improves WUE

Cattivelli *et al.*, 2008.

Response of Transgenic Tomato Plant under Drought Condition

C repeat/dehydration-responsive element binding factor 1 (CBF1) driven by a cauliflower mosaic virus 35S promoter, was transformed into the tomato genome. These transgenic tomato plants were more resistant to water deficit stress than the wild-type plants.The stomata of the transgenic CBF1 tomato plants closed more rapidly than the wild type after water deficit treatment with or without gibberellic acid pretreatment. The transgenic tomato plants contained higher levels of Proline than those of the wild-type plants under normal or water deficit conditions.Catalase activity increased and hydrogen peroxide concentration decreased in transgenic tomato plants compared with the wild-type plants.

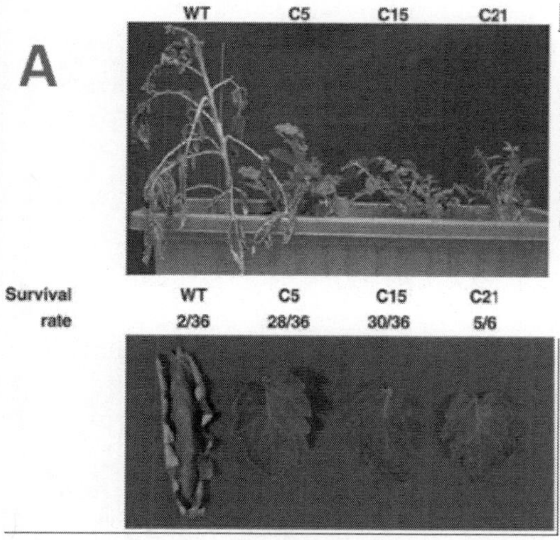

Wild-type and three transgenic T1 plants (WT, C5, C15, and C21) were grown at 24°C without watering for 21 d.

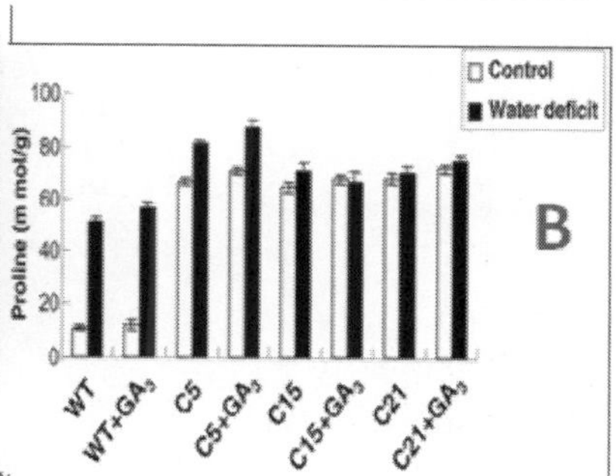

Transgenic tomato plants contain more Proline than wild-type plants. Wild-type and transgenic T1 plants with or without GA3 treatment were grown at 24°C with daily watering (control) or without watering for 28 d (water deficit).

(Hsieh *et al.*, 2002)

Engineering for Osmoprotectant Accumulation

Osmoprotectants are small neutral molecules that are non toxic to the cell at molar concentration and that stabilize proteins and cell membranes against the denaturing effect of stress conditions on cellular functions.The genetic engineering of metabolic pathways for the production of osmolytes such as mannitol, fructans, trehalose, ononitol, proline and glycine betaine increase resistance to drought.

Biochemical Indices

Different biochemical compounds get accumulated in plant in response to water stress conditions to give tolerance to plant, the different compounds involves:

Proteins and amino acids: Proline, aspartic and glutamic acid.

Methylated quaternary ammonium compounds: Glycine betaine, alanine betaine.

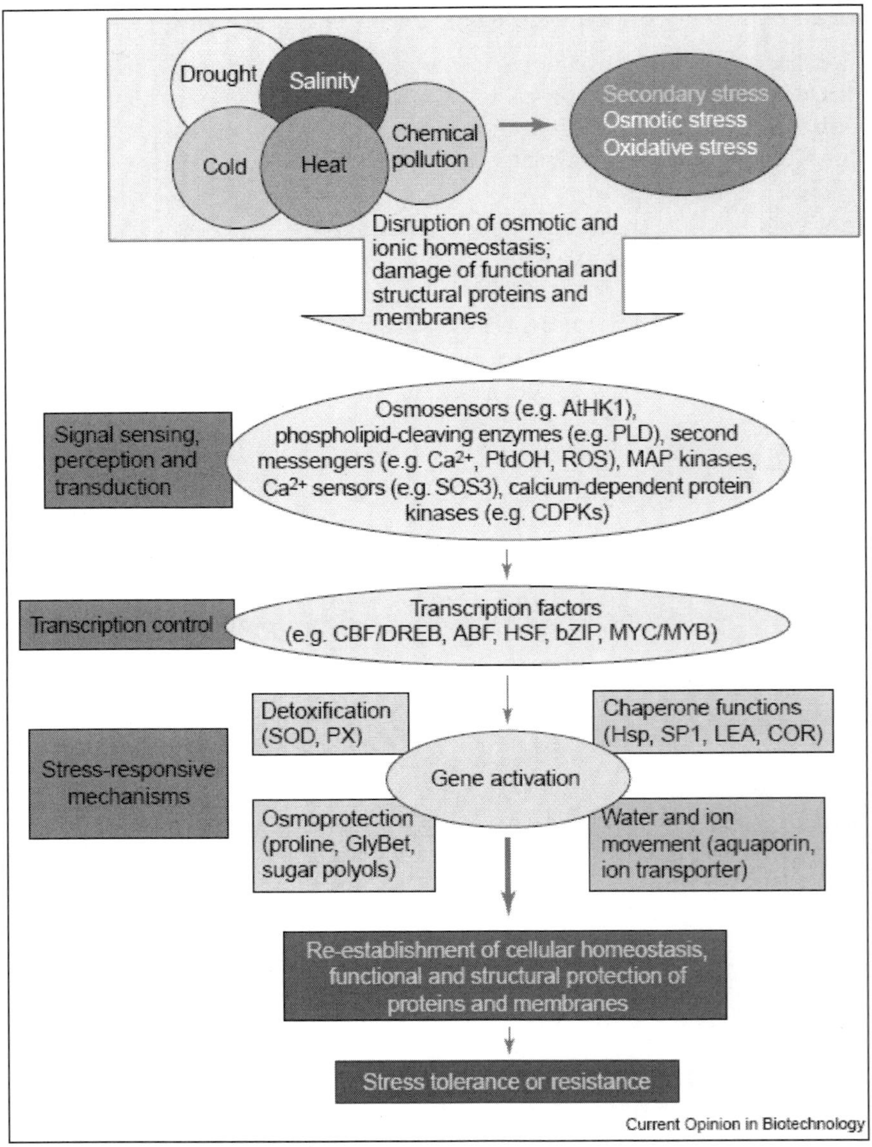

Vinocur and Altman, 2005
suggested molecular mechanisms associated with drought tolerance.

Hydrophilic proteins: LEA (dehydrin).

Growth hormone: ABA accumulation, ethylene.

Carbohydrate accumulation: fructans and sucrose.

Cyclitols: D-pinitol, mannitol.

Proline Content

This compound is produced instroma and cytoplasm in response to drought involves two step process in which Glutamate to Pyrroline- 5 –carboxyl ate enzyme involved is P5C synthase and P5C to Proline by P5C reductase. Many scientist reported its production in plant under drought conditions,up regulated expression of P5C under water and osmotic stress. Proline accumulation increases several stress related genes in rice, it is involved in prevention of protein denaturation and preservation of enzyme structure and activity, Protection of membranes from damage by ROS produced under drought by accumulation of Proline.

Glycine Betaine

This compound is produced in cytoplasm in two step process from choline to betaine aldehyde and from betaine aldehyde to Glycine betaine the enzymes involved are choline monooxygenase and betaine aldehyde dehydrogenase respectively. it is an amphoteric quaternary methylated protein, Protective effects results either from direct interaction with macro-molecules or through formation of protective shells around macro-molecules, Creates thermodynamic status to prevent unfolding and denaturation.

LEA (Dehydrin)

These are the hydrophilic globular proteins accumulate in organs in response to drought involved in seed maturation and desiccation that's why there name late embryogenesis proteins, Stabilizes membrane structures and enzyme complexes and promote ion sequestration in wheat, celery.

Cyclitols

These are the polyol found in plants synthesized from glucose 6-phosphate, Constitutes 80 per cent of total solutes involved in osmotic adjustment process *i.e.* major chemical involved in osmotic adjustment is mannitol, Works as osmoprotectant and thiol regulated enzyme against hydroxyl radicals.

ABA Accumulation

Accumulation of ABA under water deficit conditions may result from enhanced biosynthesis and\or a decrease in breakdown. it is synthesized in roots and shoots, the key regulatory step in ABA biosynthesis is catalysed by 9-cis- epoxycarotenoid dioxygenase (NCED), an enzyme that converts epoxycarotenoid precursor to xanthonin in the plastids, xanthonin is then converted into ABA by two cytosolic enzymes via abscisic aldehyde. ABA effects on stomatal closure may be mediated by a chemical signal originated in roots that may leads to changes in apoplastic ABA levels in in the leaves which may then cause stomatal closure. The signal transduction of ABA results in expression of different stress related genes which in turn gives osmoregulation, protection and stabilization to membranes, the different proteins reported in stress treated plants includes DREBP, ABAREBP, ethylene, *etc.*

Molecular Indices

- ☆ QTL identification

- MAS
- Proteomics
- Transgenic approach
- RNA Interference.
- TILLING and Eco- TILLING
- Insertional mutagenesis study
- Microarray technology *etc.*

Transgenic Approach

Genetic Engineering for Drought Tolerance

Methods of Transformation

1. Agrobacterium mediated
2. Particle bombardment (gun)
3. PEG-mediated
4. Electroporation
5. Silicon carbide fibers (WhiskersTM)

Measurement of Drought Resistance

1. **Leaf water retention** : In this method leaves are excised from the plant and are allowed to dry.
2. **Rate of photosynthesis** : The rate of photosynthesis during and after moisture stress is an important index of drought resistance.
3. **Yield performance** : Superior yield performance under moisture stress condition is an important and reliable index of drought tolerance.
4. **Root length of seedlings** : The root length during seedling stage is also used as a measure of drought resistance. In more recent study, it was observed that root mass after 30 days was reliable index of root mass at maturity. Thus, those genotypes which have longest root during seedling stage also exhibit extensive root system at maturity. This is a simple and quick method of measuring drought resistance.

Screening Procedure for Drought Tolerance

Sl.No.	*Screening for the Purpose of*	*Instruments/Techniques Used*
1	Efficient water uptake	Infrared thermometry
2	Root growth	Banding herbicide metribuzin at a certain depth of soil, and use of iodine-131 and hydroponic culture under stress of 15 bar
3	Evaluation of osmosis	Adaptation of psychometric procedure
4	Leaf water conductance	Diffusion porometry technique

Sl.No.	Screening for the Purpose of	Instruments/Techniques Used
5	Root penetration, distribution and density in the field	Mini-rhizotron technique
6	Total yield and number of fruits	Drought index measurement
7	Maturity, leaf molding, leaf length, angle, orientation, root morphology and other morphological characters	Visual scoring or measurement

Kumar *et al.*, 2012.

Screening of Plants for Drought Resistance

Kulkarni and Deshpande (2007) worked on screening of tomato germplasm under in vitro condition using polyethylene glycol (PEG) at four concentrations (0, 20, 40 and 60 g/l).Important seedling characters like root (length and weight) and shoot (length and weight) were recorded.Based on results, Hy-3 and MTG 1-4 were found to be drought resistant due to their remarkable performance at all levels of water stress.This *in vitro* screening method is potential and cost effective method to screen large set of germplasm within very less time period and accurately.

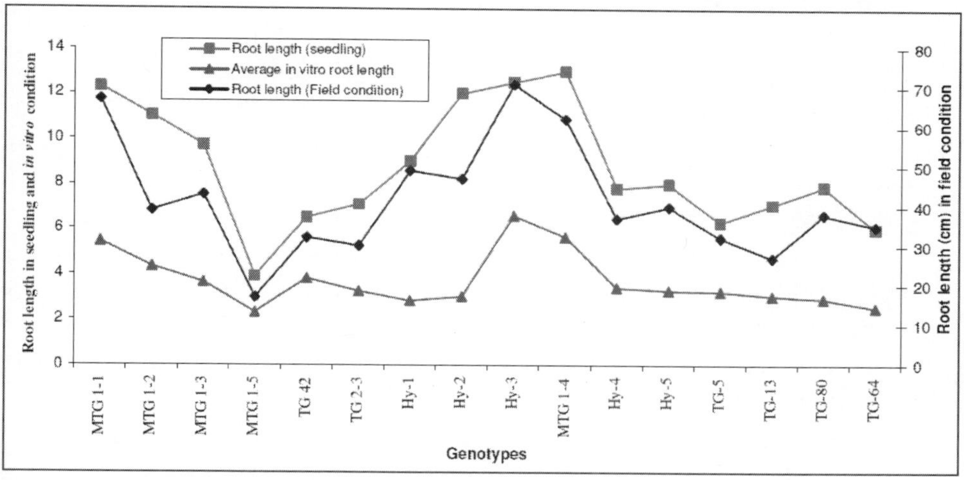

Comparative Root Growth Studies of Drought Resistance of Tomato Genotypes using Polyethylene Glycol (Kulkarni and Deshpande, 2007).

Work Related to Drought Resistance at Pantnagar

Bhatt *et al.* (2011) studied the impact of drought stress on five finger millet varieties (PR202, VL146, VL315, PES400 and VR708).Drought stress induced increase in the activity of superoxide dismutase, ascorbate peroxidase and glutathione reductase was higher in PR202 and VL315, while the activity was lower in the varieties PES400 and VR708.The results clearly indicate that better drought tolerance of the variety PR202 is positively related to the capacity of its antioxidant system to scavenge reactive oxygen species, resulting in a reduced incidence of oxidative damage.

Gusain *et al.* (2015) tested plant growth promoting rhizobacterial (PGPR) strains *Pseudomonas fluorescence* strain P2 for their role in enhancing plant growth and induction of stress related enzymes in Sahbhagi (drought tolerance) and IR-64 (drought sensitive) cultivars of rice (*Oryza sativa* L.) under different level of drought stress.Quantitative analysis of antioxidant enzymes indicated that both varieties showed higher proline content, higher activity of superoxide dismutase (SOD), catalase (CAT), peroxidase (POD), ascorbate peroxidase (APX) and lower level of hydrogen peroxide (H_2O_2), Malondialdehyde (MDA) in leaves at all the level of drought stress.

NASA's Tool to Identify Drought-Resilient Plants

The US space agency is developing a new space based instrument to study how plants react to heat and water stress and identify drought resilient plants. The instrument called the ECOsystem Spaceborne Thermal Radiometer Experiment on Space Station (ECOSTRESS) will monitor one of the most basic processes in living plants, the loss of water through the tiny pores in leaves. It is high resolution thermal infrared radiometer, which works like a giant thermometer from space to measure the temperature of plants and amount of heat radiating from earth surface (http://www.jpl.nasa.gov/news/news.php).

Do's and Don'ts for Vegetable Crops

1. Establishing vegetation-free strips under the trees and between tree rows before growth begins.
2. In crop like onion, drum seeder may be used for direct sowing.
3. Postpone transplanting of seedlings in the main field and also fertilizer application till the favorable soil moisture is prevailed.
4. Once the soil moisture condition becomes favorable transplanting of the seedlings may be taken up.
5. Resorting to foliar application of (water soluble) major nutrients.
6. Protection of young plants with partial shade.
7. In the inter spaces of crops weeding and inter-culture practices may be followed.
8. Thinning may be taken up to reduce the plant population.
9. Alternate furrow Irrigation may be taken up based on the availability of water.
10. Drip Irrigation may be followed. Pitcher irrigation wherever drip is unavailable for protective maintenance.
11. Plastic mulching and drip irrigation may be followed for better soil and moisture conservation and weed control.
12. Adopting the conjunctive use of surface and ground water as well as the use of non- conventional sources such as brackish water,
13. Waste water should not be utilized without pre treatment and safe reuse may be ensured.

14. Minimise use of those fertilizers which promote vegetative growth like nitrogen, use K and B as foliar spray to maintain plant turgor.
15. Reducing water losses during conveyance and distribution,
16. Use of super absorbent polymers such as Luquasorb for water absorption and slow release.

Constraint

1. Lack of efforts through multidisciplinary approach.
2. Incomplete knowledge of indices, selection criteria and influence ofenvironment on drought-related traits.
3. Genetic basis of many of the physiological and biochemical indices is unknown.
4. Drought reduces nutrient uptake and is associated with temperature stress and higher elevation with cold, makes breeding more complicated.
5. Limitation in application of genetic engineering is lack of information on availability of the most appropriate gene.

Future Strategies

1. There is an urgent need for exploration of the plant genetic resources with attributes related to drought resistance in different crop plants and their characterization.
2. Many different genes responsible for biosynthesis of different solutes conferring drought resistance should be considered for transfer in a crop plant at a time.
3. Identification of protein marker to produce drought resistant plants.
4. A multidisciplinary approach involving genetics, biochemistry, biotechnology, physiology, plant breeding will be appropriate to find out superior drought genotypes.

Web Resources Related to Drought

- ✰ http://www.generationcp.org/
- ✰ http://www.plantstress.com/
- ✰ http://rarge.gsc.riken.jp/
- ✰ http://rootgenomics.missouri.edu/

Conclusion

Now a day, population pressure and industrialization cause scarcity of water and land for agricultural use as well as change in climate which leads to erratic precipitation. So, using knowledge of all the sectors of agriculture we can improve crop performance sustainably which will help in overcoming food scarcity problem under drought conditions.

REFERENCES

Anonymous, 1985. Drought Basics. National Drought Mitigation Center, University of Nebraska-Lincoln, Nebraska, United States.

Anonymous, 2014. Preparing for a poor monsoon". *The Hindu*. 26 April 2014. Retrieved 27 April 2014.

Begg, J.E. and Turner, N.C. 1976. Crop water deficits. *Adv. Agron.,* 28: 161-217.

Bhatt, D., Negi, M., Sharma, P., Saxena, S.C., Dobriyal, A.K. and Arora, S. 2011. Responses to drought induced oxidative stress in five finger millet varieties differing in their geographical distribution. *Physiol. Mol. Bio. Plants,***17**.4: 347–353.

Cattivelli, L., Rizza, F., Badeck, F.W., Mazzucotelli, E., Mastrangelo, A.M., Francia, E., Mare, C., Tondelli, A. and Stanca, A.M. 2008. Drought tolerance improvement in crop plants: An integrated view from breeding to genomics. *Field Crops Research,* 105: 1–14.

Giorio, P., Sorrentino, G. and Andria R. 1999. Stomatal behaviour, leaf water status and photosynthetic response in field-grown olive trees under water deficit. *Environ. Exp. Bot.,* 42: 95-104.

Gonzales, L. and Gonzales-Vilar, M. 2001. Determination of relative water content. ***In***: Reigosa, M.J. (ed.) Handbook of Plant Ecophysiology Techniques, Dordrecht: *Kluwer Academic Publishers,* 207-212.

Gusain, Y.S., Singh, U.S. and Sharma, A.K. 2015. Bacterial mediated amelioration of drought stress in drought tolerant and susceptible cultivars of rice (*Oryza sativa* L.). *African J. Biotech.,***14**.9, 764-773.

Hall, A.E. 2004. Breeding for adaptation to drought and heat in cowpea. *Europ. J. Agron.,* 21: 447-454.

Holbrook, N.M., Shashidhar, V.R., James, R.A. and Munns, R. 2002. Stomata control in tomato with ABA deficient roots: response of grafted plants to soil drying. *J. Exp. Bot.,* **53**: 373, 1503–1514.

Hsieh, T., Lee, J., Charng, Y. and Chan, M. 2002. Tomato plants ectopically expressing arabidopsis CBF1 show enhanced resistance to water deficit stress.*Plant Physiol.,*130: 618-626.

http: //www.jpl.nasa.gov/news/news.php

Isendahl, N. and Schmidt, G. 2006. Drought in the Mediterranean-WWF policy proposals, A WWF report, Madrid. 5p.

Keyantash, J. and Dracup, J.A. 2002. The quantification of drought: an evaluation of drought indices. *Bull. Am. Meteorol. Soc.,* 83: 1167-1180.

Kulkarni, M. and Deshpande, U. 2007. *In Vitro* screening of tomato genotypes for drought resistance using polyethylene glycol. *African J. Biotech.,* **6**.6: 691-696.

Kumar, K.K., Rajagopalan, B., Hoerling, M., Bates, G. And Cane, M. 2006. Unraveling the mystery of Indian monsoon failure during *El Niño, Science,*314: 115–119.

Kumar, R., Solankey, S.S. and Singh, M. 2012. Breeding for drought tolerance in vegetables. *Veg. Sci.,* **39**.1: 1-15.

Mitra, J. 2001. Genetics and genetic improvement of drought resistance in crop plants. *Curr. Sci.,* **80**.6: 758-763.

Pena, R.D.L. and Hughes, J. 2007. Improving vegetable productivity in a variable and changing climate. *AVRDC,* **4**.1: 1-22.

Rivero, R.M., Kojima, M., Gepstein, A., Sakakibara, H., Mittler, R., Gepstein, S. and Blumwald, E. 2007. Delayed leaf senescence induces extreme drought tolerance in a flowering plant. *Proc. Natl. Acad. Sci.,* 104: 19631-19636.

Rouphael, Y., Mariateresa, C. and Giuseppe, C. 2008. Yield, mineral composition, water relations, and water use efficiency of grafted mini-watermelon plants under deficit irrigation. *Hort. Sci.,***43**.3: 730–736.

Satisha, J., Prakash, G.S., Bhatt, R.M. and Kumar, S.P. 2007. Physiological mechanisms of water use efficiency in grape rootstocks under drought conditions. *Int. J. Agric. Res.* 2: 159–164.

Schwarz, D., Rouphael, Y. Colla, G. and Venema, J.H. 2010. Grafting as a tool to improve tolerance of vegetables to abiotic stresses: Thermal stress, water stress and organic pollutants. *Scientia Horticulturae,*127: 162–171.

Turner, N.C. 1979. Stress Physiology in Crop Plants. ***In.*** Mussell, H. and Staples, R.C. (eds.). *Wiley,* New York, 343-372.

Ugherughe, P.O. 1986. Drought and tropical pasture management. *J. Agron. Crop Sci.,* 157: 13-23.

Vinocur, B. and Altman, A. 2005. Recent advances in engineering plant tolerance to abiotic stress: achievements and limitations. *Curr. Opin. Biotech.,* 16: 123–132.

Wang, C.J., Yang, W., Wang, C., Gu. C., Niu, D.D., Liu, H.X., Wang, Y.P and Guo, J.H. 2012. Induction of Drought Tolerance in Cucumber Plants by aConsortium of Three Plant Growth-PromotingRhizobacterium Strains. *Plos One,***7**.12: 1-10.

Chapter 9

Breeding Commerical Vegetable Cultivars

Introduction

Vegetables are considered essential for well balanced diets. The production and marketing of vegetables crops are undergoing continuous change globally. This is mainly due to the growing demands of consumers for safe and healthy vegetables, increased urbanisation of societies, and the growth in scale and influence of supermarkets chains. Horticultural science can respond to many of these challenges through research, breeding and innovation that can seek to gain more efficient methods of crop production, refined postharvest storage and handling methods, newer and higher value vegetable cultivars and demonstration of their health benefits. Vegetable breeding has to address and satisfy the needs of both the consumer and the producer. Innovation in vegetable breeding depends on specific knowledge, the development and application of new technologies, access to genetic resources, and capital to utilise them. The driving force behind this innovation is acquiring or increasing market share. Access to technology, as well as biodiversity, is essential for the development of new vegetable cultivars. A few multinational corporations, whose vast economic power has effectively marginalized the role of public sector breeding as well as local, small/medium-scale seed companies, dominate the global vegetable seed trade. For most vegetable crops, only a few multinational seed corporations are controlling large part of the world market. This situation makes a growing part of the global vegetable supply dependent on a few seed providers. The multinational seed corporations ensued from merging some small or medium vegetable breeding programs to reduce costs. There may be fewer vegetable breeders in the future and growers will rely on seeds with a narrow genetic base. In order to meet future needs of vegetable breeders it is important that educacional programs incorporate rapidly changing new technologies with classical content and methods. Active and positive connections between the private and public breeding sectors and large-scale gene banks are required to avoid a possible conflict involving breeders' rights, gene preservation and erosion. Horticulturists will need to develop cultural practices and vegetable breeders to breed vegetables for a multifunctional horticulture (diversity, health promotion, postharvest , yearround suply, *etc.*) and to cope with harsher climate conditions and lower inputs than they have come to expect. Improved production systems that can cope with climate extremes must allow vegetables to produce under high temperatures, greater drought stress, increased soil salinity, and periodic flooding. This will involve a combination of improved vegetable cultivars and modified production systems.

Vegetable growing offers more employment opportunity because of being labour intensive, short duration, high return and high tonnage per unit area. India is bestowed with varied agro-climatic conditions which allow growing of all types of vegetables in open in one part of the country or other. Export potential of vegetable to generate valuable foreign exchange required to be fully tapped; thus far it is mainly confined to onion. India is the second largest vegetable producer next only to China. However, vegetables are grown in hardly 2 per cent of the total cultivated area of the country which is very low in view of national need.

The vegetable improvement work in India, started about three decades ago, resulted in the development of a large number of improved varieties. These efforts were further streamlined and strengthened with the start of the All India Coordinated Vegetable Improvement Project (AICVIP) in 1970-71. So far research work has been concentrated only on 30 vegetable crops and out of these tomato, brinjal, okra, cauliflower, cabbage, onion, pea, melons, chilli and bell pepper are the important crops on which adequate emphasis has been given. Under AICVIP a number of varieties of vegetable crops were identified and recommended for release in different zones of the country. For the last two decades, vegetable breeders in India diverted their attention towards the development of hybrids and disease resistant vars/hybrids. Vegetables have great potential for export and after value addition these can become an important commodity of agricultural export out of India.

Germplasm Collection, Utilization and Conservation

Crop improvement is an unending process and it always requires new genes and their new recombination. Vegetables have tremendous strength in terms of natural resources and biological assets especially genetic resources. A large number of wild taxa and indigenous germplasm are available in the country and many of them have not been fully capitalized. Introduction of germplasm from abroad has also made significant impact on vegetable improvement. Several promising introductions made in the past were directly released for commercial cultivation in the country. Diverse introductions were also utilized as donor types for desired traits. Looking at the national scenario, India is endowed with tremendous wealth of biodiversity with respect to genetic material. The extent of diversity is immense in crops like egg plant, chilli, cauliflower, muskmelon, bitter gourd, cucumber, onion *etc.* The mountainous area, eastern region and tribal areas are the important regions of genetic diversity in a number of vegetable crops. Still many wild, semi wild, land races and old varieties are being grown under natural conditions in several parts of the country especially in tribal belts which has tremendous potential for their collection, maintenance utilization and conservation. Conservation of threatened species requires special attention. So there is a need to undertake intensive research programme to make best use of available germplasm material in the country.

Production of High Yielding Varieties/Hybrids

With the start of the All India Coordinated Vegetable Improvement Project in 1970-71, the work on vegetable crop was streamlined through research network spread over the agricultural universities and ICAR institutes. So far 155 open pollinated varieties in 14 vegetable crops have been identified for cultivation under different agroclimatic zones of the country. For the past one and half decade, vegetable breeders of India paid more attention towards the development of F_1 hybrids in important vegetables particularly tomato, brinjal, bell pepper, watermelon, muskmelon *etc.* The hybrids have been found more suitable, stable and tolerant to major diseases under varied agro-climatic conditio ns. The credit for popularization of hybrid vegetables in India goes to the seed companies and first tomato and bell pepper hybrids were marketed by Indo-American Hybrid Seed Company in 1973. A major break through in the past few years have been realized in tomato production from F_1 hybrids. In the wake of liberalization of imports under Open General License (OGL), a number of private companies have come forward to and introduce/develop hybrids in vegetable crops. Many of these hybrids are highly susceptib le to a number of diseases and pests. Further many new diseases have been introduced which require additional research backup to develop package for controlling these diseases. Under these circumstances, we have to look into the fresh areas like developing multiple disease resistant hybrids. This is a long term strategy in vegetable research which will require an effective collaboration with pathologists along with variable breeding lines/sources of resistance to various pathogens. Such programmes also need good facilities like disease resistant laboratory, growth chamber, greenhouse *etc.* During coming years, the major thrust area will be to develop hybrids in a number of vegetable crops. Also the main strategies in coming years will be to generate all kind s of requisite production technology of hybrids. This will go a long way in increasing production of hybrid varieties of vegetable crops. In the coming years, strategies have to be developed for large scale production of hybrid seed at low cost. For this hybrids based on male sterility, self incompatibility, gynoecious lines and monoecious lines, in requisite, crops will have to be developed. Use of growth substances like ethrel, gibberellic acid and silver nitrate can be done in economizing hybrid seed production after proper standardization. Biotechnology can play a vital role to make the hybrid technology a success. Mass propagation of parental lines especially self incompatible lines, gynoecious lines, and male sterile lines in *vitro* is an important area for maintenance and multiplication of parental lines.

Resistance Breeding

1. Biotic Stresses

The major problem in the vegetable production is the heavy incidences of diseases and pests. Amongst the many alternatives of controlling the insect pests and disease, chemical control is being widely followed all over the world. Due to carcinogenic nature of these chemicals many countries including India are interested in the vegetables produced without using chemicals. Therefore, the breeding work has been directed toward development of insect pests and disease resistant varieties/hybrids in the country. Several promising disease resistant varieties have been developed and recommended for cultivation under disease prone areas. These varieties have made sustainable impact in the production of tomato, brinjal and okra in many parts of the country.

On the contrary the progress in the development of insect resistance is very limited. Varieties released till date are having one or more undesirable characters associa ted with them and hence have not gained the popularity. In some of the varieties of brinjal biochemical analysis have revealed high glycoalkaloid content, peroxidase and polyphenol oxidase activity than the susceptible cultivars.

Finally it can be concluded that insect pests and diseases is a major issue in vegetable production. Although there are effective chemical control measures of a number of insect pests, the cost of such chemicals is very high and many chemicals exhibit residual effects. This requires strategies to generate technology for economic control of major pests of vegetable. Host plant resistance is the economical method but such resistance against insect pest is never stable due to population pressure of insects on the host as a result there is evolution of new biotypes and breakdown of resistance. Under this situation there is a need to search tolerant lines showing low degree of incidence and application of chemicals at critical stages.

2. Abiotic Stresses

In India, approximately 70 per cent cultivable land is under dry land cultivation. Varieties which can withstand drought cold, heat salinity, alkalinity, environmental pollution or other climatic stress of growth, will have wider adaptability as well as stability. Very limited efforts have been done to develop vegetable varieties resistant/tolerant to these abiotic stresses. Since occurrence of such stresses is increasing day by day due to a number of ecological factors, a comprehensive breeding strategy will have to be developed to produce varieties/hybrids resistant/tolerant to these stresses. Further more, there is a need to standardize technology and package of practices for growing of vegetables under abiotic stress conditions.

Breeding for Export

India is the second largest producer of vegetables next only to China, yet less than one per cent of the produce is exported. The reason can be found in lack of quality, poor postharvest management and lack of market intelligence. So as to remain competitive the quality has to be maintained, which is of prime importance in horticultural crops like vegetables. The quality being most important for export, the variety chosen has to be acceptable internationally/nationally and the environment in which it is produced should be conducive for the development of inherent characters of the variety to the best. However in India no systemic breeding work has been done to produce varieties/hybrids acceptable in the international market.

Among vegetables, onion is the major item of export. Export of onion from India is primarily directed to Malaysia, Singapore, Sri Lanka and Gulf countries. Light red and dark red varieties are in demand in Gulf countries, Sri Lanka and for East while small onions are in demand in Malaysia, Singapore and Sri Lanka. Arka Bindu and Yellow onion evolved by IIHR are suitable for export. Arka Bindu has good demand in Middle-East countries. Similarly CO-4 variety of multiplier onion developed by TNAU is suitable for export to South East Asian countries. In respect of fresh vegetable export, nearly 60 per cent of the trade centres around okra. Varieties Arka Abhay, Varsha and Uphar, which are resistant to YVMV, are suitable for export. The export demand centres around fruits having 7-9 cm length. In tomato fresh fruits can be exported to Middle East. Varieties Arka Aloke and Arka Shakti from IIHR have been bred to be resistant to wilt and can be grown in sick soil in Kerala, parts of Karnataka, Maharashtra and Odisha for export. Similarly in potato, varieties Kufri Chandramukhi, Kufri Lauvkar and Kufri Sindhuri, which have oval to long sized tubers with yellow to light yellow flesh, are required in Gulf countries.

Application of Biotechnological Techniques

Although main emphasis has been laid on conventional breeding methodology to develop high yield, good quality and resistant varieties, but work in several laboratories has been initiated on biotechnological aspect also. In order to produce homozygous diploid plants, anther culture technique is being followed to produce haploids in tomato, capsicum, cucurbits and cole crops.

Salt tolerant lines can be identified under laboratory conditions by tissue culture method.

1. Virus free plants are produced with tip culture method.
2. In order to protect germplasm from extinction, the germplasm can be conserved in liquid media. Generally, germplasm lines of tomato, pea and carrot are being preserved at -195°C in liquid nitrogen.
3. RFLP facilities a practical and rapid check of seed purity of an F1 hybrid.
4. Taxonomy and origin of cole crops have been investigated based on molecular markers (RFLP) and random amplified polymorphism DNA (RAPD) markers. Broccoli, cauliflower and cabbage groups have been clustered with very little over lapping.
5. Genetic engineering allows single gene to be transferred to the target species from a wide variety of sources. it overcomes the species barriers and gives complete control over the characters of the transgenic plant.

Plant biotechnology is a rapidly growing area of plant biology and is a potential tool for increasing vegetable productivity. The approaches like *in vitro* screening for disease resistance, gene tagging, genetic transformation *etc.* will have to be used for the development of new varieties in vegetable crops. Such strategies will result in the faster development of resistant varieties in a number of vegetable crops. The greatest strides in past to develop disease resistant cultivars have been made by plant breeders and plant pathologists working together. In future, a team effort should include a molecular geneticist as well. Such a team could discuss the needs of the farmers/users, the strength and weakness of current cvs, the genetic resources available to meet those needs, and the evaluation methods available. They could then use the genes and tools that are most appropriate and cost effective under the situation.

Future Strategies

There is a need to undertake intensive research programme to make best use of available germplasm in the country and above all to conserve this valuable genetic resource. Due emphasis has not been given in breeding for integrated management of diseases, insect pests such leaf curl, TMV in tomato, fruit and shoot borer in brinjal, virus complex of sweet pepper *etc.* An effective collaboration of breeders and plant pathologists/entomologists will be of high proposition to tackle this problem. There is a need for heterosis breeding in onion, cauliflower and root crops.

Inspite of the fact that mechanisms like cytoplamic-genic male sterility, self incompatibility and suitable sex expression are available in these crops, breeders have failed to exploit them for raising the existing yield levels and quality of these crops. Similarly breeding for resistance to abiotic stress remained neglected todate. Systematic work on breeding varieties of okra, pea, tomato and onion for processing could not receive due attention of the breeders. Presently the processing industry survives mainly on the availability of surplus vegetables during the glut period in the market. Such vegetables are of poor quality from the processing point of view, since the requirements of this industry are very specific for a quality produce. Vegetable varieties with prolonged shelf life are needed for distant transportation and export. For instance in tomato, efforts should be made to improve shelf life by using slow ripening genes (*Nor* and *Rin*). Due emphasis has also not been given to the development of vegetables for export. The Agricultural and Processed Food Products Export Development Authority (APEDA) has identified traditional vegetables like onion, okra, bitter gourd, chilli and non-traditional vegetables like asparagus, celery, bell pepper, baby corn, greens and lima beans having good potential.

Improved Postharvest and Supply Chain Methods

A major trend over the past decade, possibly as a consequence of smaller households and more dedication to leisure activities, has been the shift towards the consumption of fresh rather than frozen vegetables. Modern consumers do not store vegetable products for long periods within the household and are able to discern the difference in quality (taste, flavour, and texture) between vegetables that have been stored for short versus long periods. The challenge for breeding and horticultural science is, therefore, to refine methods for shortterm storage so that premium quality is retained rather than to focus on longer-term storage for prolonged marketing. Interestingly, this potentially transforms the approaches that can be taken for chilling sensitive vegetables where long-term storage techniques have not been routinely available. The option to provide for new approaches that can be used for quality retention during short-term storage should be an absolute priority. Maturity at harvest is the most important determinant of storage-life and of final fruit-vegetable quality. Many vegetables, in particular leafy vegetables, and immature fruit-vegetables (such as cucumbers, sweet corn, green beans, peas, and okras), attain optimum eating-quality prior to reaching full maturity. This often results in delayed harvest, and consequently in produce of low quality. The method of harvesting (hand vs mechanical) can significantly impact upon the composition and postharvest quality of vegetables. Mechanical injuries (such as bruising, surface abrasions and cuts) can accelerate loss of water and vitamin C resulting in increased susceptibility to decay-causing pathogens. Most fresh vegetables are harvested by hand. Root crops (such as carrot, onion, potato, and sweet potato) and some commodities destined for processing (such as processing tomatoes) are mechanically harvested. Management of harvesting operations, whether manual or mechanical, can have a major impact on the quality of harvested vegetables. Proper management procedures include selection of optimum time to harvest in relation to product maturity and climatic conditions, training and supervision of workers, and proper implementation of effective quality control. Expedited and careful handling, immediate cooling after harvest, maintenance of optimum temperatures during transit and storage, and effective decay-control procedures are important factors in the successful postharvest handling of vegetables. Attention must be paid to all of these factors, regardless of the method of harvesting used. These factors are nevertheless more critical in the case of mechanically harvested commodities. It should be noted that any practice that reduces the number of produce handling steps will help minimize losses. Field packing (selection, sorting, trimming, and packaging) of produce at the time of harvest can greatly reduce the number of handling steps in preparation vegetables for marketing. Mobile field packing stations with adequate shading are used for vegetables (such as broccoli, cauliflower, and green beans) that do not require washing as part of their preparation for marketing. Within each vegetable there is a range of genotypic variation in composition, quality, and postharvest -life potential. Plant breeders have been successful in selecting carrot, sweet potato, and tomato cultivars with comparably high carotenoid levels and vitamin A content; onion and tomato cultivars with longer shelf-lives, sweet corn cultivars that maintain their sweetness longer after harvest; cantaloupe and watermelon cultivars with higher sugar content and firmer flesh, *etc.* These are just a few examples of how genetic manipulation has contributed to improving the quality of vegetables and postharvest potential. Breeders have also developed vegetable cultivars with improved storage characteristics, including resistance to storage fungi and pests, as well as physiological disorders. More adequate and sustained funding for this work is required, as well as improved linkages among breeders, nutritionists, health sector experts, and policymakers. Low-cost safe storage structures for small and intermediate scale farmers need to be promoted. Many opportunities exist for applying biotechnology to improve the postharvest quality and safety of fresh vegetables. Priority goals in this regard, should, be focused on: i) attaining and maintaining good flavor and nutritional quality, so as to satisfy consumer demands; and ii) introducing resistance to physiological disorders and/or decay-causing pathogens and pests, so as to reduce the use of chemicals on vegetables. For example in tomato, the first transgenic vegetable crop, there are a lot of research conducted to manipulate fruit ripening, texture and nutritional quality using transgenic approaches. Many of the genes targeted include ethylene because of its role in fruit ripening. Enzymes that regulate ethylene biosynthesis in plants are: S-adenosylmethionine (SAM) synthase, 1-aminocyclopropane-1-carboxylate (ACC) synthase, and ACC oxidase. The genes encoding these enzymes [108,109] as well as those that metabolize SAM or ACC have been targeted in order to manipulate ethylene biosynthesis, thereby regulating fruit ripening. It has been clearly shown that modulation of ethylene biosynthesis using genetic engineering can yield tomato fruits with predictable ripening characteristics. Tomato fruit ripening manipulation has been however achieved by introducing anti-ripening genes (*rin* and *nor*) in heterozygous genotypes. These genes have been incorporated in many fresh and processing tomatoes.

Outlook

The production and marketing of vegetables crops is undergoing continuous change globally. This is mainly due to the growing demands of consumers for safe and healthy vegetables, increased urbanisation of societies, and the growth in scale and influence of supermarkets chains. The changes outlined above are merely some of the factors that are impacting on current production practices for vegetable crops. They also provide a plethora of opportunities for vegetable breeding and horticultural science to solve many of the current problems facing producers and to offer solutions to those issues that are concerning consumers. Horticultural science can respond to many of these challenges through research, breeding and innovation that can seek to gain more efficient methods of crop production, refined postharvest storage and handling methods, newer and higher value vegetable cultivars and demonstration of their health benefits. Horticulturists will need to develop cultural practices and vegetable breeders to breed vegetables for a multifunctional horticulture (diversity, health promotion, postharvest, year-round supply, *etc.*) and to cope with harsher climate conditions and lower inputs than they have come to expect. Improved production systems that can cope with climate extremes must allow vegetables to produce under high temperatures, greater drought stress, increased soil salinity, and periodic flooding. This will involve a combination of improved vegetable cultivars and modified production systems. The continued globalisation of the vegetable industry will see a rapid transfer and adoption of knowledge. This will include the transfer from developed to developing countries as major enterprises move to year-round production and in response to securing lower-cost land and labour. Many of these activities will, however, be carried out by the private sector where the protection of intellectual property, the development of unique and proprietary vegetable cultivars and the advocacy of brands will, undoubtedly, see a markedly diminished involvement of the public sector. Modern trends indicate that consumers are seeking increased variety, novelty, and healthy options in their eating choices. Creation of vegetable hybrids is a key means towards the development of cultivars for modern vegetable production.

Hybrid seed production is high technology and a cost intensive venture. Only well organized seed companies with good scientific manpower and well equipped research facilities can afford seed production. Due to globalization most vegetable breeding research and cultivar development in the world are presently conducted

REFERENCES

Allard, R.W. 1960. Principles of Plant Breeding. John Wiley and Sons, New York.

Grumet, R. 1995. Genetic engineering for crop viruses. *Hort. Sci.* 30 : 449-456.

Gupta, RK. 1995. Elements of Biotechnology. Rastogi and co., Meerut.

João Carlos da Silva Dias 2014. Guiding strategies for breeding vegetable cultivars. Agricultural Sciences 5 (1): 9-32.

Kumar, J. *et al.,* 1977. Breeding for disease resistance: A review. *Crop Improv.* 4 : 123-144.

Kohli U.K. 2004. Department of Vegetable Crops University of Horticulture and Forestry Nauni, Solan, H.P. 173 230.

Vidhyasekaran, P. 1993. Genetic engineering, molecular biology and tissue culture for crop pest and disease management. Daya Publishing House, Delhi.

Chapter 10

Advances in Protected Cultivation of Vegetable Crops

Introduction

As a result of globalization of trade and liberalization of Indian economy, there is an immense scope for export of high value horticultural crops from India, besides meeting the increased demand in domestic market. The need of the time is to increase the productivity and quality of produce to meet the demand of quality conscious consumers. A breakthrough in production technology that integrates market driven quality parameters with the production system, besides ensuring a vertical growth in productivity is required. One such technology is "Protected cultivation", or generally called greenhouse technology. In the present scenario of perpetual demand of fruits, flowers and vegetables, protected cultivation is the best alternative for using land and water resources more efficiently and around 25,000 ha area is under protected cultivation in different parts of the India and this technology is sustainable and suitable for different parts of India (Paroda, 2013). Greenhouse technology provides optimum conditions of light, temperature, humidity, CO_2 for the best growth of plant to achieve maximum yield with best quality (Ngouajio and Ernest, 2004).

Why Protected Cultivation?

- ☆ Crops could be grown under inclement climatic conditions when it is not possible to grow in open field.
- ☆ In greenhouses having complete environmental control certain crops could be grown year round to meet the market demands.
- ☆ Off- season production of nursery and crops.

- ☆ Early nursery and early cropping.
- ☆ Higher productivity – enhanced crop duration.
- ☆ Superior quality of the produce.
- ☆ Efficient utilization of precious inputs like water and nutrients.
- ☆ Effective control against diseases, insect pests.
- ☆ Reduced expenditure on weed control.
- ☆ Hardening and acclimatization of tissue cultured plants.
- ☆ Hybrid vegetable seed production.
- ☆ Protection against heavy rains, hails, birds *etc.*

Principles of Protected Crop Production

The productivity of a crop is influenced not only by its heredity but also by the microclimate around it. The components of crop microclimate are light, temperature, air composition and the nature of the root medium. Under open field conditions, it is not possible to control over light, temperature and air composition. The only possibility under open-field conditions is to manipulate the nature of the root medium by tillage, irrigation, fertilizer applications, *etc.* Even here, the nature of the root medium is being modified and not controlled. A greenhouse, due to its closed boundaries, permits the control over any one or more of the components of microclimate. A greenhouse is covered with a transparent or a translucent material such as glass or plastics. Depending upon its transparency, the greenhouse cover admits a major fraction of sunlight. The sunlight admitted to greenhouse is absorbed by the crop, floor, and other objects in the greenhouse. These objects in greenhouse in turn emit long wave thermal radiation for which the cover material has lower transparency, as a result, the solar energy is trapped in greenhouse raising its temperature. This phenomenon is generally known as greenhouse effect. It is this natural rise in the greenhouse air temperature which is utilized under cold climates to grow successful crops. The same natural phenomenon during summers, however, requires greenhouse cooling to maintain favourable temperatures. There are innumerable studies quantifying the effect of the environmental parameters individually as well as collectively on crop growth. The crop photosynthesis at optimum levels of environmental parameters follows a significantly higher curve.

Present Status of Greenhouse Technology in India

- ☆ The technology is still in its nascent stage.
- ☆ The total area under protected cultivation under greenhouse cultivation was about 1000 ha while under low tunnels it was 100 ha in India (Singh *et al.*, 2006).
- ☆ This figure is quite significant when compared with the total area under greenhouse in the world which was 6,82,050 ha (Singh *et al.*, 2006) and presently, China is the leading country area-wise 2,760,000 ha under

greenhouse (Kacira, 2011), while India is far behind with 25,000 ha in all forms of protected cultivation (Paroda, 2013).

- Thus it can be safely stated that there exists a vast scope for expansion for greenhouse technology in India.

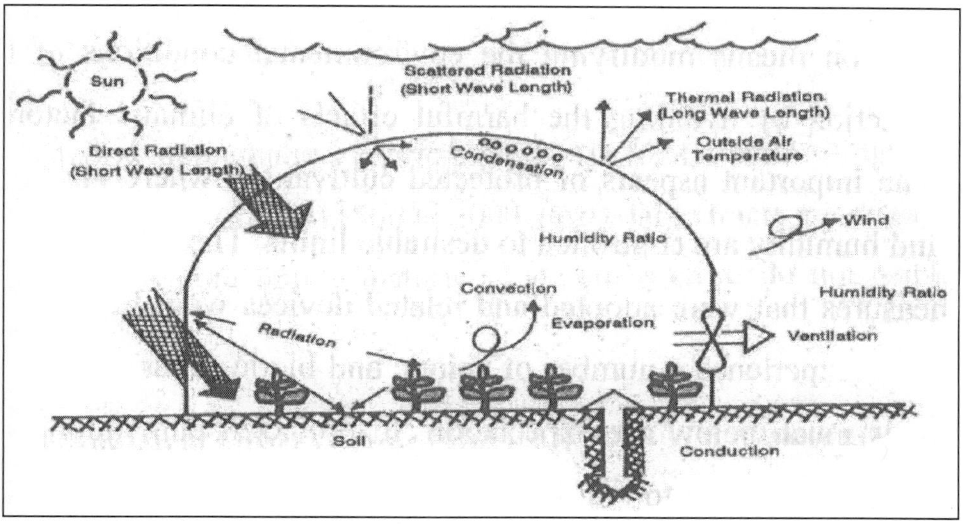

Figure 10.1: Schematic Diagram of Energy Exchange in a Greenhouse.

Protective Structures for Vegetable Crops

- Mulch
- Row cover
- Low tunnel
- High tunnel
- Greenhouse
- Net house

Mulch

Anything used to cover the soil is known as mulch and the technique in which any organic or inorganic material is laid over the soil surface is known as mulching. It conserves soil moisture and maintains soil micro-environment by increasing soil temperature and also prevents weed growth. It is of 2 types:

a) **Organic:** Straw, hay, coco peat, grass clippings, pine needles, green twigs, *etc.*

b) **Inorganic:** Plastic film- Transparent or coloured- black, white, silver, green, yellow, bi-coloured, *etc.*

Coloured plastic films have different properties as well like trapping of soil heat, moisture, prevent light to enter the soil so as to reduce weed growth, entrance, reflection of light to distract insects,

Row Cover

A row cover is to simply cover the crop with the help of a polythene or net structure to protect it from harsh sunlight, wind and insect pests attack.

Low Tunnel

Low tunnels and small walk-in tunnels are actually miniature greenhouses. A variety of types have been developed comprising of a semi-cylindrical supporting framework covered with plastic film. The tunnel protects the crop in bad weather against low temperatures, hail and also from birds and insects.

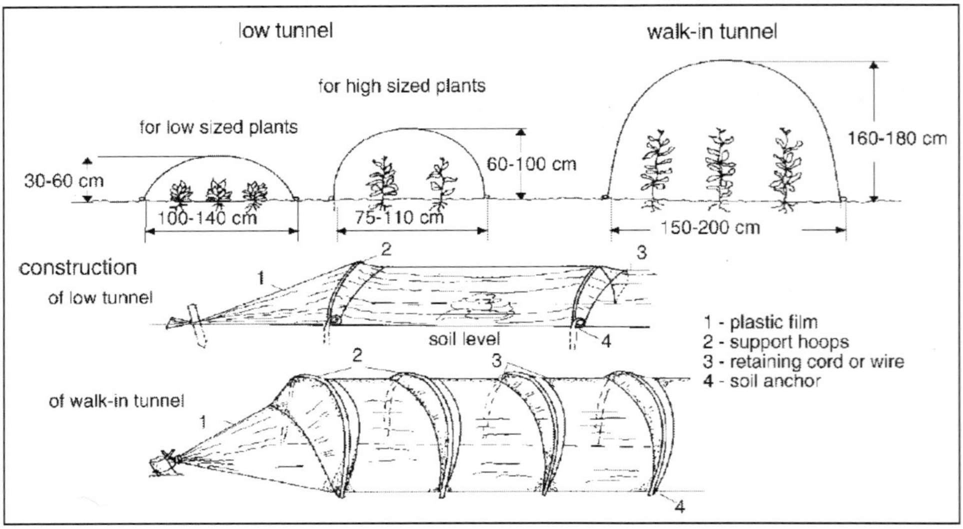

Figure 10.2: A Low Tunnel Framework with some Measurements.

High Tunnel

Man-sized tunnels covered with plastic film are high enough for working in and for accommodating taller crops such as tomatoes and cucumbers. They offer a crop, some protection against the cold and, especially for tall and vulnerable crops, protection against the wind and rain also.

Net House

These are also called shade halls. In regions with a dry sunny climate or in the dry season of a monsoon climate it is essential that the crops are protected against the blazing sun. A shade screen is usually placed above young plants, especially after potting or for cuttings. If this is going to be for a longer period, then a permanent screen will need to be placed. Shade halls are used mainly in regions with prolonged

Figure 10.3: A Low and High Tunnel.

blistering sunshine. Ventilation (cooling) occurs via the open netting of the cover on the sides. They provide the opportunity for growing a diversity of crops without the need for escaping to the more complicated cooled greenhouses.

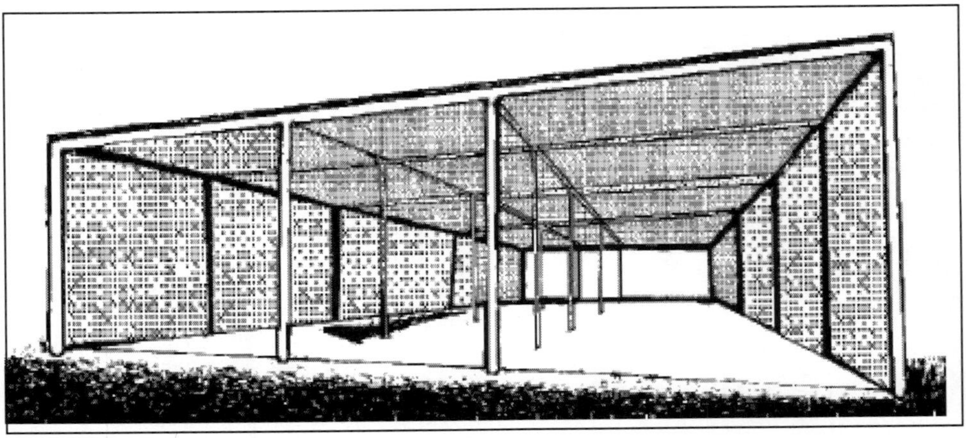

Figure 10.4: Net House.

Greenhouse

A greenhouse can be defined as a "framed or an inflated structure with a transparent or translucent material in which crops could be grown under at least partially controlled environment and which is large enough to permit persons to work within it to carry out cultural operations". The greenhouse is now better understood as a system of controlled environment agriculture (CEA), with precise control of air, temperature, water, humidity, plant nutrition, carbon dioxide and light. The inside environment (microclimate) of the greenhouse is controlled by growth factors like light, temperature, humidity and carbon dioxide concentration. They are scientifically controlled to an optimum level throughout the cultivation period, thus increasing the productivity by several folds.

Greenhouse Design

India has varied climatic conditions in different regions, so the greenhouse and the supporting facilities have to be developed accordingly. Design of the greenhouse should vary as per the local agro-climatic conditions keeping in view

the economic constraint. The southern plateau and the coastal regions need naturally ventilated poly houses and northern plains with composite climate require both cooling and heating facilities. The initial cost of the greenhouse generally depends upon the cost of the structure, cladding and temperature control mechanism and where as the operational cost relies upon mainly upon the maintenance of temperature and humidity in the greenhouse.

Classification of Greenhouses

Various types of greenhouse structures are used for crop production. Although, there are advantages in each type for a particular application, in general there is no single type greenhouse, which can be considered as the best. Different types of greenhouses are designed to meet the specific needs. The different types of greenhouses based on shape, utility, material and construction are briefly given below:

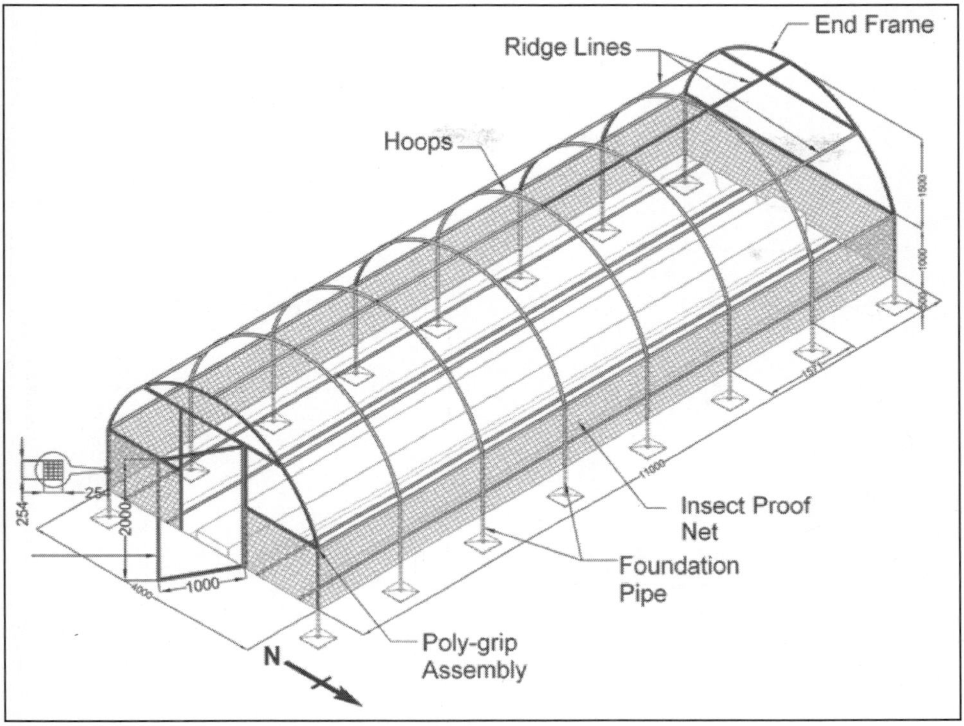

Figure 10.5: A Greenhouse Design.

1. Greenhouse Type Based on Shape

For the purpose of classification, the uniqueness of cross section of the greenhouses can be considered as a factor. The commonly followed types of greenhouses based on shape are:

- ☆ **Lean to type greenhouse**- made against a wall or support.
- ☆ **Even span type greenhouse**- made in plain areas.
- ☆ **Uneven span type greenhouse**- made in hilly or slopy areas.
- ☆ **Ridge and furrow type or gutter connected**- inner walls are absent but, if drop walls or polythene curtains are used that can be raised or lowered between sections, then suitable for taking two or more crops at a time.
- ☆ **Saw tooth type**- more common in high temperature places and those places that receive prevailing winds since design allows free movement of hot air.
- ☆ **Quonset greenhouse**- for areas having less sunshine hours.
- ☆ **Interlocking ridges and furrow type Quonset greenhouse**- for high wind prone areas.
- ☆ **Ground to ground greenhouse**- for snow prone areas.

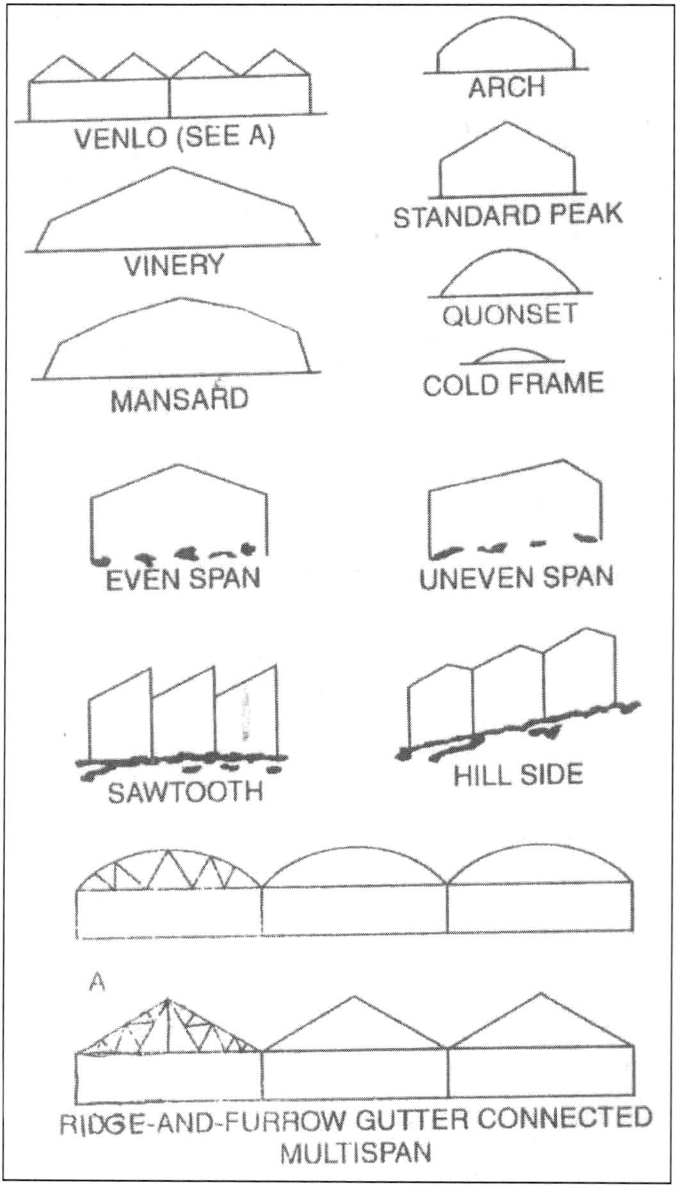

Figure 10.6: Different Shapes of Greenhouse.

2. Greenhouse Type Based on Utility

Classification can be made depending on the functions or utilities. Of the different utilities, artificial cooling and heating are more expensive and elaborate. Hence based on this, they are classified in to two types.

- Greenhouses for active heating.
- Greenhouses for active cooling.

3. Greenhouse Type Based on Construction

The type of construction predominantly is influenced by structural material, though the covering material also influences the type. Higher the span, stronger should be the material and more structural members are used to make sturdy tissues. For smaller spans, simple designs like hoops can be followed. So based on construction, greenhouses can be classified as:

- ☆ Wooden framed structure.
- ☆ Pipe framed structure.
- ☆ Truss framed structure.

4. Greenhouse Type Based on the Cost of Construction Involved

i. High cost Greenhouse
ii. Medium cost Greenhouse
iii. Low cost Greenhouse

The structural requirements and the cost per unit area for different models of low cost greenhouses for cultivation of vegetables are detailed below with diagrams to enable an interested entrepreneur to construct a low cost greenhouse on his own accord. However, the local weather conditions and the individual's necessity play a major role in the selection of the model.

Fabrication Materials

Frame

- ☆ Angle iron
- ☆ G.I. Pipe
- ☆ Bamboo
- ☆ Wood

Covering Material

Glass, acrylic, polycarbonate, fiber glass reinforced polyethylene film, weather able polyester film, poly-vinyl fluoride film.

Site Selection for Greenhouse

Following things are taken into account:

- ☆ The selection site should be free from pollution.
- ☆ Polyhouse should be established away from water logging condition.
- ☆ Polyhouse can be established in full sunshine area.
- ☆ Area should be well protected to interference of animal and human being.
- ☆ Good quality irrigation water should be available regularly.
- ☆ Supply of electricity should be regular.
- ☆ Soil should be properly leveled and drained.

- Polyhouse should be near to road side means proper approachable road must be there for the transport of product and materials to and fro.
- Some space should be there nearby for further extension.
- For surface drainage, gutters (outflow drains) or pipes are necessary with sufficient slope to lower areas from where water can be discharged to canals or rivers.
- Expertise and labours should be available when required

Orientation for Greenhouse Construction

- Orientation of the greenhouse is kept in basic consideration for two important factors, namely, light availability and shading effects are mainly considered for uniform crop growth.
- As per sunlight availability is concerned, an east- west orientation of ridge of the polyhouse is preferable in the winter for northern regions. In case of east-west orientation, shadow line developed in some area of the greenhouse. It causes the loss of production in the shade area.
- At other time in northern region and at all time for the southern region, a north-south orientation of ridges is preferable. In north-south orientation the shade moves during day time and so the crops are not much affected.
- Wind direction also may influence the orientation.

Nursery Preparation in Polyhouse

- In open field during winters as well as in cool season or adverse situations the preparation of nursery is very difficult job.
- In poly house the main crops are grown - as tomato, sweet pepper, cucumber, brinjal, chilli, cucurbits, *etc.*
- To grow early crops under adverse situation of the environment and weather conditions outside the poly house.
- Early crop provide higher price in the market.
- Some time due to heavy and continuous rainfall it is very difficult to produce nursery in open field, on those situation polyhouses are beneficial use-full to grow the seedlings.

Advantages of Polyhouse Technology

- Protection from excess rainfall, wind current, scorching sunlight and extreme cold conditions
- Under minimum space one can have maximum production of crop plants
- Humidity is maintained
- Efficient use of CO_2.
- Minimum use of water and fertilizers.
- A single person can have control over thousands of plants.

- ☆ Diseases and pests can be controlled easily.
- ☆ Production of crop throughout the year.
- ☆ Protection from birds, animals and human activities.
- ☆ Labour cost is reduced.
- ☆ Quality of product is best.

Constraints of Protected Cultivation

- ☆ Lack of location specific polyhouse designs.
- ☆ Absence of local competitive entrepreneurs.
- ☆ Non availability of quality polyethylene sheet.
- ☆ Inadequate financial assistance to growers.
- ☆ Insurance facility against natural calamities lacking.

Future Strategies

- ☆ Development of need based polyhouse designs for different areas.
- ☆ Ensuring easy availability of U.V. stabilized plastic sheet and nets.
- ☆ Development of suitable varieties specifically for polyhouse cultivation.
- ☆ Work on ecofriendly nutrient and pest management to be taken up.
- ☆ Government incentives for popularization of the technology.

Government Assistance

For adoption of Greenhouse Technology by farmers, Government of India has been providing subsidy @ 50 per cent of the total cost with a maximum ceiling upto 4000 m^2 per beneficiary under National Horticulture Mission (NHM) and Horticulture Mission for North East and Himalayan States (HMNEH).

Subsidy given by Government to the Farmers

Items	Pattern of Assistance (Rs/m^2) upto 4000 m^2 per beneficiary		
	Tubular structure	Wooden Structure	Bamboo Structure
Greenhouse with Fan and Pad system	1465	-	-
Naturally ventilated greenhouse	935	515	375

Iyengar *et al.* (2011).

Conclusion

The protected cultivation technology is still in its preliminary stage in India and concerted efforts are required from all concerned agencies to bring it at par with the global standards. Globalization coupled with economic liberalization will help in achieving the desired results. Greenhouse Technology has got a tremendous role in keeping up the pace of precision farming in Indian Agriculture. Protected cultivation of vegetable not only increases the sustainability of agricultural production but also improves the standard of living.

In future, it is essential to develop appropriate cost effective greenhouse technology and organize special training program and demonstrations for enhancing the protected cultivation of vegetable crops.

REFERENCES

Anonymous. 2010. State-wise area, production and productivity of vegetables. *Indian Horticulture Data Base*, pub. By NHB Gurgaon. pp. 6-10.

Chadha, K.L., 2003. Polyhouse vegetable production in sub-tropics ***In***: Hand Book of Horticulture. *ICAR Publication*, New Delhi. pp. 478-481.

Chakrabarti, A.K., Munshi, A.D. and Kumar, R. 2006. Protected cultivation of high value vegetables in low cost polyhouses ***In***: Protected cultivation of horticultural crops, *Department of Floriculture and Landscaping*, IARI, New Delhi. pp. 55-62.

Iyengar, K.S., Gahrotra, A., Mishra, A., Kaushal, K.K. and Dutt, M. (2011). Greenhouse-A Reference Manual. *NCPAH*, New Delhi. pp. 23.

Kacira, M. 2011. Greenhouse production in US: status, challenges, and opportunities. ***In***: CIGR 2011 conference on Sustainable bio-production WEF 2011, September 19-23, 2011 at Tower Hall Funabori, Tokyo, Japan.

Nair, R. and Barche, S. 2014. Protected cultivation of vegetables: Present status and future prospects in India. *Indian Journal of Applied Research* 6.**4**: pp. 245-247.

Ngouajio, M. and Ernest, J., 2004. Light transmission through coloured polythene mulches affects weed population. *Horti. Sci.* 39**(6)**: pp. 1302-1304.

Paroda, R.S. 2013. Strategies for protected cultivation. ***In***: National seminar on advances in protected cultivation, March 21, 2013 by Indian Society for Protected Cultivation, CPCT, IARI, New Delhi, India. pp. 1-12.

Singh, B. 2005. Protected cultivation of vegetable crops. Kalyani Publishers. New Delhi. 350p.

Singh, R., Patel, V.B. and Singh, S.K. 2006. Protected cultivation of fruits ***In***: *Protected cultivation of horticultural crops*, by Department of Floriculture and Landscaping, IARI, New Delhi. 28p.

Chapter 11

Novel Use of Plastics in Profitable Horticultural Production

No technological development has modified so much the course of controlled environment agriculture in the production of fruits, vegetables, flowers, and ornamentals as the recent widespread use of plastic films and related materials. Plastic films are used extensively for the design and covering of new greenhouses; the covering of old conventional glass greenhouses; for air-inflated, self-contained, or supported bubble houses; as interior curtains and external barriers to reduce heat loss in conventional greenhouses; and for the containment of CO_2-enriched atmospheres. Plastic films also are used for constructing high and low tunnels or covers for many row crops, protective covering of seed beds, and for soil mulches. Plastic tubes, laterals, and drip lines are important components of drip irrigation systems for high-value horticultural crops, which now cover 300,000 ha world-wide. Drip irrigation is often a component with plastic soil mulches, crop row covers, and plastic greenhouses. Recent introductions using plastic films include peat modules, bag cultures, rock wool, the nutrient-film technique, and non variable root environments for field-grown tomatoes (Geraldson, 1982; Wittwer, 1981). Flats, pots, and even labels for growing plants in greenhouses involve plastics. Plastic components contribute to the precise control of top and root environments of plants. In many modern greenhouses, all plant growing structures, other than the root media itself are plastic.The modern-day plastic revolution for horticulture is manifest in the precipitous rise and expansion of cultivated areas during the past 2 decades under plastic greenhouses, row tunnels, row covers, and soil mulches. The most intensive crop-producing systems are those in greenhouses or other protective structures, and the most widely used protective structures world-wide are now predominately plastic. The end product is stable and extended crop productivity-at high levels. Plastic films of various composition, types, and structural designs help circumvent most of the hazards of climate and weather. Among the greatest constraints in crop production are adverse temperatures; moisture and light deficiencies; destructive winds, rains, snow and hail; the growth of weeds; deficiencies in soil nutrients; and atmospheric CO_2. With plastic film covers or mulches, near-optimal conditions of temperature, moisture, nutrients, air movement, and atmospheric composition are possible. One of the most sophisticated is the nutrient film technique (NFT), which employs a variety of plastic structures, films, and materials. NFT is promotive of plant growth to near-optimal levels if combined with or enclosed in a plastic greenhouse. It offers the potential of maximizing control of both the top and root environments and optimizing both water and nutrient uptake (Cooper, 1976; Rudd-Jones, 1977; Spensley *et al.*, 1978). On the negative side, plasticulture needs financial capital, intensive management, and extensive resources, including human capital. It is a labor-intensive production system. Disposal of used plastic in ways that are environmentally friendly is also a challenge. Significant developments in the production of horticultural crops linked with new technologies and the most efficient uses of resources are occurring world-wide in the current plastic revolution. Plastics provide an intensified expansion in both the vertical and horizontal dimensions for high-value crops (vegetables, cut flowers, fruit, bedding plants, potted plants, nursery stock, ornamentals). The technology is especially appealing where population densities are high, constraints of land and water resources are serious, and where the climatic endowments are most favorable for plasticulture. The potential is equally good for advanced as well as agriculturally developing countries. Plastic greenhouses, high tunnels, low tunnels, row covers, and plastic soil mulches now can be observed from the equator to the Arctic and Antarctic regions. One may well ask how it all begain.

The word 'PLASTIC' is derived from the Greek words *'PLASSIEN'* and *'PLASTIKOS'* meaning to mould or shape a soft substance permanent or temporary. Plastic encompasses a wide variety of resins or polymers with varied characteristics. While there are natural polymers but only synthetic polymers are referred as plastics. Plastic has become a popular material in our daily life due to its structural integrity, chemical property and versatile nature. Plastic has many valuable applications in high-tech horticulture includes drip irrigation, plastic mulches, packaging and storage for superior quality of produce and in postharvest management.

The term plasticulture is defined as the use of plastics in agriculture. This broad term would include plastic film mulches, drip irrigation, row covers, low tunnels, high tunnels, silage bags, hay bale wraps, and plastic trays and pots used in transplant and bedding plant production. Use of plastic in horticulture crop production has increased dramatically in the last ten years even though the number of agricultural plastic manufactures has been reduced by 40 per cent over the same period. The use of plasticulture in the production of horticultural crops (vegetables, small fruits, flowers, tree fruits, and ornamentals) helps to mitigate the sometime extreme fluctuations in weather, especially temperature, rainfall and wind, which occurs in many parts of our country

India has adopted some of the newer techniques for agriculture, but modern techniques involving the use of plastic is still lagging behind. The comparison with China is very apparent. While China's agricultural sector uses modern techniques and consumes plastic to a very great extent, agricultural sector in India uses a very small percent of the total plastic consumed in the country (about 5 million tons in 2005).

Plastic has become a popular material in our daily life due to its structural integrity, chemical property and versatile nature. Plastic has many valuable applications in high-tech horticulture includes drip irrigation, plastic mulches, packaging and storage for superior quality of produce and in postharvest management. (Agrawal and Agrawal, 2005). Use of plastic mulches accelerates plant growth by increasing soil temperature, establishing soil moisture, weed control and production of quality produce and reduction in leaching of fertilizer (Das *et al.*, 2007; Pande *et al.*, 2005). Use of low plastic tunnels help in reducing the impact of frost and low temperature to a great extent in winter and high temperature during summer (Singh and Asrey, 2007).

Greenhouse technology provides optimum conditions of light, temperature, humidity, CO_2 for the best growth of plant to achieve maximum yield with best quality (Ngouajio and Ernest, 2004). To make use of plastic in packaging and storage of horticultural produce for extending storage life includes plastic bags and plastic sacks, plastic blow moulded containers, plastic food packaging, plastic films and plastics for transit packaging (Sharma *et al.*, 2007). Use of low gauge polyfilm of 100 gauge thickness improves the vase life and maintains the flower quality (Jawaharlal *et al.*, 2006).

Plastic has wide variety of uses in nursery *viz.*, for material glazing, seeder trays and cell pack for propagation, container carrying trays, container for propagation and growing labels for proper identification, ground cover and packing of planting material for long distance transportation. Therefore plastic has immense application in horticulture to increase the productivity by optimizing natural resource and use of inputs.

Beneficial Properties of Plastics

- ☆ Extreme versatility
- ☆ Lighter weight than competing materials, reducing fuel consumption during transportation
- ☆ Extreme durability
- ☆ Resistance to chemicals, water and temperature
- ☆ Good safety and hygiene properties for food packaging
- ☆ Excellent thermal and electrical insulation properties
- ☆ Relatively inexpensive to produce
- ☆ One tonne of plastics is equivalent to 20,000 two litre drinks bottles or 120,000 carrier bags

Plasticulture

The term plasticulture is defined as the use of plastics in agriculture. This broad term would include plastic film mulches, drip irrigation tape, row covers, low tunnels, high tunnels, silage bags, hay bale wraps, and plastic trays and pots used in transplant and bedding plant production. Use of plastic in horticulture crop production has increased dramatically in the last ten years even though the number of agricultural plastic manufactures has been reduced by 40 per cent over the same period.

The use of plasticulture in the production of horticultural crops (vegetables, small fruits, flowers, tree fruits, and ornamentals) helps to mitigate the sometime extreme fluctuations in weather, especially temperature, rainfall and wind, which occurs in may parts of our country. Many growers experience some extreme in weather conditions during the growing season that can kill or injure the crops, or reduce marketable yield. Row covers, low tunnels and high tunnels all have the potential to minimize the effect of these extreme weather events on the crop and optimize plant growth and development in a protected environment.

Use of Plastics in Horticulture

1. Drip irrigation
2. Mulching
3. Plastic for raising planting material
4. Greenhouse
5. Low Tunnel polyhouse
6. Shading net house
7. Packaging
8. Floating row cover

1. Drip Irrigation

Drip irrigation is the most efficient method of irrigating. While sprinkler systems are around 75-85 per cent efficient, drip systems typically are 90 per cent or higher. Water is supplied through a network of pipe using dripper/emitters. Water is supplied at a regular interval and at a required time/quantity. Since evaporation and conveyance losses are negligible, water use efficiency under DMI is over 90 per cent. Productivity gains through DMI vary from 20 per cent to about 50 per cent depending upon the crop. Mostly useful to wide spaced crops and importantly, under DMI system, water is supplied to the crop but not to the land. What that means is much less wasted water! For this reason drip is the preferred method of irrigation in the desert regions. But drip irrigation has other benefits, which make it useful almost anywhere. It is easy to install, easy to design, can be very inexpensive, and can reduce disease problems associated with high levels of moisture on some plants.

Drip irrigation (sometimes called trickle irrigation) works by applying water slowly, directly to the soil. The high efficiency of drip irrigation results from two primary factors. The first is that the water soaks into the soil before it can evaporate or run off. The second is that the water is only applied where it is needed, (at the plant's roots) rather than sprayed everywhere.

New Approaches to Drip Irrigation

The future for drip is bright due to a growing emphasis on water conservation in many areas, as well as a move toward growing crops on marginal ground with less attractive soil types and terrain. Using fertigation through drip, the grower can supply everything the plant needs through the drip system. "Soil becomes just a media to anchor the plant". "What's found in the field is of less importance." New and coming advances in drip systems include products that allow crops to grow on terrain not traditionally associated with drip irrigation, tape products that are biodegradable or trigger degradable, tape products that work well with recycled water, tape products that can be retrieved and reused, and controllers that allow more customized water and fertilizer inputs. Pressure compensating drip tape makes it possible for drip to reach new places. A well-designed drip system with pressure compensating tape can distribute water evenly up a hill and mitigate the effects of differing soil types and textures, making it possible to grow vegetables on a hillside. "A future generation of tapes will be made of materials that will decompose into the soil when the crop is harvested". The new drip products will have to handle recycled water, new chemicals and new types of biological. Many of the advances coming to drip are in products that can be removed and reused increasing the life of the systems and reducing the overall cost of drip irrigation.

The Basic Parts of a Drip System

- **Valve**: They can be automatic or manual. If an anti-siphon valve is used it has a built-in backflow preventer, which saves money.
- **Pressure Regulator**: Most drip systems will need a pressure regulator. If water pressure is over 2.8 bars (40 PSI). If in doubt, install one. The regulator can go before or after the valve. Traditionally it is installed after the valve.
- **Filter**: Drip emitters have very small openings that are easily clogged. Use a 150-mesh screen or one with a higher mesh number like 200 mesh. The filter may be installed before the valve or pressure regulator, but the inexpensive plastic filters often sold for drip systems should be installed after the pressure regulator. Most valve failures result from sand or rust particles clogging of the tiny passages inside the valve. Use a filter that is the same size as, or larger than, the valve.
- **Emitters**: Most emitters emit 4 liters/hour (4.0 l/hr) of water. That's about 1 gallon per hour (1 g/ph). Use pressure-compensating emitters if irrigating a hilly area. There are many different types and brands available. Multi-Outlet emitters are very popular. Use single outlet emitters for a less troublesome drip system.
- **Mainline**: The mainline is the pipe that goes from the water source to the valves. In the illustration of a very simple drip system above the gray

colored vertical pipe under the valve is a mainline. The mainline may be made of galvanized steel, copper, SCH 40 PVC, SCH 80 PVC, Cl 315 PVC, and Heavy Wall Polyethylene (SDR 7 or SDR 9). Polyethylene has a low burst pressure and should only be used for mainlines where local conditions are appropriate.

- ☆ **Sub-Main**: The sub-main is the pipe that goes from the valves to the connection point of the drip tube. Many small drip systems do not have a sub-main, in those systems the drip tube connects directly to the valve. The illustration of a very simple drip system above shows a system without a sub-main. Sub-mains are usually 200 PVC pipe or standard weight polyethylene (poly) pipe. Use a sub-main when multiple drip tubes are needed.
- ☆ **Drip Tubing**: Drip tubing is a thin wall polyethylene tube, and is generally produced in metric sizes. Common sizes are 12 mm (0.455″ or 3/8″), 16mm (0.620″ or 1/2″), 18mm (0.720″ or 1/2″), and 24mm (0.940″ or 3/4″).
- ☆ **Adapters and Fittings:** Used to attach the drip tube to the other parts. Important- make sure the fittings are the exact right size. Using fittings made for a different tubing size will result in the tube blowing out of the fitting. 9 times out of 10, when a tube blows out of a fitting it is because the fitting is the wrong size.
- ☆ **End Cap**: The end cap is important. Without it the water all runs out the end of the drip tube.

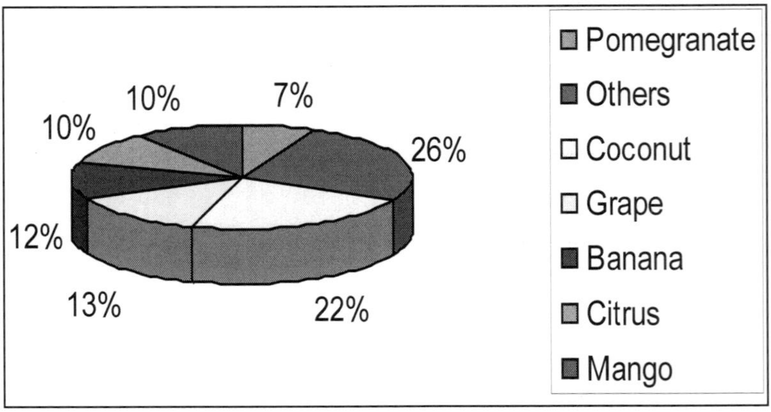

Fruit Crop [Area (per cent)] Covered under Drip Irrigation.

Irrigation water management and system maintenance are also extremely critical in order to succeed with drip irrigation. A simple and highly effective water management technique using tensiometers will be described in this publication. Clogging and prevention and use of chlorine as a means of preventing clogging by biological and chemical contaminants will also be discussed.

Although many advantages favor installation of a drip system, there are some limitations as well.

Relative Performance of Crops with Drip Irrigation in Comparison with that of Traditional Irrigation

Crop	*Location*	*Yield (q/ha)*		*Irrigation Water (cm)*		*WUE (q/ha/cm)*		*Advantage of Drip Irrigation*	
		Surface	*Drip*	*Surface*	*Drip*	*Surface*	*Drip*	*Saving of Water (Per cent)*	*Increase in Yield (Per cent)*
Banana	Jorhat	447.0	720.0	185.0	107.0	2.41	6.72	42.0	61.1
Ber	Belvatgi	13.7 kg/tree	18.0 kg/tree	15.4 m^3/plant	12.5 m^3/plant	0.9	1.4	18.8	34.1
Grapes	NCPA	264.0	325.0	53.0	28.0	5.0	11.6	47.2	23.1
Guava	Allahabad	0.16/pl	.22/pl	6.4 m^3/pl	5.21 m^3/pl	0.03	0.04	18.8	28.0
Kinnow	Delhi	68	98	22.1	17.3	3.1	5.7	21.7	44.1
Lemon	Delhi	15	27	23	17.5	0.65	1.54	23.9	80.0
Papaya	Coimbatore	130.0	230.0	228.0	73.0	0.6	3.20	68	77.0
Pomegranate	Hyderabad	15.0	37.0	183.0	178.0	0.08	0.21	27	147.0

Source: CAZRI, Jodhpur, TNAU Coimbatore, IARI New Delhi, IIT Kharagpur, GBPUA&T Pantnagar, AICRP(WM) Annual Reports 2002-03, 2003-04, 2004-05, 2005-06.

Plastics in Mulching

Mulching is a practice of covering the soil around the plant with an organic or inorganic material/synthetic material which make condition more favourable for plant growth and development.

Why Plastic Mulch?

- ✰ Excellent weed control within the planted row.
- ✰ Holds moisture in the soil (and) it makes drip irrigation more efficient as it virtually eliminates evaporation of the irrigation water.
- ✰ But the most powerful feature of plastic mulch is the impact it has on light.

Colours of Plastic Mulch

Colours of plastic mulch films have been investigated for their impact on crops. Each colour film reflects the wave-length that gives it the colour we perceive.

- ✰ Yellow has been shown to attract insects so using yellow-mulched rows to attract insects to a location where they can be killed,
- ✰ Black plastic has been the standard plastic using worldwide,
- ✰ Silver-reflective plastic mulch associated with higher reflectance cause insect disorientation and repels aphids,
- ✰ Blue attracts thrips but has been very effective in greenhouse

There also appears to be some reduction in disease pressure with crops grown on specific colours.

Types of Plastic Use in Mulching

1. **Reflective Plastic Mulches**: Painting the plastic with aluminum paint or white paint increases its reflectivity and cools late planted crops resulting in better fruit quality. The reflective properties of aluminum-faced plastic interfere with the movement of aphids, which spread the watermelon mosaic virus II, which causes the green streaking in the autumn yellow squash.
2. **Infra-Red Transmitting (IRT) Mulches**: These plastics transmit the warming wavelengths of the sun, but not those that allow weeds to grow. These materials result in warmer soils than black plastic, but cooler soils than clear plastics. The IRT mulches retard the growth of weeds. Crops grown on IRT mulch will develop 7 to 10 days earlier than crops grown on black plastic.
3. **Biodegradable plastic mulches**: Plastic mulches do not break down so should never be incorporated in the soil. New photodegradable or biodegradable mulches have been developed, which will solve this problem of plastic removal or disposal after completion of the cropping season. In first stage the film is reduced to a fine powder, which is totally

inert and physiologically harmless to plants so it also known as eco-friendly plastic

Weed Density and Light Transmission through Coloured Plastic Mulches

Film Colour	*Weed Density (no./m²)*	*Light Transmission (per cent)*
White	155	48
Black	20	1
Gray	44	17
IRT green	24	42
IRT brown	18	26

Ngouajio and Ernest, 2004.

Plastics in Greenhouses

Greenhouse technology is the most intensive form of commercial cultivation and could be called as food factories.

Greenhouse film technology has improved significantly compared to 10 years ago, giving commercial growers access to plastic covers that last up to twice as long, improve light transmission, and are specifically engineered to lift crop production. This has followed a demand for technological improvements worldwide within the expanding greenhouse industry. Unique among these covering materials are multi-layered polyethylene films, often referred to as 'smart films' that include UV inhibitors and colourants to filter or enhance light quality, and additives that offer anti-drip and anti-disease properties, as well as cooling and thermal benefits.

In order to understand how smart films work, the effect of the solar spectrum on plant growth needs to be understood. Plant growth is stimulated by the presence of water, nutrients, temperature, carbon dioxide, and photosynthesis. During the process of photosynthesis, plants depend on the total amount of visible light, or more specifically, photosynthetically active radiation (PAR), the group of wavelengths of light between 400-700 nanometers (nm). The distribution of individual wavelength intensities, not only the total combined PAR intensity, influences plant growth and development responses (photo- morphogenesis). Wavelengths of non-visible energy known as infra-red (600-700 nm) can inhibit stem elongation and branching of plants, and leaves are sometimes smaller and thicker. This results in a lessening of flowering in short-day plants, but promotion of flowering in long-day plants. Far-red radiation (700-800 nm) leads to an increase in stem elongation, and eliminating the far-red part of the solar spectrum can produce shorter plants. Flowering can also be inhibited in some plants. At the other end of the light spectrum, UV wavelengths below 380 nm have detrimental effects on plant growth and cause blackening and burning. Ultraviolet (UV) light and excessive infra-red (IR) or heat radiations reduce the longevity and performance of plastic covers. The challenge for plastic manufacturers is to develop greenhouse films that limit UV degradation and IR heat radiation absorbency without interfering with light quality and the development of plants. The light transmission, performance and longevity of films can also be affected by placing inhibitors, stabilisers, colourants and other additives in the plastic, making them a less virgin resin base.

Anti-dripping Effects

Droplets that form on the inside of greenhouse plastics due to condensation reduce light transmission by 15-30 per cent and have negative impacts on plant quality and growth. Condensation also increases the risk of disease. Plastic Kritis manufacture anti-dripping films that eliminate droplets by forming a continuous thin layer of water running down the sides of the greenhouse. Some greenhouses capture this condensate for reuse. These films are mainly recommended for well-ventilated and/or heated greenhouses with adequate inclination of the roof. The anti-dripping effect only lasts about two years, because the additives function by migrating to the surface of the film and are slowly washed out by water. Under certain circumstances, there is a heavy fog (mist) formation in greenhouses, which usually occurs at sunset and dawn. However, this fog is undesirable and could damage plants. Growers using these films need to ventilate and/or heat the greenhouse to remove the fog.

Disease Control Films

There are several "types" of disease control films targeted at certain pests and diseases. All of them contribute to better IPM management inside the greenhouse. An important type is a UV-blocking film that works by blocking UV light up to 390 nm. These films reduce populations of whiteflies, thrips, aphids and other greenhouse pests by omitting those wavelengths needed for insects to thrive and survive. Disease control films are sometimes called anti-insect films because of this feature. They are also called anti-viral films, because they reduce viruses vectored by these pests. Yet another type of disease control film is the manufacturer's latest release, a clear film that is 98 per cent resistant to sulphur. It is well known that sulphur, halogen and other substances contained in pesticide residues that are diffused in film, react with UV stabilisers and deactivate them. Hindered Amine Light Stabilisers (HALS), a class of UV stabilisers widely used in greenhouse films, is particularly sensitive to such attack. Even nickel, which is relatively inert to attack from sulphur, is known to be sensitive to chlorine. "Sulphur is a major contributor to plastic degradation and the life of the plastic is reduced by at least 50 per cent. While most films use a standard class of UV stabilisers or nickel, this new film uses an additive that is almost completely resistant to sulphur. "breakthrough" film is expected to cost up to 20 per cent more than other sulphur-resistant films on the market. However, replacement costs for film damaged by sulphur and other agrochemicals, will mean a short payback period. There are also crop health and productivity factors to be considered from covers that perform under specification owing to agrochemical damage. As sulphur condenses out, it also accumulates around greenhouse gutters, causing rust.

Photo-selective Films

Plastic manufacture a range of special films that incorporate colourants (pigments) to modify the light spectrum entering the greenhouse. These photo-selective films make it possible to promote or retard plant growth, causing elongation or dwarfing of the stems. Flower growers to improve colouration and promote special characteristics demanded by market fashions, such as long-stem roses, mainly use them. Tomato and capsicum growers to enhance fruit colour and quality sometimes use them. Monbulk Rural Enterprises was the first Australian company to trial films with red pigments for rose production. The Australian distributor offers a range of red and blue photo-selective films manufactured by Plastic Kritis, including a specific rose film.

Polyane

Polyane is the first company to develop bubble film and has developed a new family of smart films under the concept they call "The Plant Effect" with an emphasis on improving the parameters for plant growth. Of special note is the Celloclim clear bubble plastic, a three-layer film manufactured to suit Australia's harsh climate with its large temperature differences between day and night (the diurnal range). "The clear Celloclim is durable and perfectly adapted to all types of climate and every type of crop that we can find in greenhouses here. Celloclim has been specially engineered with multi-layer co-extrusion technology that sandwiches an expanded polymer layer with gas micro bubbles between two plain polymer layers. This film favours photosynthesis by improving the light diffusion inside the greenhouse. Light passing through the bubbles breaks up the light inside the greenhouse into a multitude of light rays, bathing plants in intense but not direct light. According to David Ribot, the patented bubble film improves light quality. "The gas bubbles diffuse the light to give more uniform light radiation throughout the greenhouse, and the shadows below the plant canopy become less distinct,"he said. Polyane call this "util" (from utility) or "useful"light. Instead of giving 90 per cent of available light on only 20 per cent of the crop surface, the diffusing effect gives 85 per cent of light on 80 per cent of the crop surface. The multi-directional spread of light also eliminates growth towards the light source (phototropism). Clear Celloclim includes a proprietary system of UV absorber additives that cuts the light wavelengths from 300 up to 375nm, which helps to minimize the blackening of rose petals. The same wavelengths that burn sunbathers. Importantly, the additive doesn't block those UV wavelengths responsible for plant colouration (375-400 nm). "These wavelengths are responsible for brighter colours and better contrast in bicolour flowers, including roses. The introduction into Australia of the clear Celloclim bubble film follows six years experience by Polyane across a wide range of vegetable and flower crops, and in diverse climates - from north Ukraine to Spain, and from north to southern Africa. Polyane also produce their own resin granules and proprietary additives, and have the ability to "formulate" greenhouse films for different climate conditions. Polyane is a part of the ADELPRO group, one of the largest plastic extruders in Europe, manufacturing 65, 000 tonnes of polyethylene film per year, representing a turnover of 100 million Euros. Fifty-five percent of their market is agribusiness. Polyane was also the first company to develop sulphur resistant films. This followed three years experience in the Kenyan rose market where growers burn sulphur for 12 hours during the night to minimize fungal diseases. "When the sulphur evaporates in the greenhouse atmosphere, it combines with humidity to form sulphurous acid, which destroys the UV stabilization system of greenhouse film over a short period of time. Sulphur burning also causes leaf yellowing, damages the quality of the crop, and eliminates the option of using biological pest controls.

Packaging Techniques for Fruits and Vegetables

"If you package it right, you can sell just about anything." The main functions of a produce container are to prevent and reduce injury to the crop during transit and handling. It provides ventilation to hasten coolin, escape of heat caused by respiration and reduce water loss from the crop. India is a land of large varieties of fruits and vegetables due to its vast soil and climatic diversity. With 38 and 71 million tons of production of fruits and vegetables, India is the second largest producer of fruits and vegetables next to Brazil and China respectively. It is also a matter of concern that there is a wide gap between availability and the per capita nutritional requirement of fruits. The low availability of quality fruits and vegetables is mainly due to considerably high postharvest losses, poor transportation facilities, improper storage and low processing capacity coupled with the growing population. Around 20-30 per cent losses take place during harvesting, grading, packaging, transportation and marketing of fruits. The fruits of increased production of fruits and vegetables and other agricultural produce will be realized only when they reach the consumer in good condition and at a reasonable price. The existing postharvest loss of fruits and vegetables could be considerably reduced by adopting improved packaging, handling and efficient system of transport. Packaging of fruits and vegetables is undertaken primarily to assemble the produce in convenient units for marketing and distribution

Fresh fruits and vegetables harvested seasonally in large quantities from different areas are mostly stored in suitable environments until marketed and consumed. During storage and transportation, the appropriate maintenance conditions should be practiced since fresh fruit and vegetables are living systems and very sensitive to deteriorative effects. Packaging of a food product is an operation aimed to prevent most of the possible kinds of degradation that render it unsuitable for consumption or of a lower sensorial value. Stability of a packaged foodstuff greatly depends on the characteristics of the packaging material and proper conditions of harvesting, storage and distribution.

Plastics Material Use in Packaging

- ☆ Cellulose film (cellophane)
- ☆ Cellulose acetate
- ☆ Polyethylene (HDPE and LDPE)
- ☆ Polystyrene
- ☆ Ethyl cellulose
- ☆ Polypropylene
- ☆ PVC
- ☆ Edible plastic

Use of Plastics in Packaging

- ☆ Plastic bags and plastic sacks
- ☆ Plastic blow moulded containers
- ☆ Plastic food packaging
- ☆ Plastic plant packaging
- ☆ Plastic films
- ☆ Plastics for transit packaging

Trays

Product is placed on trays made of foam plastic or chipwood and wrapped in plastic. This method keeps the produce clean during handling.

Boxes

Small boxes ranging from half quart to two quart capacity and can be open or covered Boxes are often used by farmers because they Can hold stems, leaves, buds *etc.* Examples: Strawberries and blueberries.

Shrink Wrap

Wrapping plastic around product and then cooling. It Helps to reduce damage in handling and prevents loss of water. If product emits ethylene after harvest this should not be used. It will cause fruit to over-ripen and spoil. Avoid using with pears, peaches, plums, avocados, and bananas.

Containers

Containers are as important as the plants they hold. It can be madeup of plastic or pressed cardboard. It is easier to keep adequate moisture and plant is removed from container when ready to plant.

Row Covers

They literally "float" or lie directly over the crop, whether direct seeded or transplanted. Materials include perforated plastic, spunbonded polyester, and spunbonded polypropylene; they do not impede seedling emergence or subsequent growth of the crop.) To secure the cover against wind, all the edges are buried or weighted down with sandbags, rocks, or other materials. For most crops, floating row covers require no support because they are lightweight

There are two types of these covers: perforated polyethylene which is about 1 mil thick and spunbonded polyester or polypropylene which is available in several weights (rather than in thickness).

Perforated polyethylene has a uniform pattern of 3/8-inch holes (74 holes/ sq ft) for ventilation. However, the holes allow for heat loss at night and are an entry point for insects. Overall, many growers have found these covers to be very beneficial for growth enhancement.

Spunbonded covers are comprised of a thin mesh of white synthetic fibers which entrap heat and serve as a barrier to wind, insects, and varmints. Water from rain or overhead irrigation freely passes through. The weight of these covers range from 0.3 to about 2.0 oz/sq yd (10 to 68 grams/sq meter). The lightest covers are used primarily for insect exclusion while the heaviest of the covers are used for frost protection. The most common weights are 0.5 to 1.25 oz\sq yd (17 to 42 grams/sq meter). With covers under 0.5 oz there is minimal heat retention at night; and over 1.75 oz, there is a significant reduction in light transmission. The heavy covers are used for night time's frost protection only since they do not transmit sufficient light for optimum crop growth. Spunbonded row covers in the 0.5 to 1.25 oz range provide 2° to 4° F frost protection in the spring. In the fall, there is more protection because there is a larger reservoir of heat in the soil in the fall than in the spring. These covers perform very well in protecting late-season tomatoes and pepper from early frosts.

Floating covers require much less installation labor than hoop supported covers. The wider and longer the covers, the less labor required per unit area since only the edges are secured. These covers vary in width from 6 to 50 feet and up to about 800 feet long. One way to evaluate labor needs is to compare the time that it takes to apply one piece of cover 50 feet wide x 200 feet long (500 perimeter feet) versus the time it takes to apply 5 pieces 10 feet wide x 200 feet long (2100 perimeter feet). Regardless of width, the cover is secured by weighting down the edges (sides and ends) with soil, sand bags, stones, or long pins. In extremely windy areas, additional weighting in the middle of the cover is advisable.

Insect control is effective with spunbonded covers when all of the edges are completely sealed. For example, maggots in radish (and in other crops in the cabbage family) are controlled when a cover is applied at seeding with a complete seal around the edges. When the adult maggot flies search out the young seedlings for laying eggs, the flies will be unable to get under or through the cover. A continuous furrow of soil along the edges is probably the best method.

It is feasible, however, that row covers could actually increase insect damage on some crops. The environment under the cover is pretty "cozy" for insects, so it is important that all transplants that are to be covered are free of insects at transplanting. To prevent a heavy population of Colorado potato beetles under a cover, do not plant potatoes in the same place in successive years and use a cover the second year. Overwintering adult beetles could emerge from the soil under the cover and lay an abundance of eggs which would soon hatch into a dense population of larvae. There are a couple of disadvantages of floating covers. One is the weed pressure under the covers. Between strips of plastic mulch or with crops such as sweet corn where plastic mulch is not used, weeds grow rapidly and competitively. When using herbicides, the highest labeled rate is generally needed to adequately control weeds. There is also some inefficiency in covering the space between strips of plastic, but here again the trade-off is reduced installation labor of wide covers versus narrow covers.

Low Tunnel Polyhouse

Low tunnels are miniature form of greenhouses to protect the plants from rains, winds, low temperature, frost and other vagaries

Shading Net House

Shading nets are used to provide relief to the plants from the scorching sunlight, hot winds, direct rainfall as well as insects and pests. Shading nets are being used for raising nursery, indoor plants, hardening of tissue cultured plantlets and growing of vegetable.

Plastic for Raising Planting Material

- Polythene bags
- Plug trays
- Grower pots
- Growing media pots

Plug Trays

Available with round, square or hex cells and choice of wide or narrow lip. Common Element or standard dimensions. Perfectly suited for seed germination or vegetative propagation. Accurate die-cut holes ensure consistent performance in drainage and air pruning. Stacking notches on many trays for easier denesting in automated equipment.

Uses for Specific Crops

Strawberries

World-wide, the most extensively grown crop with the aid of plastic film (greenhouses, tunnels, rowcovers, or soil mulches) is the strawberry. Production is from October to May in California, Japan, China, Israel, Egypt, and throughout Europe- especially in the Mediterranean area. Strawberries may be grown in greenhouses, under rowcovers, with plastic mulches, or a combination of the three along with drip irrigation. All-season varieties, first developed in California, are found throughout the world (Voth and Bringhurst, 1959), along with plastic mulching and rowcovers. Plastic mulches were first used in California in 1958. There are 8000 ha of strawberries in California that are mulched with clear polyethylene plastic. The mulch is applied very snugly over the soil surface as soon as possible after transplanting. Associated with high soil temperature is a 50 per cent increase in total yield and double the early yield. Drip irrigation, introduced in 1957, is used with the plastic (Voth and Bringhurst, 1990).

Plasticulture for strawberries with suitable varieties is used for winter production, either in the open or in greenhouses throughout the northern hemisphere. Row covers along with the plastic mulches were next introduced in the Mediterranean countries and in China and Japan.

Cucumbers

The cucumber also is welladapted to growth in plastic greenhouses and tunnels. Cucumbers rank first for culture in plastic greenhouses in Japan, China. Korea, and Russia, and is second only to tomatoes in Greece. Different varieties are grown throughout all European countries, especially those in the eastern and northern parts. Production is high, the crop matures earlier and is less exacting than the tomato in cultural requirements, and production may be carried through winter months. Two crops a year may be grown in many countries bordering the Mediterranean. Aside from growth in greenhouses, cucumbers are highly productive under rowcovers and with plastic soil mulches.

Muskmelons and Watermelons

Melons are among the most responsive of all crops to plasticulture. They are sensitive to both low soil and air temperatures and to wind, but are very tolerant to high temperatures. With perforated or slitted rowcovers and spunbonded floating rowcovers, there is some frost protection (Wells and Loy, 1985b). Both watermelons (5000 ha) and muskmelons (1500 ha) are grown under rowcovers in Greece and, to a lesser extent, in greenhouses. Watermelons and muskmelons are two of the leading crops for row tunnels in Spain and Portugal. Melons are grown in the greenhouses of Japan, China, and in most northwestern European countries, as well as those near the Mediterranean. Rowcovers and black plastic soil mulches are seen in Egypt and Israel and in dispersed areas of the northern United States and Canada. Early, as well as total, yields may be increased for muskmelons. The use of black plastic mulches, often coupled with transparent or slightly opaque rowcovers, is common in California, Arizona, Michigan, New York, New Jersey, and Essex County, Ont., Canada. Watermelons in China are especially responsive to clear plastic soil mulching (Wittwer *et al.,* 1987). They are grown extensively in all provinces, autonomous regions, and municipalities. The progressive use of plastic soil mulches for watermelons in China is given below. At present, 360,000 ha of watermelons are mulched with plastic annually in China. This accounts for 18 per cent of the 2 million ha of mulched crops, being exceeded only by cotton and equal to that for peanuts. In the northern, northeastern, and northwestern regions of China, 75 per cent of the total watermelon area is mulched with plastic. There is also an increase in the use of plastic row covers combined with the soil mulches. Transparent soil mulches increase soil temperatures and prevent surface evaporation of soil moisture.With plastic, the melons in northern China mature 20 days earlier, and are the main source of supply for all of China during late August and through September. In southern China, the plastic mulch reduces soil erosion and prevents compaction from heavy rains. The mulch promotes the growth and fruiting of watermelons and increases total yields by 29 per cent to 30 per cent (Runfang, 1990). Plastic tunnels often are combined with plastic mulch. This is the most popular method of forcing culture in watermelon production. Such a "double layer" of film cover is used widely in northern China and Korea to take advantage of sunny spring weather for early maturity and to give wind and frost protection. In the lower reaches of the Yangxi river valley and the suburbs of Shanghai, the growing of watermelons in plastic tunnels promotes early fruit set, early maturity, and results in enormously high yields. Watermelon production in small to medium-sized plastic houses has progressed rapidly in central China. The structures are simple, with flexible bamboo frames. Sometimes a tunnel with mulch is prepared within the plastic house to increase warmth This results in a "three-layer" film cover. The area oftunnels and plastic houses in Tongshan County of Jiangsu Province now totals 1800 ha (Runfang, 1990).

Advantages of Plasticulture

The initial driving forces for the use of plastics in horticulture were, first, to increase earliness and total crop productivity of highvalue horticultural crops (Abdul-Baki and Spence, 1992); second, to take advantage of out-of-season production; and third, to use something as effective, but much less expensive, than glass as a protective covering. This latter advantage was the primary stimulus for Emmert's (1955) pioneering studies in Kentucky. The promotion ofearliness, coupled with more-productive and predictable total yields, holds for most all field-grown horticultural crops where plastics are used. The effectiveness of plastic covers in compensating for low soil temperatures and the reductions in wind damage has been phenomenal for vine crops, especially watermelon, muskmelon, squash, cucumber, sweet corn, strawberry, yam, and sweetpotato and cassava in the tropics. Harvest may be hastened by a few days, a week, or months, depending on the structures and the combinations of covers used. Earliness is especially important in the response to plastic covers for tomato, cucumber, pepper, eggplant, melon, sweet corn, and cut flowers.

The improvement of cut flower quality is often a compelling factor for using plastic covers. Extending the geographical areas for successful production applies to a wide range of vegetables, flowers, and fruit crops from the equator to the arctics. Earlier maturity is promoted. Most successful has been the plastic greenhouse for cucumber, tomato, pepper, eggplant, strawberry, melon, green bean, and green onion; and for tomato, cucumber, melon, and sweet corn in the field. Modern greenhouses, constructed with double-layer plastic with an air space between, are more retentive of heat and CO_2 than are glass greenhouses. Protection against short-term frosts and cold waves with temperature depressions ranging from 1 to 3C is possible in the open field with some types of spunbonded and floating rowcovers of polypropylene (Wells and Loy, 1985b;.

Other beneficial effects of plasticulture with row crop mulching and/or covers in the field are the conservation of water through reductions in surface evaporation; a reduction in the loss of soil nutrients by leaching (Wein and Minotti, 1987); weed control (especially important for vine crops); alleviation of soil compaction by the beating action of rain; protection of plants against wind, rain, hail, and insects; and an increase in atmospheric CO_2. One, several, or all of the above advantages of plasticulture may accrue, depending on the crop, where it is grown, and the plastic structures employed.

In summary, plasticulture provides one of the few options for further expansion of both the horizontal and vertical dimensions of horticultural crop production and for the most-effective management and use of land, water, fertilizer, sunlight, and atmospheric CO_2 as essential crop inputs. There are also new vistas for marketing the improved quality virtues of fresh fruits, vegetables, and cut flowers.

Disadvantages of Plasticulture

Cost is a chief constraint in the use of plastics for horticultural crops. While rowcovers are intermediate in cost between plastic soil mulches and plastic greenhouses, they are seldom used alone. A usual combination with row covers is a plastic soil mulch and drip irrigation, as is used for strawberries in Israel. In fact, drip irrigation often is combined with plastic soil mulching and plastic bag culture inside a plastic greenhouse, sometimes with the addition of rowcovers as well. Each input requires an additional expenditure. A further cost, which must be factored in, is the annual or periodic replacement of plastic coverings for greenhouses.

Plastic culture demands high-production technology and significant human resource inputs. Those engaged in growing crops with the aid of plastic mulches, covers, or greenhouses should receive technical training as to factors controlling plant growth and the art of plant growing. Heating, ventilating, cooling, and condensation difficulties still exist with crops grown inside plastic enclosures. Programming inputs of mineral nutrients, and meeting optimal requirements for temperature, light, and atmospheric CO_2 levels are desirable and should be considered. Plasticulture involves a series of production technologies, beginning with plant growing through to harvest, that relate to one of the most intensive types of agricultural production coupled with the most efficient use of human and natural resources. It is also one of the most labor- and management-intensive agricultural production systems. The cost of labor along with the cost and availability of other inputs could be prohibitive. A final problem is disposal of used plastic. Plastic pollution is unsightly and is recog- nized as an environmental hazard and a constraint wherever plasticulture has flourished.

A possible approach for the future is the use of photo- or biodegradable plastic. Several products of biological origins have been introduced that show some promise. Degradability, however, has not been sought after for plastic greenhouse covers until recently.

Durability has rather been the primary concern. Recycling agricultural plastics is another option for disposal. The presence of foreign particles is, however, an obstacle for reprocessing.

Future Thrust

- ☆ Encouragement of environmentally degradable material in horticulture
- ☆ Promotional policies for packaging like shrink packaging
- ☆ Greenhouse design to suit different crop and climatic condition along with energy efficient environment control system
- ☆ Availability of Low cost polyhouse/greenhouse construction material
- ☆ Retrieval, reuse and recycling of used agriculture plastic
- ☆ Design of equipment and system for precise application of water, fertilizer and agrochemical to meet crop requirement

- ☆ Plastic based system for storage and handling of horticultural produce
- ☆ Biotechnology for production of ecofriendly plastics and ecofriendly disposal of waste plastic.

REFERENCES

Abdul-Baki, A. and C. Spence. 1992. Black polyethylene mulch doubled yield of fresh-market field tomatoes. *HortScience* 27(7): 287-289.

Agrawal, N. and Agrawal, S. 2005. Effect of drip irrigation and mulches on the growth and yield of banana cv. Dwarf Cavendish. *Indian Journal of Horticulture,* 62 (3): 238-240.

Asnani, V.L., J.A. Otoo, and S.K. Hahn. 1985. Seed yam production-an improved technology. Intl. Seminar on Modern Technol. for Agr. In Jamaica and the Caribbean. Kingston, Jamaica. Jan. 27-31 Jan. 1985. IITA, Ibaden, Nigeria.

Bonanno, A.K., and W.J. Lamont. 1987. Effect of polyethylene mulches, irrigation method and rowcovers on soil and air temperature and yield of muskmelon. *J. Amer. Soc. Hort. Sci.* 112(5): 735- 738.

Brown, S.L. and J.E. Brown. 1992. Effect of plastic mulch color and insecticides on thrips populations and damage to tomato. *HortTechnology* 2(2): 208-211.

Carolus, R.L. and L.S. Downes. 1958. Studies on muskmelon and tomato responses to polyethylene mulching. *Mich. Agr. Expt. Sta. Quart. Bul.* 40 (4): 770-785.

Castilla, D.N. 1991. Protected cultivation in Spain. *Colture Protette* 104-15.

Cooper, A.J. 1976. Nutrient film technique of growing crops. Grower Books, London.

Cotter, D.J. and C.E. Chaplin. 1967. A review of plastic greenhouses: The problems, prospects and possibilities. *HortScience* 2(1): 7-9.

Dalrymple, D.G. 1973. Controlled environment agriculture: A global review of greenhouse food production. Econ. Res. Serv., Washington, D.C. *USDA Foreign Agr. Econ. Rpt.* 89.

Das, B.; Nath, V.; Jana, B. R.; Dey P.; Pramanik, K. K. and Kishore D. K. 2007. Performance of strawberry cultivars grown on different mulching materials under sud-humid subtropical plateau conditions of Eastern India. *Indian Journal of Horticulture,* 64 (2): 136-143.

Dhillon, P.S. and P.J. Kirschling. 1971. Profitability of tomato productions under plastic greenhouses. *Rutgers Univ., A.E.* 355.

Dubois, P. 1978. Plastics in agriculture. Applied Science Publ., London.

Emmert, E.M. 1955. Low-cost plastic greenhouses. *Kentucky Agr. Expt. Sta. Prog. Rpt.* 29.

Emmert, E.M. 1957. Black polyethylene for mulching vegetables. *Proc. Amer. Sot. Hort. Sci.* 69: 464 469.

Fontes, MR. 1973. Controlled environment horticulture in the Arabian Desert at Abu Dhabi. *Hort-Science* 8(1): 13-16.

Geraldson, C.M. 1982. Stabilization of the root environment with a high moisture level for maximum vegetable yields. *21st Intl. Hort. Congr.* 29 Aug.-4 Sept. 1982 Hamburg, Germany.

Hall, B.J. and S.T. Besemer. 1972. Agricultural plastics in California. *HortScience* 7(4): 373-378.

Hodges, C.N. 1981. New options for climatic defensive food production, p. 181-205. In: L.E. Slater and SK. Levin (eds.). Strategies and technologies for climate-defensive food production. Westview, Boulder, Colo.

Hopen, H.J. 1965. Effects of black and transparent polyethylene mulches on soil temperatures, sweet corn growth and maturity in a cool growing season. *Proc. Amer. Soc. Hort. Sci.* 86: 415-420.

IITA. 1984. Root and tuber improvement program. Inst. of Trop. Agr., Ibaden, Nigeria. Jensen, M.H. (ed.). 1977. Proc. Intl. Symp. On controlled environment agriculture. 7-8 Apr. Environ. Res. Lab., Univ. of Arizona, Tucson.

Jawaharlal, M.; Dinesh, B. M. and Indhumathi, K. 2006. Postharvest packaging techniques of Dendrobium Hybrid Sonia-17. *Journal of Ornamental Horticulture,* 9(1): 16-19.

Lawson, G.E. 1981. Plasticulture in Japan. *Amer. Veg. Grower* 29 (10): 14,20-21.

Makus, D.J. and A.R. Gonzalez. 1991. Production and quality of white asparagus grown under opaque rowcovers. *HortScience* 26(4): 374-377.

Marr, C., W.J. Lamont, Jr., and M. Allison. 1991. Rowcovers improve seedless watermelon yields in an intensive vegetable production system. *Hort- Technology* 1(1): 103-104.

Moore, E.L. 1972. Tomato varieties suited for greenhouse forcing. *Mississippi Agr. Expt. Sta. Info. Sheet* 768.

Motsenbocker, C.E. and A.R. Bonanno. 1989. Rowcover effects on air and soil temperatures and yield of muskmelon. *HortScience* 24(4): 601-603.

Nerd, A., A. Karady, and Y. Mizrahi. 1989. Irrigation, fertilization, and polyethylene covers influence bud development in prickly pear. *HortScience* 24(5): 373-375.

Ngouajio, M. and Ernest, J. 2004. Light transmission through coloured polythene mulches affects weed population. *Horticulture Science,* 39(6): 1302-1304.

Olympios, C.M. 1991. The situation of protected cultivation in Greece. *Plasticulture* 91(3): 5-16.

Pande, K. K.; Dirmi, D. C. and Kamboj, P. 2005. Effect of different mulches on growth, yield and quality attributes of apple. *Indian Journal of Horticulture,* 62(2): 145-147.

Plucknett, D.L. and H.L. Beemer, Jr. 1981. Vegetable farming systems in China. Westview, Boulder, Colo. Porter, W.C. 1991. Bed covers alter temporal distribution of production of sweetpotato transplants. *HortScience* 26(3): 252-253.

Pritts, M., K.A. Worden, and M. Eames-Sheavly. 1989. Row-cover material and time of application and removal affect ripening and yield of strawberries. *HortScience* 24: 531-536.

Rudd-Jones, D. 1977. Root environment control: Nutrient film culture. *Proc. Intl. Symp. on Controlled Environ. Agr*. p. 216-224.

Runfang, X. 1990. Watermelon production and variety improvement in the Peoples Republic of China. *Jiangsu Acad. Agr. Sci.*, Nanjing, China.

Scott, S.J., P.J. McLeod, F.W. Montgomery, and C.A. Handler. 1989. Influences of reflective mulch on incidence of thrips (Thysanoptera: Thripidae: Phaeothripidae) in staked tomatoes. *J. Entomol. Sci*. 24 (4): 422-427.

Shadbolt, C.A. and O.D. McCoy. 1960. Temperature and plant responses to paper and plastic protectors on cantaloupes. Hilgardia 30: 247-266. *HortTechnology* l Jan./Mar. 1993 3(l)

Shales, F.D. and P.H. Massey, Jr. 1968. Tomato production in plastic greenhouses. Virginia Polytech. *Inst. Ext. Div. Publ*. 154.

Sharma, R. K.; Kumar, J. and Pal, V. 2007. Effect of polythene and natural plant extract on self-life of kinnow. *Indian Journal of Horticulture*, 64 (1): 87-89.

Singh, R. and Asrey, R. 2007. Cultivating strawberry the plasticulture way. *Indian Horticulture*, 52 (2): 6-7.

Sirjacobs, M., A. Nisen, and Ch. von Zabletitz. 1988. Protected cultivation in the Mediterranean climate greenhouses in Egypt. United Nations Food and Agr. Org., Rome.

Spensley, K., G.W. Winsor, and A.J. Cooper. 1978. Nutrient film technique-crop culture in flowing nutrient solution. *Outlook Agr*. 9: 299-305.

Spice, H.R. 1959. Polyethylene film in agriculture. Faber and Faber, London.

Stevenson, D.S., G.H. Neilson, and A. Cornelsen. 1986. The effect of woven plastic mulch, herbicides, grass sod, and nitrogen on 'Foch' grapes under irrigation. *HortScience* 21(3): 439-440.

Tesi, R. 1989. Dipartimento of orloflorofritticoltura. Universita di Firenze Vin Donezelli, 6 (CP 50144). Firenze, Italia.

U.S. Department of Agriculture. 1988. Census of horticultural specialties. Census of Agriculture, USDA, Washington, D.C. Voth, V. and R.S. Bringhurst. 1959. Polyethylene over strawberries. *Calif. Agr*. 13(5): 5-14.

Voth, V. and R.S. Bringhurst. 1990. Culture and physiological manipulation of California strawberries. *HortScience* 25(8): 889-892.

Wein, H.C. and P.L. Minotti. 1987. Growth, yield, and nutrient uptake of transplanted fresh-market tomatoes as affected by plastic mulch and initial nitrogenrate. *J. Amer. Soc. Hort. Sci*. 112(5): 759- 763.

Wells, O.S. and J.B. Loy. 1985a. Rowcovers: A changing landscape. *HortScience* 20(5): 800.

Wells, O.S. and J.B. Loy. 1985b. Intensive vegetable production with row covers. *HortScience*, 20(5): 822-826.

Wittwer S.H. and R.E. Lucas. 1956. Celery production in Michigan. *Michigan Agr. Ext. Bul.* 339.

Wittwer, S.H. 1963. Tomato production in plastic greenhouses-opportunity with problems. *Proc. 1963 Agr. Plastics Conf.*

Wittwer, S.H. 1971. Report of an UNDP/FAO mission for research and training in environmental control for growth of high value crops in Israel, New York, UN/FAO, Rome.

Wittwer, S.H. 1981. Advances in protected environments for plant growth. Advances in food producing systems for arid and semi-arid lands. Academic, New York.

Wittwer, S.H. 1986. UNDP/FAO World Bank mission report-review of technical assistance requirements in the agricultural and food security sector in Egypt, Jan. 7 Jan.-6 Feb. *Proc. Matl. Wkshp. on Protected Agr*. Cairo, Egypt, 8-15 Dec.

Wittwer, S.H. and S. Honma. 1979. *Greenhouse tomatoes, lettuce, and cucumbers.* Michigan State Univ. Press, East Lansing.

Wittwer, S.H., S. Han, and W. Lianzheng. 1987. *The plastic revolution. Feeding a billion, frontiers in Chinese agriculture*. Michigan State Univ. Press, East Lansing. p.381-390.

Chapter 12

Production of High Value Vegetable Crops Under Protected Cultivation

Indian Horticulture has attained a pride status in the field of modern agriculture as horticulture crops contribute 30.4 per cent to GDP of agriculture from merely 8.5 per cent of area and have a high potential for value addition and foreign exchange earnings. Hi-Tech production of high valued horticulture crops under protected conditions adopting modern technology is the recent development in this field. With changing life styles and increased urban affluence, floriculture has assumed a definite commercial status in recent times and during the past 2-3 decades particularly. Appreciation of the potential of commercial floriculture has resulted in the blossoming of this field into a viable agri-business option. Availability of natural resources like diverse agro-climatic conditions permit production of a wide range of temperate and tropical flowers, almost all through the year in some part of the country or other. Improved communication facilities have increased their availability in every part of the country. The commercial activity of production and marketing of floriculture products is also a source of gainful and quality employment to scores of people.

Protected cultivation, which enables some control of wind velocity, moisture, temperature, mineral nutrients, light intensity, and atmospheric composition, has contributed and will continue to contribute much to a better understanding of growth factor requirements and inputs for improving crop productivity in open fields. Protected cultivation is a unique and specialized form of agriculture. Devices or technologies for protection (windbreaks, irrigation and soil mulches) or structures (greenhouses, tunnels and row covers) may be used with or without heat. The intent is to grow crops where otherwise they could not survive by modifying the natural environment to prolong the harvest period, often with earlier maturity, to increase yields, to improve quality, to enhance the stability of production, and make commodities available when there is no outdoor production. The primary emphasis is on producing high-valued horticultural crops (vegetables, fruits, flowers, woody ornamental, and bedding plants).

Protected Structures

A greenhouse is a framed or an inflated structures covered with a transparent or translucent material in which crops could be grown under the condition of at least partially controlled environment and which is large enough to permit persons to work within it to carry out cultural operations.

Classification

Based on Shape

1. **Lean to type:** This type of design is used when a greenhouse is to be constructed against the side of an existing building. It is constructed on the south side of the building so that it can get maximum sunlight during winter when it is required most. Since it is constructed against the southern wall of the house, its three sides are made with glass structure. Slope is made towards south side.
2. **Even span type:** Greenhouse is constructed with the two roof slopes of equal length on both the sides from the center. These type of greenhouses are very popular and more than 80 per cent of this type are being constructed. There may be of several single and multiple span types.
3. **Uneven span type:** In these type of greenhouses one side of roof is linger than the other. It makes a small angle with the horizontal and thus a lower pitch. The shorter arm is normally one third of longer arm. They are well adaptable to the hilly regions not soled for automation.
4. **Ridge and Furrow type greenhouse:** The green hoses are connected to another along the length of the eave. The eave serves as a furrow or gutter to carry rain and melted snow away, the side wall is eliminated between the greenhouses.

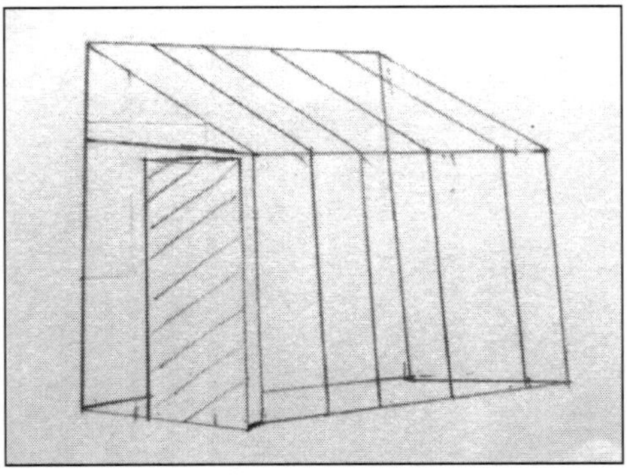

Lean to Type

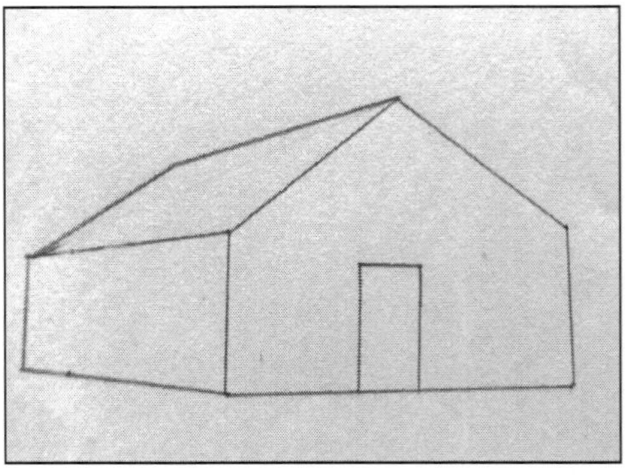

Even Span

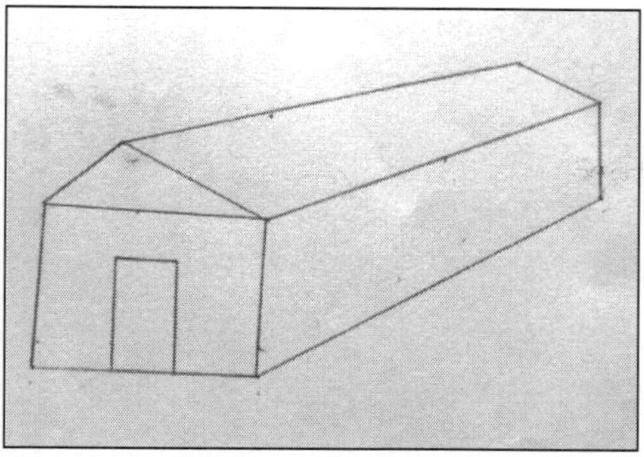

Uneven Span

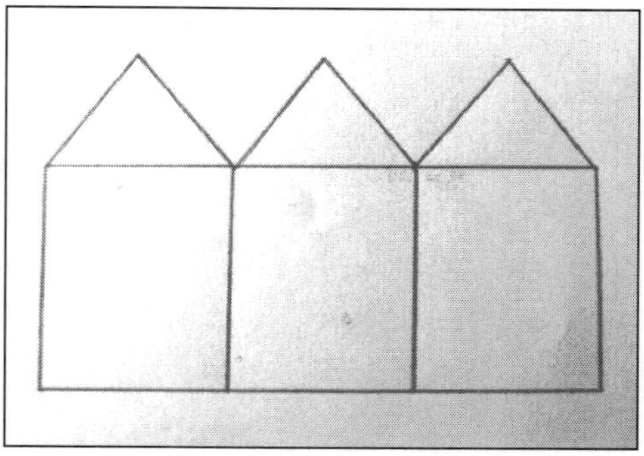

Ridge and Furrow

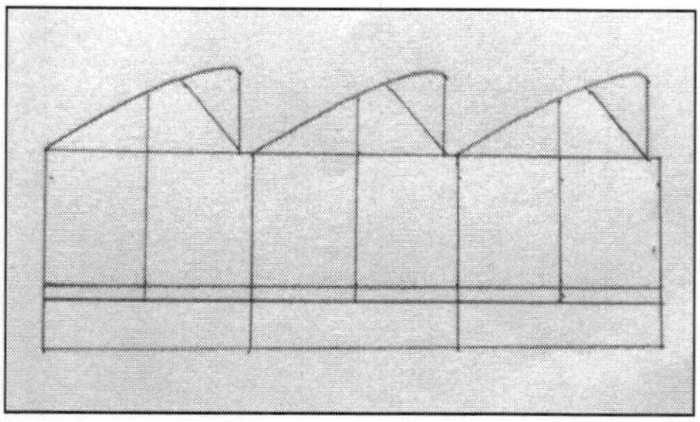

Saw Tooth

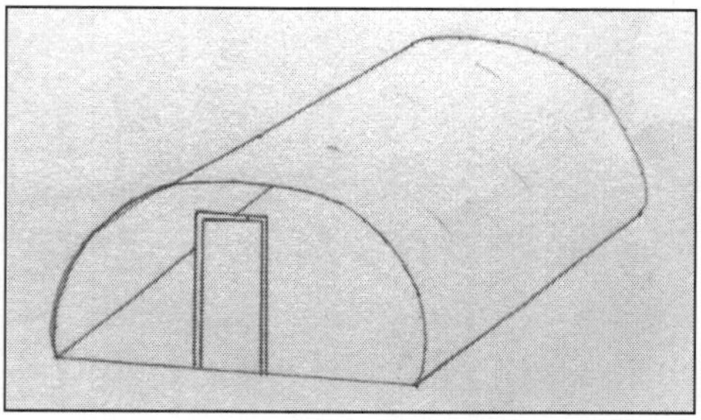

Quonset

5. **Saw tooth types greenhouse:** The structure is similar to ridge and furrow type greenhouses except that, there is provision for natural ventilation in this type specific natural ventilation flow path develops in a saw tooth types greenhouse.
6. **Quonset greenhouse:** Constructed by using pipe arches or trusses fir support. The pipe purlins run along the length of the greenhouse. The greenhouse is covered by polyethylene sheet, hence it is less expensive.

Greenhouse Type Based on Utility

1. **Greenhouse for active heating:** In winter, air temperature inside greenhouse decreases during the night time, therefore, to avoid the cold bite to plants (freezing), some amount of artificial heat has to be supplied to compensate the heat less, various methods have been adopted to reduce that heat losses, *viz.*, using double layer polyethylene, thermo pane glasses (two layers of factory sealed glass with dead air space) or to use heating systems, such as unit heaters, central heat, reactant heat and solar heating system.
2. **Greenhouse for active cooling:** In summer for plant survival, it is necessary to reduce the temperature of greenhouse for effective crop growth. Suitable modification is made so that large volumes of cooled air could be drawn into greenhouse. Either evaporative cooling pad with fan

or log cooling is utilized. This greenhouse is designed in such a way that it permits a roof opening of 40 per cent and in some cases nearly 100 per cent.

Greenhouse Type Based on Construction

1. Wooden framed structures
2. Pipe framed structure
3. Trees framed structure

Greenhouse Type Based on Covering Materials

1. **Glass greenhouses:** Glass sheers are used as cladding materials. Higher air infiltration rate which leads to lower interior humidity and better disease prevention. Lean to type, even span, ridge and furrow types of design are used for construction of glass greenhouse.
2. **Plastic film greenhouses (Polyhouses):** There greenhouses are covered with flexible plastic films in which polyethylene, polyester, and polyvinyl chloride materials are used. The polyhouses are most popular and cheap cost wise. The best quality Ultraviolet (UV) stabilizer film can last for four to five years. Quonset design or gutter connected design is suitable.
3. **Rigid panel greenhouses**: Polyvinyl chloride (PVC) rigid panels, fiber glass reinforced plastic, acrylic and polycarbonate rigid panels are used as cladding materials. Quonset type frame or ridge and furrow type frames are used. It is resistant to breakage and the light intensity is uniform throughout the greenhouse, which have long life even up to 20 years. But, the disadvantage is that the panels trend to collect dust as well as to harbor algae, which results in darkening of the panels and light reduction and there is more danger of fire hazard.

Factors to be Considered before the Construction of Greenhouse

1. Topography of land
2. Land area prediction
3. Climate
4. Labour availability
5. Accessibility of the site
6. Available water
7. Orientation

Mechanisms for Control of Light

Sun is the primary source of light in the greenhouse. The structures is designed so that it will admit the maximum amount of sunlight as usually required for the crops. The reduction in the amount of light during summer is achieved by screening material. Cotton fabrics such as tobacco cloth, cheese cloth, and tight weight muslins are less durable than synthetic fabrics – polypropylene polyester.

Selection of Media for Greenhouses

- ☆ Root media should support plant growth.
- ☆ It serves as a reservoir for plant nutrients.
- ☆ It holds water in a way that it is available to the plant.
- ☆ It facilitates the exchange of gases between roots and the atmosphere.
- ☆ It provides an anchorage or support for the plant.

Properties of a Root Medium for Greenhouse

Good soil structure should be available in pot when seeds are sown or plants are potted. It is important that decomposition of organic matter in the root medium to be used in pots must be minimum. Decomposition of the organic aggregates helps to develop finer texture and consequently poorer aeration. Straw and sawdust, except redwood sawdust decomposes rapidly therefore are not desirable in a root medium used for pot crops.

Fertigation

It is defined as a field technique which precisely delivers the plant nutrients via irrigation system in the root zone of the crop according to the demand during the crop growing season.

Characteristics of Fertilizers Suitable for Fertigation

- ☆ High nutrient content in a form readily available
- ☆ Fully water soluble at field temperature conditions
- ☆ Fast dissolution in irrigation water
- ☆ No clogging of filters and emitters
- ☆ Low content of insoluble (< 0.002 per cent)
- ☆ Minimum content of conditioning agents
- ☆ Compatible with other fertilizers
- ☆ Minimal interaction with irrigation water
- ☆ No drastic changes in water pH
- ☆ Low corrosives for control head and system

Carbon Dioxide Injection

A higher level of CO_2 will be required to support higher photo synthetic rate. Proper threshold levels of CO_2 are crop specific. For example, 3200 ppm for tomato, 1500 for cucumber and 1200 for gerbera are recommended. The commonly injected level of CO_2 in greenhouses around the world today is at 1000-1500ppm for most of greenhouse crops.

Advantage of Greenhouse

- ☆ Crops can be grown throughout the year.
- ☆ Increased crop productivity and superior quality.
- ☆ Efficient utilization of water, fertilizer, seeds and plant protection chemicals.
- ☆ Cropping programme can be planned according to the market need.
- ☆ Non cropping season – drying of produce can be taken up with entrapped head.
- ☆ Automation and artificial intelligence technologies could be used.

Disadvantages of Greenhouse

- ☆ Very costly- high initial expenditure.
- ☆ Required skilled person to manage.
- ☆ Intensive and difficult cultural operations.
- ☆ Only high returns crops can be grown.

Protected Cultivation of Vegetable Crops

1. Tomato

Tomato is the most popular vegetable crop grown under protected condition throughout the world. It is consumed either as salad, cooked or as processed food. In India tomato is grown in 4.7 lakh hectares with an average yield of 18.0 t/ha. This yield level can be enhanced to a substantial level by using hybrids with improved production practices/technologies.

Climate: Day temperature of 28°C and night temperature of 18°C is ideal for its growth. Fruit set is affected at temperature higher than 35°C and a relative humidity of more than 90 percent.

Hybrids: Tomato hybrids with indeterminate and semi determinate growth habits are the best suited for shade net cultivation.

Nursery: For preparation of healthy seedlings vermin-compost + sand (1:1) or composted, sterilized coco-peat as growing media can be used for nursery production. Pro-trays (98 cells) are filled with the growing media and the seeds treated with Thiram (0.3g/100g seed) are sown one per cell, to a depth of 0.5 cm. The seeds are covered with thin layer of growing medium and watered lightly. About 150 g seeds are required to plant one hectare area. Seeds germinate within 4-6 days and the seedlings will be ready within 30 to 40 days.

Growing medium: Sandy loam soil and well-decomposed farmyard manure mixed in 1:1 ratio is the best suited for tomato cultivation. After uniform leveling, raised beds of one meter width were formed with a furrow of 20 cm between two beds. FYM @ 20 kg per square meter of bed area is added for the first crop. For subsequent crops, FYM@ 5 kg/square meter has to be applied.

Transplanting: Thirty to forty days old healthy seedlings with a ball of earth are used for planting. The seedlings are planted in paired row system on both the sides of laterals adopting a spacing of 80 x 40 x 60 cm between pairs, rows and plants, respectively.

Fertilizer application to the growing beds: The recommended dose of NPK @ 250:250:250 kg/ha is followed. Entire amount of P and 20 per cent recommended N and K will be applied as basal through straight fertilizer at the time of planting and remaining 80 per cent will be applied through fertigation with straight fertilizers.

Drip irrigation: At the center of the bed, one inline dripper lateral has to be placed. Inline dripper with laterals should have an emitting point for every 30 cm interval with a discharge of 2 liters per hour. Drip irrigation is given daily to replenish 50 per cent of open pan evaporation.

Pinching: The tomato plants are pinched to get more value, only two stems per plant are retained. Pinching usually starts from 20 to 30 days after transplanting. Four weeks after transplanting, both the stems of plants are twined along the plastic twine. Separate plastic twine has to be provided for each branch.

Harvesting and yield: Harvesting of tomato fruits starts at 70 to 80 days after transplanting and continues until 150 days. Harvesting of fruits is done at weekly intervals. Fruits should be harvested at breaking stage. A marketable fruit yield of 96 t/ha can be realized from the crop of 6 months duration.

2. Capsicum

Capsicum (Sweet Pepper or Bell Pepper) also popularly called as Shimla Mirch in India is one of the leading vegetables grown in open conditions as well as under protected conditions. Because of its economic importance as a high value vegetable crop both in domestic and overseas markets due to more consumer preferences and use in various culinary products, quality production of capsicum is the need of the day. This has led to production of capsicum under protected conditions to meet the standards of different markets prompting popularity of this crop as an enterprise in urban and peri urban areas.

Selection of cultivars: Growing of capsicum hybrids in greenhouse is useful to obtain continuous and regular flower and fruit setting relatively for a long period of 8 to 10 months. Most of the capsicum hybrids produce green fruits that mature

to red, orange or yellow depending on the hybrid. The fruits should have characters such as uniform size and shape preferably four lobes, fruit weight of >150g, uniform coloring after attaining complete maturity, with a better shelf life of more than 5 days under ambient conditions. Selected hybrid should be high yielding, with potential yield of >40t/acre. Hybrids should have shorter intermodal lengths (7 to 10 cm), attaining maximum height of 10 feet in a crop period of 10 months. Popularly grown commercial hybrids in India include Indra, Yamuna (Green); Bomby, Triple star, Natasha, Inspiration, Pasarella (Red); Sunnyez, Swarna, Orobelle, Bachata (Yellow). Capsicum hybrids with high yield potential (>100 t/ha) and having uniform size and shape needs to be selected. Hybrids preferably should have long growing period of 8- 10 months. Fruits should have characters such as four lobes, uniform colour and maturing with better shelf life.

Nursery raising: Good quality seeds are required for producing better seedlings. The seedlings are raised in pro-trays of 98 cells or cavities. About 16,000 to 20,000 seedlings are required to plant one acre for which 160-200 gm of seeds is required. The pro-trays are filled with sterilized cocopeat and seeds are sown, one seed per cell to a depth of ½ cm and covered with the same media. The filled trays are staked one above the other and covered with plastic sheets till germination of seeds. Seeds germinate in about a week's time after sowing. The trays are shifted to net house/playhouse and lightly watered. After 15 days of sowing, Mono ammonium phosphate (12:61:0) (3g/l) and 22 days after sowing 19:19:19 (3g/l) solution has to be drenched. The seedlings in portrays are drenched with COC (Copper Oxy Chloride) 3g/l before transplanting. The seedlings will be ready for transplanting in 30-35 days. Spray imidacloprid @ 0.2 ml/l and chlorothelonil @ 1g/l before transplanting of seedlings. Always add about 0.3 ml/l of wetting agent per liter of water with each spray of pesticide.

Land preparation: The land should be thoroughly ploughed and soil should be brought to fine tilth. Well decomposed organic manure at the rate of 20-25 kg per sq. meter is mixed with soil. One application is sufficient to grow three capsicum crops successively. Raised beds are formed after bringing soil to fine tilth. The bed size should be 90-100 cm wide and 15-22 cm height. Between the beds walking space of 45 cm to 50 cm need to be provided.

Fumigation: The crop beds are drenched using 4 per cent formaldehyde (@4 l/ m^2 of bed) and covered with black polyethylene mulch sheet. While treating with formalin, care should be taken to wear mask, gloves and apron. Four days after formalin treatment, the polyethylene cover is removed; the beds are raked repeatedly every day to remove the trapped formalin fumes completely, prior to transplanting. Formalin treatment can be repeated after three crop cycles or whenever necessary.

Fumigation with formaldehyde helps to minimize the soil borne diseases. Basamid can also be used for soil sterilization.

Fertilizer application: A basal fertilizer dose of 20:25:20 NPK is required per acre and is applied to the beds uniformly before transplanting in the form of 80 kg calcium ammonium nitrate, 125 kg super phosphate and 32 kg murate of potash or 40 kg sulphate of potash. Application of neem cake and Microbial Bio-control Agents fifteen days before transplanting, neem cake has to be enriched with bio agents like *Trichoderma harzianam* and *Pseudomonas lilacinous*. Neem cake of about 200 Kg is powdered and slightly moistened. *Trichoderma harzianam, Pseudomonas lilacinous* and *Paecilomyces chilmdosporia* each of two kg are mixed thoroughly to the neem cake. The mixture is covered with wet gunny bags or dry grass and left for 8-10 days. Avoid direct exposure to sunlight and rainfall. After 10 days, this enriched mixture of neem cake and bioagent along with 600 kg of neem cake has to be applied uniformly to the beds for an area of one acre. This is highly useful to reduce the problem of soil borne pathogens and nematodes. Azospirilllum or *Azoctobacter* or VAM which is a nitrogen fixing bacteria can also be applied to the growing bed.

Laying of drip line: Place one 16mm inline drip lateral at the center of the bed having emitting points at every 30 cm interval with discharge rate of 2 l/hr or 4 l/hr run the drip system to check each emitting point for uniform discharge before covering the beds with polythene mulch.

Mulching and Spacing: Black polyethylene non-recycled mulch film of 30-100 micron thick, 1.2 m wide, is used to cover the planting beds. Holes of 5 cm diameter are made on the polyethylene film as per the recommended spacing (45cm x 30cm). The planting beds are covered with the film by securing the edges of the sheet firmly in the soil. Mulching practice conserves water, controls weeds, reduces infestation of pests and diseases and results in higher yield and good quality produce.

Transplanting: The planting beds are watered to field capacity before transplanting. Seedlings of 30-35 days old are used for transplanting. Care should be taken to see that no damage is occurred to roots, while taking out the seedlings from individual cells of protray. Seedlings are transplanted into holes made in polyethylene mulch film at a depth of 5 cm. After transplanting, seedlings are drenched with 3 g/l Copper Oxy Chloride (COC) or 3 g/l captan or 2 g/l copper hydroxide solution to the base of seedlings at the rate of 25-30 ml per plant. Watering the mulched beds daily during afternoon by using hose pipe for a week continuously is essential to avoid mortality due to heat trapped by mulch sheet.

Pruning: Capsicum plants are pruned to retain four stems. The tip of the plant splits into two at 5th or 6th node and are left to grow. These two branches again split in to two giving rise to four branches. At every node the tip splits into two giving rise to one strong branch and one week branch. The pruning is done after 30 days of transplanting at an interval of 8 to 10 days, resulting in bigger fruits with better quality and high productivity. The capsicum plants can also be pruned to two stems and same level of yield can be maintained.

Training: The main stem of plant is tied with four plastic twine to train along and tied to GI wire grid provided on the top of the plants. This is practiced after four weeks of transplanting. The new branches and plants are trained along the plastic twines.

Drip irrigation and Fertigation: Drip irrigation is given to provide 2-4 liters of water per square meter per day depending on the season. Water soluble fertilizers are given through fertigation for entire crop growth period, starting from third week after transplanting. Fertigation is to be given twice a week as recommended in the table below. Capsicum crop is sprayed with water soluble fertilizers like potassium nitrate and calcium nitrate at every 3 week interval after 2 months of transplanting @ 3g/l as foliar application.

Sl.No.	*Required fertilize dosage per fertigation (kg/ac)*
1	19:19:19 4 kg
2	Potassium Nitrate 1.5 kg
3	Calcium Nitrate 1.5 kg

Harvest: Large sweet peppers usually are picked while they are still green in colour but fully grown when sold in the market. Sweet peppers are picked with an upward twist which leaves a piece of stem attached with the fruits. Young immature peppers are rather soft and yield readily to mild pressure of the fingers. Green fruits ready for harvest are relatively firm and crisp. The yield of capsicum varies depending upon variety and the cultivation practices.

3. Cucumber

Cucumber is a widely cultivated plant in the gourd family Cucurbitaceae. It is a creeping vine that bears cylindrical fruits that are used as culinary vegetables. There are three main varieties of cucumber: slicing, pickling, and burpless. Botanically cucumbers are classified as accessory fruits. Much like tomatoes and squash they are often also perceived, prepared and eaten as vegetables. Cucumbers contains usually more than 90 per cent water. The crop requires a shorter growing season with warm climate. Sandy loam soil rich in organic matter with good drainage and pH range from 6.5-7.5 is preferred.

Varieties: There are two major types of cucumbers that can be grown in the greenhouse for both home and commercial production. The most popular are the long, seedless varieties often referred by European, Japanese or English. The older, traditional varieties have seeds and white spines. Seedless varieties have parthenocarpic fruit, or fruit that do not develop seed. A major benefit of these varieties is they do not require pollination. The skin is smooth and often has longitudinal ridges. Fruit are long, ranging from 12 to 24 inches when ready for harvest. Seeded varieties require pollination to form fruit. They produce both male and female flowers; pollen from the male flowers must be transferred to female flowers. Outdoors under good weather conditions, insects typically do an adequate job of pollinating. In protected condition, however, it is the grower's responsibility to transfer pollen. When cucumbers are not properly pollinated, the fruit will be misshapen and poorly developed, especially on the blossom end of the fruit. Cucumbers are very sensitive to imbalances or changes in growing conditions. Growers should carefully monitor fertilizer salts, light, air temperature, humidity, carbon dioxide and moisture. In attention to these details can result in decreased production and poor-quality fruit, such as bitter tasting cucumbers.

Seedlings: Sow seeds in sterile media. Members of the Cucurbita-ceae (squash) family, such as cucumbers, are sensitive to root disturbance. If planting only a few plants, sow seeds directly in the garden or in individual pots to reduce root disturbance during transplanting. For large-scale production, sow in flats and use care not to damage roots when transplanting.

The optimum germination temperature for seedless varieties is 25° to 27°C, but seeded varieties germinate at 21° to 23°C. The seed will often come with the specific germination temperature printed on the pack. Cover the seeded flats with glass or plastic to reduce heat loss and to prevent drying out. Remove the cover as soon as the seeds have germinated and emerged. Maintain daytime soil temperatures between 21° to 23°C and night tem-perature at 18°C. Keep seedlings moist. When the cotyledons (seed leaves) have expanded, transplant to individual pots containing a potting mixture with good water holding capacity and adequate drainage. Peat, vermiculite and coconut fiber are popular amendments added to improve water-holding capacity. Perlite and horticulture-grade sand are commonly used to improve drainage.

Begin fertilizing three days after potting or when true leaves have emerged. Plants should be watered frequently with a fertilizer solution. A minimum of 14 hours of direct light is required for developing seedlings.

Planting in the Greenhouse: In two to three weeks after seeding the plants will be ready to transplant into their permanent location in the greenhouse. Prior to planting, moisten the media with warm water. Plant one seedless cucumber plant per 10 square feet. Allows 5 square feet of bed space for each seeded cucumber plant. This will insure good air circula-tion and adequate light for fruit production.

Fertilizing: As the plants grow and have more tissue to support, their fertilizer requirements will increase. When plants are small, start with one quart of fertilizer solution per plant per day. As plants mature and increase in size, adjust feeding volumes upward. A mature plant will require 3.5 to 7.5 liter of solution per day. Warm the fertilizer solu-tion to room temperature before using. Nitrogen is the most important element during the growing season. Be sure to apply continually through the irrigation water. It is often more convenient to purchase a premixed complete fertilizer with micronutrients. If you choose a commercial fertilizer mix, start with a weak strength and increase the concentration as the plant grows. Most commercial producers will want to mix their own fertilizer tailored to specific crop requirements and water analysis. Water can vary in pH, calcium, sodium and micronutrient levels and should be tested to de-termine fertilizer formulations. If the water is alkaline (high pH level), phosphoric acid may added as a source of phosphorous and to adjust the pH down.

Pruning, Thinning and Training: Branches, leaves, flowers and fruit should be pruned to maintain a proper balance between the vegetative and reproductive growth to maximize production. Proper training increases the plant's ability to access the sun-light needed for growth. Too dense a canopy of leaves will shade fruits from sunlight, causing them to be pale. Flower production depends on the amount of branch growth and the number of leaf axils. Removing fruit stimulates vegetative growth.

When too many fruits set at any one time, a large proportion may abort — or experience what is of-ten called fruit drop — due to insufficient nutrients. Likewise, when a heavy load of fruit sets, many will be malformed or poorly colored. Fruit loads should be thinned to one fruit per leaf axil. Cucumbers are often trained on a string or wire system. The umbrella system, which is best used for seedless varieties, is straightforward and not too demanding in labor. Seeded cucumber varieties perform best with the tree trellis system.

Pollination: Pollination is the process of transferring pollen from male to female flowers. Seeded cucumbers are mone-cious, meaning that they have both male and female flowers on the same plant. While both sexes of flower have the same size yellow petals, they are physically dif-ferent. Male flowers are attached to the stem by a thin stalk and contain the stamen. Female flowers are identified by the small, spiny, immature cucumber between the yellow flower petals and the flower stem, and they also contain the pistil. In protected cultivation, because of the elimination of natural pollinators, it becomes the grower's responsibility to "play pollinator" by transfer-ring pollen from the male to female flowers. This is best done by removing the male flower petals, exposing the anthers, which are covered in pollen, and touching them to the center of the female stigma (center of the flower). This can also be done with a small, soft bristled brush.

Harvesting: The picking size of cucumbers varies according to the type and desired use, but they should always be harvest-ed before the seeds fully enlarge and harden. A cucum-ber is of the highest quality when the fruit is firm, bright and green in color with no dullness or yellowing to the skin. If mature fruit are left on the plant, they decrease future production. When harvesting, cut fruit from the plant with a sharp, clean knife to reduce damage and disease. Cucumbers have thin skin and lose moisture quickly, often softening in storage. To avoid losses from spoilage, store harvested fruits in cool, moist conditions at 7°F to 10°F and 80 to 90 per cent humidity.

REFERENCES

Anonymous (2013). National Horticulture Database (2012-13). Published by National Horticultural Board, Gurugram, Haryana.

Bose.U.S. (2012). Commercial Protected Floriculture. Oxford Book Company Jaipur and New Delhi.

Chadha, K. L. (2010). Hand Book of Horticulture. Directorate of Information and Publications of Agriculture, I.C.A.R., New Delhi.

Sylvan H, Wittwer and Nicolas Castilla (1995). Protected Cultivation of Horticultural Crops World Wide. *HortTechnology*. Jan./Mar.1995 5(1).

Shankara S Hebbar; Balakrishna.B; Prabhakar.M; Srinivas.V; Anil Kumar Nair; Ravikumar.G.S; Girija Ganeshan; Debi Sharma; Sudhakar Rao.D.V; Doijode.S.D; Hegde.M.R and M.S.Rao.(2011) *Protected Cultivation of Capsicum*. Technical Bulletin No. 22 (Revised Edition).

Chapter 13

Postharvest Management of Vegetable Crops: Bulb and Cole Crops

Introduction

India is the second major producer of vegetables after China. It grows a wide range of vegetables due to different agro climatic conditions. As per NHB data (2012-2013) vegetables are grown in India in about 9.2 million ha with annual production of 162.18 million tones. It is estimated that 30 to 35 per cent of India's total vegetable production is lost due to improper postharvest handling, but just about 2 per cent of this goes for processing. Onion potatoes and green vegetables like okra, bitter gourd, green chilies also have good export potential. Reducing the postharvest losses is very important; ensuring that sufficient food, both in quantity and in quality is available to every inhabitant in our planet.

Why Postharvest Losses Occur?

Vegetable and flower are living dynamic system even after detachment from parent plant. As living biological entities, they respire and transpire. (Brosnan and Sun, 2001)

Causes of Losses

1) Primary Cause

Mechanical Losses

Mechanical loss to the fruits is caused by careless handling during harvesting, packing, transportation, storage *etc.* Some insects and birds are also responsible for the mechanical injury in fruits and vegetables. Mechanical injuries like bruising and cracking render them more prone to attack by organisms and significantly increase the rate of water loss and gaseous exchange. Many a times the mechanical injury received by vegetables due to the pressure thrust during transportation, though sometimes invisible, leads to the rupturing of inner tissues and cells. Such produce is degraded faster during the natural ageing process. Produce become unmarketable.

a) **Microbial losses**: Like any other food, fruits and vegetables are also prone to microbial spoilage caused by fungi, bacteria, yeast and moulds. A significant portion of losses of fruits and vegetables during postharvest period is attributed to diseases caused by fungi and bacteria. The succulent nature of fruits and vegetables makes them easily invaded by these organisms. Besides attacking fresh fruits and vegetables, these organisms also cause damage to canned and processed products. Many serious postharvest diseases occur rapidly and cause extensive break down of the commodity, sometimes spoiling the entire package. It is estimated that 36 per cent of the vegetable decay is caused by soft rot bacteria. As far as vegetables are concerned, naturally the source of infection is from the field, water used for cleaning the surface, contact with equipment and storage environment. The most common pathogens causing rots in vegetables and fruits are fungi such as *Alternaria, Botrytis, Diplodia, Monilinia, Phomopsis, Rhizopus, Pencillium, Fusarium, etc.* Among bacteria *Ervinia, Pseudomonas, etc.* cause extensive damage.

c) **Physiological losses:** Different Physiological processes continue in vegetable even after harvest. Some are natural but detrimental. Market price is reduced.

d) **Physical losses:** Loss in weight- If vegetables are stored at higher temperature then transpiration and evaporation may cause loss to weight. The vegetables which are stored in air conditioned room shows lesser loss as compared to open conditions.

2) Secondary Causes

a) Method of Harvesting

Mechanical harvesting of tomato has been reported to result in more cracking (33 per cent) than hand picking (10 per cent). In bulb and cole crops harvesting is done at particular maturity indices, if it is done at overripe stage then harvesting losses is more.

b) Time of Harvesting

Harvesting should be done in cooler part of day *i.e.,* at morning or evening hours. The produce should be shifted in shade as soon as possible. Harvesting during hotter part of the day results in faster senescence, shriveling and wilting of fruits and vegetables as compared to those harvested in the early morning or later afternoon. Harvesting of fruits and vegetables during rain or immediately after rains creates conditions favourable for decay.

c) Absence of Legal Standards

The presence or absence of legal standards can affect the eventual retention or rejection of a vegetable or fruit for human consumption. Legal standards vary from country to country and are influenced by the economic status of the population and pressure of the population on the fruit or vegetable consumption. Strict legal standards will give better prices to farmers and superior quality to the consumers.

India is a major producer of vegetable crops, although many Indians are unable to obtain their daily requirement of vegetables and the Human Development Index (HDI) is very lôw. Considerable quantities of vegetables produced in India go to waste due to improper postharvest operations and the lack of processing. This results in a considerable gap between gross production and net availability.

It should be noted that the production of vegetables is of significance only when they reach the consumer in good condition and at a reasonable price. The concept of placing exclusive emphasis on increased production of vegetables is self-defeating. It is important to see how much of the produce goes through marketing channels and finally reaches the consumer. Efforts should be made to integrate production with postharvest management since postharvest loss reduction and utilization have considerable bearing on food availability. It is known that food loss reduction is normally less costly than equivalent increases in food production. Reduction of postharvest losses is essential in increasing food availability from existing production. The success of production lies in the proper distribution of produce and its subsequent utilization by the consumer with zero waste in the process *i.e.*, 100 per cent utilization of production in one form or another should be the motto. Opportunities exist in both domestic and international markets for fresh and processed vegetables.

So we need proper postharvest management.

What is postharvest management?

Postharvest management involves all treatments or processes that occur from time of harvesting until the foodstuff reaches the final consumer.

Or

Postharvest Management (PHM) can be defined as methods and techniques applied to increase the shelf – life and retain quality of fresh or processed horticultural produce. Efficient techniques for harvesting, conveying/transportation, handling, storage, processing/preservation, packaging, *etc.* are components of the postharvest chain.

Bulb Crop Include

Common Name	*Botanical Name*
Onion	*Allium cepa*
Garlic	*Allium sativum*
Leek	*Allium porrum*

Onion and garlic are required every day in the kitchen; however, they are harvested once or twice in a year. To maintain steady supply for domestic as well as export market they need to be stored. Onion is harvested during *Kharif* (Oct-Nov. 20 per cent), Late *Kharif* (Feb-March 20 per cent) and *Rabi* (April-May 60 per cent) seasons. However garlic is harvested in rabi only. *Kharif* and Late *Kharif* onion harvest is consumed within one or two months as there is heavy demand during those months and therefore does not require storage. Rabi harvest is in high quantity and available across country. These bulbs need storage to ensure availability till next Oct-Nov and also gain more profit over a period of storage. In case of garlic, it is harvested during March - April and the same material is used for daily consumption for almost a year.

Harvesting

Maturity standards have been determined for many fruit, vegetable and floral crops. Harvesting crops at the proper maturity allows handlers to begin their work with the best possible quality produce. Produce harvested too early may lack flavor and may not ripen properly, while produce harvested too late may be fibrous or overripe. Numerous review point to importance of the maturity of the crop at harvest on subsequent postharvest quality and self life (Ahumada and Cantwell,1996; Lee and Kader, 2000).

Crop	*Days from Planting to Harvest*	*Visible Changes*	*Remarks*
Green onion	–	As soon as they reaches preferred size	Pencil thickness
Onion	140-150	Development of red pigments, size specific to the variety and pungency	TSS12-14° B 75 per cent of the top dry
Garlic	100-140	Break over the top to prevent too much top growth	30 per cent top dry
Leek		Relatively straight,leaf top – fresh and green	Not exceed 5 cm in diameter

Curing

The only postharvest treatment required for the long storage of bulb onions is a thorough curing of the bulbs. Curing is a drying process intended to dry off the necks and outer scale leaves of the bulbs to prevent the loss of moisture and the attack by decay during storage. The essentials for curing are heat and good ventilation, preferably with low humidity. This dries out the neck and the two or three outer layers of the bulb. The outermost layer, which may be contaminated with soil, usually falls away easily when the bulbs are cured, exposing the dry under-layer, which should have an attractive appearance. Onions are considered cured when neck is tight and the outer scales are dried until they rustle. This condition is reached when onions have lost 3 to 5 per cent of their weight. If onions cannot be dried in the field, they can be collected in trays, which are then stacked in warm, covered area with good ventilation. In cool, damp climates, onions in bulk ventilated stores are dried with artificial heat blown through the bulk at a duct temperature of 30 degrees Celsius. Onions can also be cured by tying the tops of the bulbs in bunches and hanging them on a horizontal pole in a well-ventilated shade. Curing in shade improves bulb colour and reduces losses significantly during storage.

Grading

Onions after curing are graded manually before they go in to storage or for marketing. The thick neck, bolted, doubles, injured and decayed bulbs are picked out so also misshapen small bulbs. Sorting and grading is done after storage also to fetch better price. The outer dry scales usually rub off during the grading process, giving the onions a better appearance for market. It has been experienced that if storage is arranged after proper sorting and grading, losses in storage are reduced.

For local market the onions are graded based on their size.

1. Extra large onion (>6 cm dia.)
2. Medium (4-6 cm dia.)
3. Small (2-4 cm dia.)

The extra large onions have great demand and fetches very good price.

General Characteristics

The Bulbs Shall

1. Be reasonably uniform in shape, size colour and pungency of the variety/ type.
2. Be mature, solid in feel, reasonably firm with tough clinging skins.
3. Be throughout cured and dried.
4. Be free from dust and other foreign material.
5. Be free from defective, diseased, decayed and damaged bulbs caused by seed stems, tops.
6. Moisture, dry sun scald burn, sprouting, mechanical or other injuries and staining.
7. Be free from moulds, soft rot and insect attack.
8. Per cent of seed stem or bolted bulbs shall not exceed 20 per cent in Nasik kharif onions.

Packaging

Packing should be small for easy handling during transit and may vary according to market demand. Onions are packed in jute (hessian) bags for transporting to yard or brought as loose. For safe handling, 40 kg open mesh jute bags having 200-300 g weight should be used in domestic market. For export, common big onions are packed in 5-25 kg size open mesh jute bags. Bangalore Rose and multiplier onions are packed for export in 14-15 kg wooden baskets. Nylon net bags, when used for packing have resulted in less storage loss because of good ventilation.

Storage

Proper storage of bulbs is necessary both for consumption and also for seed production. Onions should not be stored unless adequately dried either in the field or by artificial means. It is necessary to dry the neck tissue and outer scales until they rustle when handled otherwise the bulbs will rot in storage. Sprouting in onion is controlled by temperature. The temperature between 10-25°C increases sprouting. Rooting is influenced by relative humidity (RH). More the relative humidity, more is rooting. Weight loss is more when temperature is above 35°C. Under ambient conditions the onions are stored at a temperature of 30-35°C with RH of 65-70 per cent. In cold storage, temperature is maintained at 0-2°C while the RH is kept at 60-75 per cent.

Sprouting is checked effectively if Maleic Hydrazide at 2500 ppm is sprayed at 75-90 days after transplanting. Effect is, however, more pronounced in kharif season than in rabi season. The storage rots could be checked if proper cleanliness is maintained in store and crop is sprayed with 0.1 per cent Carbendazim after 90 days of transplanting and just before harvest. In India, the farmers practice different storage methods. The onions are bulk stored in special houses with thatched roof and side walls are made up with bamboo sticks or wire mesh for good air circulation.

In North India, the sides are also covered with gunny cloth. Onions are stored in these sheds by spreading them on dry and damp proof floor or racks. Periodical turning of bulbs or removal of rotten, damaged and sprouted bulbs should be done. Well-ventilated improved storage structures with racks or tiers having two or three layers of bulbs would be desirable for proper storage.

Storage structures

DOGR has carried out extensive R and D on storage structures and found that 'Bottom and side ventilated two rows structure' is suitable for 25 to 50 tons capacity and 'Bottom and side ventilated single row low cost storage structure' is suitable for 5 to 10 tons capacity.

Transport

Onion stocks are transported in bullock carts, tractor trolleys and trucks as also railway wagons are used for longer distance movement within the country. Onions are transported in ventilated ships as well as sailing vessels/motorboats for export to Gulf and South-East Asian countries. It is also shipped in 3.5m containers or 7m containers by loading on ships.

Postharvest Disease of Onion

1. Neck Rot :*Botrytis allii, B. squamosa* and *B. cinerea*
2. Blue Mold Rot- *Penicillium* sp
3. Fusarium basal rot : *Fusarium oxysporum* f.sp. *cepae*
4. Black mould- *Aspergillus niger*

1. Neck Rot (*Botrytis allii, B. squamosa* and *B. Cinerea*)

- ☆ Symptoms usually appear after harvest, although infections originate in the field. Greatest epidemic development occurs when cool (50° to 75°F), moist weather prevails for some days before or during harvest.
- ☆ If the weather remains dry during harvest and curing, losses found in storage are usually small.
- ☆ Symptoms are first seen as a softening of the tissues around the neck of the bulb, or more rarely, at a wound.
- ☆ A definite margin separates diseased and healthy tissues. Infected tissues become sunken, soft, and appear brownish to grayish in color, as if they had been cooked. These symptoms progress gradually to the base of the bulb.
- ☆ Then the entire bulb may become mummified. Secondary invasion by soft rot bacteria causes a watery rot.
- ☆ Hard, irregularly shaped kernel-like bodies, sclerotia, may form between scales, especially at the neck region.
- ☆ The fungi that cause neck rot survive the winter on previously infected onion debris in the soil, in cull piles and refuse dumps, and in trash in storage sheds

2. Blue Mould Rot (*Penicillium* sp.)

- ☆ Blue mold generally appears during harvesting and storage. Initial symptoms include water soaked areas on the outer surface of scales.
- ☆ Later, a green to blue green, powdery mold may develop on the surface of the lesions. Infected areas of fleshy scales are tan or gray when cut.
- ☆ In advanced stages, infected bulbs may disintegrate into a watery rot.
- ☆ Many species of *Penicillium* can cause blue mold. These fungi are common saprophytes on plant debris and senescent plant tissue. Invasion of onion bulbs and garlic is usually through wounds, bruises, or uncured neck tissue.
- ☆ Once inside the bulb, the mycelium grows through the fleshy scales, eventually sporulating profusely on the surface of lesions and wounds.
- ☆ Optimum conditions include moderate temperatures 70° to 77°F (21° to 25°C) and high relative humidity.

3. Black Mould (*Aspergillus niger*)

- ☆ Infection usually is through neck tissues as foliage dies down at maturity.
- ☆ Infected bulbs are discolored black around the neck, and affected scales shrivel.
- ☆ Masses of powdery black spores generally are arranged as streaks along veins on and between outer dry scales.

- Infection may advance from the neck into the central fleshy scales.
- In advanced disease stages, the entire bulb surface turns black, and secondary bacterial soft rot may make the bulb soft and mushy.
- No external symptoms may be found with some bulbs.

Processed Products

- Canned onion
- Caramelized
- Frozen
- Dehydrated products-powder
- Paste- ginger onion garlic paste
- Fried products
- Pickles of onion and garlic

Next crop is cole crops, which include crop listed below

Common Name	*Botanical Name*
Cabbage	*Brassica oleracea* var. *capitata*
Cauliflower	*Brassica oleracea* var. *botrytis*
Broccoli	*Brassica oleracea* var. *italica*
Brussels Sprout	*Brassica oleracea* var. *gemmifera*
Knol khol	*Brassica oleracea* var. *gongyloides*
Kale	*Brassica oleracea* var. *acephala*

Sequence of operation in postharvest management cole crop:

a) Harvesting
b) Pre-cooling
c) Cleaning and sorting
d) Grading
e) Storage
f) Packaging
g) Transportation and marketing
h) Processing

Harvesting

Harvesting of cole crops are also done at proper maturity stages as immature crop subjected to decay whereas over mature become fibrous. Maturity indices of different cole crops is given below:

Maturity indices of cole crops

Crop	Days from planting to harvest	Visible changes	remarks
Broccoli	40–45	Cut before the buds begins to open &head remain compact	Cut before yellow petal not open
Cabbage	plains:62–110 Hills:81–125	Head solid and firm . Head colour change to lighter shades	Cut all heads with firmness and compactness
cauliflower	Plains 60–70 Hills 110–120	Lower leaves dry. Cut when the head s are compact.	Cut before the ricyness of curd
Knol khol	Plains 55–70	Harvest when knobs are light green , flesh creamy white tender	Harvest before the knobs become pithy, tough , woody & stringy

Pre-cooling

Pre-cooling is the rapid cooling process administrated in commodity for removal of heat, it has to be done immediately after harvest. It reduces the rate of respiration accompanied by reduction in metabolic activity and ultimately extend the shelf life of produce. The process of pre-cooling is the removal of field heat which arrest the deteriorative and senescence processes so as to maintain a high level of quality that ensures customer satisfaction as reported by Son and Brosnan(1999) and McDonald and Sun(2000).

Types of Pre-cooling

1. Room cooling
2. Forced-air cooling
3. Hydrocooling
4. Top or liquid Icing
5. Vacuum cooling

1. Room Cooling

Room cooling is not a true pre-cooling method, but uses the ambient temperature of a refrigerated storage facility to act as the cooling process. Cooling times in room coolers are too slow for moderate or high-respiration produce. Room cooling can be an effective method for cooling less perishable items such as potatoes, gourds, onions, and some citrus fruits; and chilling-sensitive crops, such as peppers, eggplant, watermelon, or cucumbers.

2. Forced-Air Cooling

It is similar to room cooling but adds fans to direct aimovement through pallets of produce. This method is much faster and more consistent than standard room cooling. Half-cooling times are often less than one hour. Forced-air units are also generally inexpensive and fairly easy to construct on site. Because moving air also facilitates moisture evaporation, the amount of time produce is in a forced-air unit must be carefully managed or wilting, shriveling, and shrinkage can result. During forced-air cooling the humidity of the air is not crucial for produce quality, except for some products such as mushrooms. Humid air actually slows the rate of forced-air cooling. However, the amount of time produce is in a forced-air unit must be carefully managed or dehydration can result. As soon as the product is cooled, it should be moved to a storage area that has the recommended relative humidity

3. Hydrocooling

Hydrocooling essentially is the utilization of chilled or cold water for lowering the temperature of a product in bulk or smaller containers before further packing. Hydrocooling is achieved by flooding, spraying, or immersing the product in/with chilled water. While hydrocooling is one of the fastest and most uniform pre-cooling methods available, it is not appropriate for all crops, and can quickly distribute and internalize pathogens if the produce or worker's hands are not clean, if the water is not potable (safe to drink), or if it hasn't been properly sanitized.

Hydrocooling is generally best suited for leafy greens, brassica crops (except cabbage). Hydrocooling also creates an opportunity for water-borne pathogens to reproduce readily. Additionally, because postharvest pathogens travel quickly in water and can be internalized, there is the potential for contamination of an entire load of produce.

Several important points should be considered when hydro-cooling:

1. Produce should always be cleaned before hydrocooling.
2. Water must be potable (safe to drink.)
3. Sanitizing agents should always be added to the water.
4. Good food safety practices must be used.

Sanitizers

Peroxyacetic acid (PAA) is an increasingly popular sanitizer for use on produce, particularly for organic producers. PAA can be used to reduce fruit and vegetable surface microbial activity, thus reducing product spoilage by microorganisms and reducing. PAA is available under several trade names. SaniDate 5.0 and Tsunami 100 Chlorine is an accepted disinfectant for hydrocooling water, but is subject to federal law and must be carefully monitored.

4. Top or Liquid Icing

Icing is particularly effective on dense products and palletized packages that are difficult to cool with forced air. In top icing, crushed ice is added to the container over the top of the produce by hand or machine. For liquid icing, a slurry of water and ice is injected into produce packages through vents or handholds without removing the packages from pallets and opening their tops. Icing methods work well with high-respiration commodities such as sweet corn and broccoli. One pound of ice will cool about three pounds of produce from 85° F to 40° F

5. *Vacuum Cooling*

Produce is enclosed in a chamber in which a vacuum is created. As the vacuum pressure increases, water within the plant evaporates and removes heat from the tissues. This system works best for leafy crops, such as lettuce, which have a high surface-to-volume ratio. To reduce water loss, water is sometimes sprayed on the produce prior to placing it in the chamber. This process is called *hydrovac* cooling. The primary drawback to this method is the cost of the vacuum chamber system.

Rapid cooling of horticultural produce can be carried out with vacuum cooling. Vacuum cooling is achieved by the evaporation of moisture from the produce. The evaporation is encouraged and made more efficient by reducing the pressure to the point where boiling of water takes place at a low temperature

The basic principles of the vacuum cooling process are described as follows:

1. At atmospheric pressure (1013 mbar), the boiling temperature of water is 100°C. This boiling point changes as a function of saturation pressure therefore at 23.37 mbar the water boiling temperature will be 20°C and at 6.09 mbar, it will be 0°C.
2. To change from the liquid to vapour state, the latent heat of vaporization must be provided by the surrounding medium, so that the sensible heat of the product is reduced.
3. The water vapour given off by the product must be removed.

Variable	*Ice*	*Hydro*	*Vacuum*	*Forced Air*	*Room*
Cooling times (hr)	0.1-0.3	0.1-1.0	0.3-0.2	1.0-10.0	20-100
Water contact with the product	Yes	Yes	No	No	No
Product moisture loss (per cent)	0-0.5	0-0.5	2.0-4.0	0.1-2.0	0.1-2.0
Capital cost	High	Low	Medium	Low	Low
Energy efficiency	low	high	high	Low	low

Kadar and Rosa, 2004.

Cleaning and Sorting

Sorting produce is usually done to eliminate injured, decayed, or otherwise defective produce (culls) before cooling or additional handling. Sorting will save energy in that culls will not be handled. Removing decaying produce items will limit the spread of infection to other units, especially if postharvest pesticides are not being used.

Grading

Cabbage and Cauliflower

1. Small- < 1kg

2. Medium – 1-2 kg
3. Large->2 kg

Broccoli is graded into 4 size – grades, respectively:

a. Grade 1 : 30 cm curd diameter
b. Grade 2 : 25 – 30 cm curd diameter
c. Grade 3 : 20 – 25 cm curd diameter
d. Grade 4 : 15 – 20 cm curd diameter

Storing

Cabbage is most satisfactorily stored at about 0°C and 98 per cent to 100 per cent relative humidity. In these conditions, cabbages may be stored for as long as eight months. Cabbages that are destined for storage are trimmed of their outer leaves, while careful handling is of importance to prevent injuring the wrapper leaves. Controlled atmospheres of 2.5 per cent to 5 per cent oxygen and 2.5 per cent to 5 per cent carbon dioxide may extend the storage life by several months. Avoid storing cabbage with any product that emits ethylene such as apples or pears as this can cause premature yellowing and abscision of leaves.

Cauliflower keep for 2 to 6 weeks at 0°C and relative humidity above 95 per cent. Heads should be cooled to 5°C or below soon after harvest. Both hydrocooling and vacuum cooling are effective methods to remove field heat. Cauliflower that is destined for storage is preferably cut slightly immature; otherwise the curds may separate. Perforated plastic film overwraps are effective in reducing water loss during storage and marketing. Controlled atmospheres do not extend the storage life of cauliflower and may cause off-odours, softening or discoloration.

Brussels sprouts at 0°C and above 95 per cent relative humidity will keep for 3 to 5 weeks. At -2°C, sprouts can be stored for a longer period, but have to be thawed slowly later on. Sprouts can be cooled following harvest using hydrocooling, vacuum cooling or icing. Similar to cabbage exposure to ethylene will accelerate yellowing and cause leaf abscission. Controlled atmospheres of 2.5 per cent to 5 per cent oxygen and 5 per cent to 7.5 per cent carbon dioxide will increase the storage life of sprouts held at 5 or 10°C, but have no benefit at 0°C.

Broccoli is highly perishable and should be cooled immediately following harvest by hydrocooling or packing in ice. If held at 0°C and near 100 per cent relative humidity, broccoli can be held for 3 to 4 weeks. Exposure to ethylene will accelerate the yellowing of flower buds and reduce storage life and should be avoided. Controlled atmospheres of 10 per cent carbon dioxide with or without reduced oxygen can slow yellowing of heads at temperatures above 0°C. Hot water dips of broccoli ranging from 47°C for 10 minutes to 50°C for 2 minutes prior to cooling prevents yellowing and reduces decay of flower heads.

Packing

- ✰ Wooden carets

- ☆ Wire bound wooden carets
- ☆ Plastic carets
- ☆ CFB Boxes
- ☆ Polymeric plastic films (shrink, stretch, cling, seal packing)
- ☆ The StretchPack is mainly used for packaging of the Broccoli, Cauliflower, (China) Cabbage.
- ☆ StretchPack guarantees the highest possible packing quality and product visibility at the lowest film costs.

Storage

- ☆ Mainly CA and MA storage method is used In general shelf-life of any fruits or vegetables is extended by refrigerated storage, but controlled atmosphere storage has potential to almost double the storage life of many fresh or processed fruits/vegetables
- ☆ Principal: Once produce is packed and sealed, an environment different from the ambient conditions will be established as the produce continues to respire.

  Benefits of MAP (in combination with cold storage):

  - ❒ Reduce moisture loss (reduced weight loss)
  - ❒ Delay ripening (longer marketing time)
  - ❒ Control decay (reduced postharvest losses)
  - ❒ Delay undesirable composition changes (delay loss of fruit acids and sugars

Postharvest Diseases of Cauliflower

- ☆ **Bacterial Soft Rot:** Soft rot is the most important decay of cauliflower. Symptoms are similar to those caused by Bacterial Soft Rot of Cabbage. This decay often follows bruising and freezing.

  Control: Low temperatures will keep most of this decay in check.
- ☆ **Brown Rot (Alternaria):** Brown or black spotting of the flower head or curd, size of spots varies. Develops even at low temperatures, although slowly, especially if curd is wet.

  Control: Field sanitization. Minimize mechanical injuries. Keep curds dry. Refrigerate promptly and adequately.
- ☆ **Freezing Injury:** Stem and curd become water-soaked, discolor, soften, and acquire a strong spoiled cabbage odor. Soft rot rapidly invades tissues

  Control: Protect from repeated or severe freezing by maintaining the storage temperature above the highest freezing point of 30.6°F (-0.8°C).

Postharvest Diseases of Cabbage

Bacterial Soft Rot

Bacterial soft rot is caused by various bacterial species including *Erwinia, Pseudomonas,* and *Xanthomonas.* These bacteria are typically secondary disease pathogens that enter the tissue at the time of wounding or follow primary fungal invasions. Infected tissue quickly decays and turns into a soft, slimy, foul-smelling mess at ambient temperatures. Care should be taken to avoid injury during harvest and handling. Cabbage should also be held at a cool temperature to minimize bacterial soft rot growth. Development of bacterial soft rot at the cut stem end can be prevented by spraying with a 15 per cent solution of alum (aluminium potassium sulfate) in water.

Gray Mould

Gray mould, caused by the fungus *Botrytis cinerea,* is most commonly found on stored cabbage grown under wet conditions. The fungus persists in the soil, on crop debris, and in unsanitary storage facilities. Symptoms begin as brown water-soaked areas on the outer leaf surface. Under humid storage conditions a whitish mould develops, which eventually darkens into a brownish-gray mass Once established on the leaf surface, the fungus can attack and decay healthy tissue and produce a nesting mould growth inside a packed container. The optimal temperature for growth of gray mould is 20°C (68°F). Decay can be minimized, although not completely controlled, by rapid cooling of the cabbage after harvest and storage at 0°C (32°F).

Phytophthora Rot

Phytophthora rot is caused by the soil-borne fungi *Phytophthora porri,* which is typically found in poorly drained areas of the field. This disease is most severe on cabbage produced during the rainy season. Symptoms typically begin as a dark brown firm rot of the stem end, gradually progressing into the head. Cavities tend to form in the stalk tissue and sparse white mould strands may be observed. The decayed tissue produces a distinctive sour odour. Gray water-soaked blotches may also appear on the outer leaves. The disease can be spread by contaminated cutting knives. Fungicides are largely ineffective against this pathogen. Sanitary cultural practices, well-drained soils, clean cutting knives, and refrigeration after harvest all minimize the development of *Phytophthora* rot.

Rhizoctonia Rot

Rhiz-octonia rot is caused by another common soil-borne fungus, *Rhizoctonia solani.* This disease is favoured under wet conditions, especially when there is contact between the soil and the base of the cabbage head. Symptoms begin as sunken black lesions on the lower leaf midribs in contact with the soil. Circular spots later appear on the lower leaves. In addition, small irregularly shaped lesions may develop on the tops of the heads, gradually coalescing and darkening. Eventually head rot may follow. As decay progresses, a dark mould spreads over the surface. Rhizoctonia rot can be controlled after harvest by storing the cabbage at cool temperatures.

Postharvest Disorders of Cabbage

Yellowing

Storing cabbage at ambient temperature will result in a gradual loss of green chlorophyll pigment and yellowing of the outer leaves. Cabbage is also sensitive to ethylene, which causes both leaf yellowing and leaf abscission.Adequate ventilation during storage is important to maintain very low ethylene levels in the storing area. In addition, cabbage should not be stored in close proximity with fruit which emit high amounts of ethylene.

Black Leaf Speck

Black leaf speck, also called pepper spot, is a disorder commonly observed on heads which have been in storage, although symptoms can be found in the field on over-mature heads. Symptoms begin with the development of individual specks, randomly distributed over the leaf. The black specks result from discolouration and collapse of tissue surrounding the natural openings (stomata) in the leaves. Initially the specks are minute in size, but they may develop further in storage and coalesce into lesions as large as 2 mm (0.08 in) in diameter. Symptoms can often be seen well into the center of the head promoting vigorous growth increase plant susceptibility. Low storage temperatures.

Physiological Disorders of Broccoli

Bead yellowing may occur in over-mature broccoli, when stored at higher than optimal temperatures, and/or in response to exposure to ethylene. Presence of yellow beads ends the commercial marketability of broccoli. There sometimes is confusion between senescence-associated yellow bead and yellow-light green marginal areas of floret that occur due to shading by adjacent floret tissue.

Processed Product

- ☆ Dried product
- ☆ Freeze product
- ☆ pickles

Conclusion

India is known for its rich diversity in horticultural crops. Though India ranks second producer of vegetable in world, our share in world market will not significant. Fruits and vegetables are perishable in nature. Growers do not have proper infrastructure facilities for handling or storage of produce in growing areas. Proper training of farmers in appropriate PHM activities will help in avoiding the glut of fruits and vegetables reduce losses due to spoilage, add value to the fresh and processed products. Hence, good income to the growers and better nutritious produce to consumer at a reasonable price.

REFERENCES

Ahumada, M., Cantwell, M. 1996. Postharvest studies on Pepino dulce (*Solanum muricatum*) maturity at harvest and storage behavior. *Postharvest Biol. Technol.* 7: 129-136.

Anonymous 1978. Report of the steering committee for study on Postharvest food losses in developing countries. National Research Council, National Science Foundation, Washington, DC 206.

Anonymous, 2012. Indian Horticulture production at a glance, Indian Horticulture Database, 2012. National Horticulture Board, Ministry of Agriculture, Government of India, Haryana, India pp. 2-3.

Anonymous, 2014. Packaging of broccoli. http: //www. brimapack.nl/about-us/- date of visit 17.04.2014.

Anonymous 1992. Put it on ice. American Vegetable Grower. June. p. 17–18.

Barth, M.M., Kerbel, F.L., Perry, A.K. and Schmidt, S. 1993. Modified atmosphere packaging affecting ascorbic acid, enzyme activity and market quality of broccoli. *J Food Sci.* 58.1: 140-143.

Brosnan, T. and Sun, D.W. 2001. Pre-cooling techniques and applications for horticultural products – a review. *International J Refrigeration*, 24: 154-170.

Chadha, K. L. 2010. Postharvest management, *Handbook of horticulture. ICAR*, pp. 930-940.

Chonhenchob, V. and Singh, S.P. 2003. A comparison of corrugated boxes and reusable plastic container for mango distribution. *Packaging technol. Sci.* 16: 234-237.

Howell, John C., editor. 1993. Postharvest handling. Vegetable Notes: Growing and Marketing Information for Massachusetts Commercial Growers. p. 1–5

Kader, A. A. and Rosa, R. S. 2004. The role of postharvest management in assuring the quality and safety of horticultural produce, FAO Agricultural Services Bulletin 152, pp. 36.

Lee, Brosnan, T., and Sun, D.W. 2001. Pre-cooling techniques and applications for horticultural products – a review *International J Refrigeration*, 24: 154-170.

McDonald, K., and Sun, D.W. 2000. Vacuum cooling technology for the food processing industry: a review. *J. Food Engg.*, 45: 55-65.

Nandi, R.K., Deb, M., Maity, T.K. and Sounda, G. 2002. Response of onion to different level of irrigation and fertilizer. *Crop Res.* 23: 317-20.

Rahi S. and Bahrami H, Shaeikhdavoodi M. 2013. Using Vacuum Cooling Method of Precooling Process of Cabbage. *J. Life Sci. Biomed.* 3(1): 56-59.

Rosa, S. R. 2006. Postharvest management of fruit and vegetables in the Asia-Pacific region. *Asian Productivity Organization*, pp. 131-151.

S.K. and Kader, A.A 2000. Pre-harvest and postharvest factor influencing vitamin C content of horticultural crops. *Postharvest Biol. Technol.* 20: 207-220.

Shinde, K.G., Warade, S.D. and More, T.A. 2001. Storage of onion under ambient condition- a review. *Indian J. Hort.* 64: 340-44.

Sun, D.W., and Brosnan, T. 1999. Extension of the vase life of cut daffodil flowers by rapid vacuum cooling. *International Journal of Refrigeration,* 22: 472-478.

Talbott, M.T., Sargent, S.A.,and Brecht, J.K. 1991. Cooling florida sweet Corn. L Univ. Florida Coop. Ext. Serv. Circular 941, FL, USA.

Tetteh, M.K., Prussia, S.E., Mc Smith, D.S., Verma, B.P. and Aggarwal, D. 2004. Modeling blueberry firmness and mass loss during cooling delays and storage. *Trans ASAE,* 47: 1121-1127.

Tripathi, P.C., Shankar, V., Mahajan, V.M. and Lawande, K.E. 2011. Response of gamma irradiation on postharvest losses in some onion varieties. *Indian J. Hort.* 68.4, 556-560.

Index

E

F

G

H

I

K

L

M

N

O